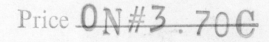

Logic and Contemporary Rhetoric:
The Use of Reason in Everyday Life

Logic and Contemporary Rhetoric:
The Use of Reason in Everyday Life

Howard Kahane

University of Kansas

Wadsworth Publishing Company, Inc.
Belmont, California

Ignorance is preferable to error;
and he is less remote from the truth who
believes nothing, than he who believes
what is wrong.

—*Thomas Jefferson*

It ain't so much the things we don't
know that get us in trouble. It's the things
we know that ain't so.

—*Artemus Ward*

ISBN–0–534–00057–6
L. C. Cat. Card No. 79–165934
Printed in the United States
of America

  3 4 5 6 7 8 9 10—
76 75 74 73 72

For Bonny sweet Robin . . .

Preface

Today's students demand a marriage of theory and practice. That is why so many of them judge introductory courses on logic, fallacy, and even rhetoric not relevant to their interests.

In class a few years back, while I was going over the (to me) fascinating intricacies of the predicate logic quantifier rules, a student asked in disgust how anything he'd learned all semester long had any bearing whatever on President Johnson's decision to escalate again in Vietnam. I mumbled something about bad logic on Johnson's part, and then stated that *Introduction to Logic* was not that kind of course. His reply was to ask what courses did take up such matters, and I had to admit that so far as I knew none did.

He wanted what most students today want, a course relevant to everyday reasoning, a course relevant to the arguments they hear and read about race, pollution, poverty, sex, atomic warfare, the population explosion, and all the other problems faced by the human race in the second half of the twentieth century.

This book is designed for exactly that kind of course. Most texts use examples that are hoary with age, such as the standard example of *amphiboly,* "If Croesus went to war with Cyrus, he would destroy a mighty kingdom." This text instead uses examples from current sources, material on topics of vital interest to today's students. (*Amphiboly* itself is not discussed, because of its relative unimportance in daily life.)

The focus of this text is the avoidance of false belief, and in particular *fallacy,* because today as always, most public rhetoric deceives by means of fallacious argument. So the first four chapters are devoted to fallacious reasoning. Almost all of the examples are taken from recent political speeches, newspapers, and magazines, and concern political topics of current interest.

But spotting fallacies is only part of the process of critical analysis. Chapter Five deals with the analysis of lengthier passages: editorials, political columns, and a presidential speech.

Political campaigns are one of the most important political institutions in a democracy. In America, they have traditionally featured slogans, Fourth-of-July-type oratory, and a generally low level of rhetoric. They still do; but now a new, or at least refined, wrinkle has to be contended with: the professional ad man. Chapter Six deals with the candidate as product. I hope that the person who understands how modern political campaigns are waged, and understands the devices and ploys used in campaign oratory, will be better prepared to cope with them.

Good thinking does not occur in a vacuum. Successful critical analysis cannot be done with an empty head, or worse, a head stuffed with falsehoods. So Chapter Seven is concerned with the ways in which the standard mass media (newspapers, mass circulation magazines, etc.) manage the news; it tries to explain to the reader why and how the mass media present a distorted image of the current state of the world.

The gap between theory and practice in our political and social system is hardly reported at all by the mass media. Every perceptive adult American knows the gap exists; what we tend to overlook is the extent to which it continues *because* it goes relatively unreported. But how can young people reason well about political and social issues if they are ignorant of this vital fact? We can't realize the American dream unless we are aware of the specific ways in which we now fall short of its realization.

Newspapers, magazines, and TV are not the only villains by any means. After TV, public school textbooks constitute perhaps the most important part of the mass media, and they too are guilty of the errors of omission and distortion just mentioned. Chapters Eight and Nine give examples of this distortion; they discuss how it arises and what we can do to guard against it. Again, the problem is vitally related to cogent reasoning about political issues, because the ill-informed reasoner (no matter how intelligent) is much more easily taken in by clever fallacious argument.

And then there is valid argument, the focus of most introductory courses on logic and correct thinking. The majority of introductory texts (including the author's own *Logic and Philosophy*) concentrate on *deductive* validity. But the crucial steps in most arguments in daily life are not deductive: they rarely claim the kind of certitude characteristic of valid deduction. So this text concentrates on nondeductive (inductive) arguments and contains a very brief account of inductive validity (as well as a short description of the difference between deduction and induction) in Appendix A.

This more formal material on inductive logic is placed at the end of the text, rather than at some earlier point, in order to avoid interrupting the generally informal and practical discussion that characterizes the greater part of the book. But some teachers will no doubt want to assign portions of this formal material along with (or even prior to) some of the informal matter in the main body of the text. For instance, they may want to assign the section on inductive logic along with the sections of Chapter Three that deal with the fallacies of *questionable cause, questionable classification,* and *questionable analogy.*

Finally, exercises have been included at the end of each chapter (but *no busy work!*). Only a few of these exercises are of the standard clearcut-answer variety. We all like exercises with definite unarguable answers, but examples from daily life seldom fit that mold. So most of the exercises in this text are of the messy variety over which reasonable men may differ. With respect to these, the way in which a student defends his conclusion often will be more important than his conclusion itself. (Appendix B contains answers to selected exercise questions, to be used by students as a guide. Needless to say, these answers are *not* presented as the revealed truth; reasonable men are likely to differ over them.)

Textbooks must be objective. But what sort of objectivity is required? In a sense, what is true, what is the case, must count as objective fact. Hence anyone who makes a true statement is in some way within the bounds of objectivity.

However, for our purposes, a different kind of objectivity is required, although it is not clear exactly what it consists in. The man who luckily utters the truth on the basis of outrageous prejudice has not achieved this kind of objectivity. Nor has someone failed to achieve it who unluckily utters falsehoods based on intense research and cogent reasoning. Roughly, we want assertions based on *sufficient evidence* (and cogent reasoning) to count as objective in this sense, whether or not they later turn out to be true.

But most political arguments, like most arguments about religion and morals, concern problems for which sufficient evidence rarely is at hand, one of the main reasons these topics are so controversial. We therefore must settle for *good* rather than sufficient evidence, although it is not always clear what constitutes good evidence in specific cases.

So good evidence (plus cogent reasoning) is the criterion of objectivity used in this text. For instance, the text takes it to be an objective fact that

Negroes in the United States never have received and still do not receive the treatment they are entitled to by law and by the lofty standards stated in our Declaration of Independence. The text assumes it to be an objective fact that *in general* there is a tremendous gap in the United States between ideals, standards, and the law, on the one hand, and day-to-day actual practice, on the other. This assumption is made on the basis of what the author takes to be good (although certainly not conclusive) evidence.

Yet these unfortunately are matters of great controversy. In the past, textbook writers have tended to shy away from controversial topics of this kind, or to pussyfoot around them, taking care not to contradict established dogma, no matter how much contrary evidence there might be. The result has been the pablum with which we are all familiar and to which today's students, with good reason, greatly object.

The opinion is widespread that objectivity requires the omission from textbooks of all value judgments, moral or otherwise, because such judgments are subjective. But has there ever been a satisfactory textbook in the humanities, or even in certain areas of the social sciences, completely devoid of value terms and value judgments? [1]

Nor, in my opinion, is such a strict admonition against value judgments proper. In the first place, it begs philosophical questions about the objectivity or subjectivity of value judgments; the view that value judgments can be objective (not all are, obviously—any more than are all factual judgments) is a time-honored one, including among its adherents Plato, Aristotle, Aquinas, Spinoza, Kant, and Hegel, to name only a few.

And further, a text completely free of value judgments, if such a thing is possible in the humanities or social sciences, would be a crippled entity, incapable of dealing satisfactorily with anything related to the political or social problems of the day. It simply is impossible to deal with these topics effectively except against a backdrop of moral values.

Then why should we require textbooks dealing with topics such as *practical* reasoning, reasoning about political and social problems, to be divorced from the value realm? The vast majority of moral, rational men believe that murder, slavery, rape, racial discrimination, and grand theft are morally wrong. Why then object to textbooks' stating that slavery and the racial discrimination which followed it in the United States were, and are, morally wrong? Why object to their stating the moral evil of the white man's grand theft of the North American continent from its prior owners, the American Indians?

---

[1] Imagine a psychology text which tried to do without value terms such as *healthy, normal,* or *sane.* A whole discipline within psychology—abnormal psychology—is defined in terms of values; merely odd behavior, remember, is not thereby abnormal.

But this textbook definitely is not a partisan political or moral effort. Opinions about anything other than logic intrude only when necessary to make a point of *logic,* or to illustrate devices used to con the public. Issues are never discussed merely for their own sake; nor are value judgments gratuitously introduced. Republicans and Democrats both take it on the chin quite frequently, although Democrats on the whole come in for less criticism, because a Republican administration was in power in 1970 and 1971 when this text was written. But they are attacked only by way of illustrating fallacies or points of logic.

This book was written with one and only one idea in mind; it is an attempt to raise the level of political argument and reasoning by acquainting students with the devices and ploys which drag that level down. The intent is not to move students either to the left or the right on the political spectrum, but rather to move them *up* on the scale of cogent reasoning about political issues.

The fact is that the level of most political argument in this country is and always has been extremely low. Yet if representative government is to function as it should, we must have an electorate sufficiently sophisticated to demand a high level of political argument. If this book helps even in a small way to produce a more intellectually sophisticated electorate, it will have served its purpose.

Custom dictates that only the name of the author appear on the title page of a textbook. But most texts owe a great deal more to the efforts of others than this custom would indicate, and this text is no exception. It could not have been written, or at least not written in this form, without the invaluable aid of the publisher's readers, Professors Leland Creer, Central Connecticut State College, Peter K. Machamer, The Ohio State University, Gerald Messner, College of San Mateo, Paul O. Ricci, Cypress Junior College, and in particular Ray Kytle, Central Michigan University, whose efforts went far beyond those normally associated with a reviewer. Credit also is due to students in my logic classes at the University of Kansas, who were subjected to earlier versions of portions of the text, to the nice people who work at the New Britain Public Library and at the Library of Central Connecticut State College, and to my secretarial assistant, Mrs. Carol Hubbs, especially for her great speed and accuracy.

But even beyond these debts, this book owes a great deal to the numerous invaluable comments of my wife, Judith Kahane, Central Connecticut State College.

Howard Kahane
June 1971

Contents

Appendix A: Valid Argument   218

Appendix B: Answers to Selected Exercises   230

Bibliography   244

Indexes   247

Introduction

What This Book Is About

Everyday all of us are bombarded with language and pictures intended to persuade us in one way or another. This barrage is frequently quite successful, in particular because we all are receptive to ideas favorable to what we already want to do anyway. Part of this barrage is self-inflicted; we often try to convince ourselves to do some things and avoid doing others. But a great deal is inflicted on us by others, sometimes with malice aforethought, sometimes from the best of motives.

Unhappily, the cases in which the persuasion is successful frequently are not those in which it *ought* to be. And that's what this book is all about.

People try to persuade us about many things. This book will restrict discussion to *political* persuasion, with just one interesting exception (advertising). For the most part, we'll examine actual political arguments from recent newspapers, magazines, political speeches, press conferences, and (interestingly) textbooks. Occasionally, we'll throw in examples from memory or imagination, or even from the dim past prior to, say, 1968.

Let's call uses of language or pictures intended to *persuade* anyone of anything an **argument**. In this sense, "Don't go near the edge; you might fall" is an argument. So is an advertisement. And so are the words "I love you" when intended to convince someone of the opposite sex. (But remember that we're going to concentrate on political arguments. So forget "I love you" and arguments of that kind.)

And let's call an argument which *should not* persuade a rational person to accept its conclusion a **fallacy**. (Whether it does or not is another matter.) We can then say that a person *commits* a fallacy if he is convinced

1

by a fallacious argument, and that he is *guilty* of a fallacy, or *argues* fallaciously, when he uses a fallacious argument in an attempt to convince someone else.[1]

In this book we're going to spend much more time on the avoidance of bad reasoning than we do on good reasoning. This may initially strike the reader as a somewhat negative approach. But in fact it is not. For one of the most important ways, perhaps the most important way, to improve the quality of our reasoning is to avoid being taken in by incorrect reasoning or by bad argument. By thus avoiding fallacy, we make sure that we don't get into trouble over "the things we know that ain't so."

Some fallacious arguments are so obvious that they're hardly likely to fool anybody. Unfortunately, many others are all too apt to con even the wary. This fact has not gone unnoticed. Politicians, for instance, know that getting elected requires at least a small amount of verbal con artistry.

Since we all engage in a certain amount of self-deception, we all to some extent must be classified as verbal con artists, at least able to con *ourselves* when it is comforting to do so. But few of us can compare with the professionals, the men who are paid to persuade on a large scale by means of words and pictures.

Most of the professionals are probably honest. Some may even be unaware of the fact that they employ verbal trickery. Undoubtedly, many do their work with malice aforethought. But for whatever reason, the fact is that most of the persuasion used in politics and advertising is a strange complex mixture of cogent and fallacious argument. The job of the rational man is to sort out this conglomeration as best he can, so as to fend off verbal con artistry as much as possible. Failure to do so makes rational decision-making impossible. The verbal con artist, in ourselves and others, is our natural enemy.

---

[1] It follows that a person who argues fallaciously does not automatically *commit* a fallacy (in the sense of that term just described). The charlatan who tries to convince others with reasoning which he knows to be shoddy is an example of a person *arguing* fallaciously without *committing* a fallacy.

Chapter One

Fallacious Even If Valid

> It would be a very good thing if every trick could receive
> some short and obviously appropriate name, so that when a
> man used this or that particular trick, he could at once be
> reproved for it.
>
> **Arthur Schopenhauer**

Roughly speaking, a **valid argument** is an argument whose premises, *if true,* alone provide good, or sufficient, grounds for accepting its conclusion.[1] (All other arguments are said to be **invalid**.)

Here is a made-up example of a valid argument:

All Democratic politicians are honest (first premise), *and Lyndon Johnson is a Democratic politician* (second premise). *So Lyndon Johnson is honest* (conclusion).

The premises of this argument provide good grounds for accepting its conclusion, *if its premises are true.*

But we all know from sad experience that the first premise of this argument is false, a fact which makes the argument itself **unsound**. (To be **sound** an argument must be both valid *and* have all true premises.) Nevertheless, the argument is *valid,* because *if* its premises were true, they would provide good grounds for acceptance of its conclusion.

Let's use the notions of argument validity and argument invalidity as the basis for a division of fallacious arguments into two basic categories:

---

[1] A few of the principles of formal argument validity, chiefly inductive, are discussed in Appendix A.

3

(1) arguments which are **fallacious even if valid**; and (2) arguments which are **fallacious because invalid**.

But in using these basic categories of fallacy, or any categories of fallacy for that matter, it must be remembered that the arguments of everyday life frequently cannot be placed in a particular category with one-hundred-percent certainty, because so many arguments in daily life are either *vague* or *ambiguous,* or both. (This point will become clearer later.)

This chapter deals with arguments which fall into the first category, namely arguments which are *fallacious even if valid.*

1. Suppressed evidence

When arguing, it is human nature to present every reason you can think of that is favorable to your own position, while omitting those that are unfavorable. Nevertheless, anyone who argues in this very human way argues fallaciously. Let's call this the fallacy of **suppressed evidence**. Anyone convinced by such an argument who might reasonably be expected to think of the suppressed evidence can be said to *commit* the fallacy of *suppressed evidence.*

William S. White, the well-known biographer, argued fallaciously by way of *suppressed evidence* in the following passage about Lyndon Johnson:[2]

> . . . *as early as March of 1949, as the very new and junior Senator from Texas with a plurality of less than a hundred votes in his pocket, he* [Johnson] *had gone on record* [against racial discrimination]: *"Perhaps no prejudice is so contagious or so unreasoning as the unreasoning prejudice against men because of their birth, the color of their skin or their ancestral background. . . ."*

Mr. White wanted to portray Johnson as having been a champion of civil rights in 1949, at some risk to his political career. But as pointed out by I. F. Stone,[3] White suppressed the fact that the quotation is taken from a speech in defense of a filibuster *against civil rights legislation,* in which Johnson also stated:

---

[2] In *The Professional, Lyndon B. Johnson,* Houghton Mifflin, Boston, 1964.

[3] In his book *In a Time of Torment,* Random House, New York, 1964 (also in a Vintage Books paperback edition).

I say frankly that the Negro . . . has more to lose by the adoption of any resolution outlawing free debate in the Senate than he stands to gain by the enactment of the civil rights bill. If the law can compel me to employ a Negro, it can compel that Negro to work for me.

Once pointed out, omissions of this kind often seem obvious. But it is surprising how frequently we fail to think of the suppressed fact, or even to realize that there is one to think of. This is true in particular when an argument is designed to misdirect our attention. A series of TV commercials extolling Shell gasoline and Platformate constitutes a good example. In these commercials the auto using Shell with Platformate always obtained better mileage than autos using gasoline without this ingredient. What was the suppressed evidence? Simply the fact that just about every standard brand of gasoline at the time contained Platformate or a similar ingredient. Thus, Shell pitted its gasoline against a decidedly inferior product most auto owners did not use. The viewer's attention was directed away from this fact by the way the claim was worded and also by the general presentation of the commercial.

Experts often trade on the layman's ignorance of details in perpetrating the fallacy of *suppressed evidence*. (The layman so taken in commits a fallacy only if he should have suspected that evidence was being suppressed.)

E. Laurence Chalmers, Jr., Chancellor of the University of Kansas, apparently traded on the outsider's ignorance of factual detail in an alumni question-answer session:[4]

> Alumnus: *How do you justify the reduction of ROTC credit by the faculty when the student referendum was to keep credits as they were?*
>
> Chalmers: *The answer is we don't have to justify it. There has been no reduction in credit.*
>
> Alumnus: *That's not what has been in the newspapers.*
>
> Chalmers: *I know it hasn't been published, but I can't publish it. . . . The Faculty Senate recommendation is to integrate ROTC education into the regular departments of the schools and colleges of the University.*

[4] Before the Wichita Alumni, May 20, 1970. The session is reported in the University's *Kansas Alumni*, May 30, 1970.

Integration is defined to include either (a) courses cross-listed by departments as being appropriate in their department for credit such as history of the military; (b) team teaching where faculty members will join military personnel to jointly present a course and include it in that department of the school or college. These will be implemented during the next year. They are in complete accord with the Department of Defense recommendations on ROTC, and endorsed by Secretary Laird last September.

In this case, the questioner's general impression is correct. The Chancellor mentioned the Faculty Senate recommendation, which would not remove credit from ROTC courses, but failed to mention a motion passed by the College of Liberal Arts and Sciences. The latter motion removed College credit from ROTC courses not successfully integrated into the regular offerings of academic departments by September 1971, and its likely effect was to reduce credit for ROTC courses. (In a meeting, the College Faculty hooted at a definition of course integration similar to the one given by the Chancellor in his answer.)

This omission of relevant facts very likely slipped by because of the great complexity (to the outsider) of university organization. It would have taken a sharp outsider to realize that the Chancellor had spoken of an all-University body, while the news stories which bothered the questioner were, in all probability, about the College of Liberal Arts and Sciences. This was no small omission, since the College is the tail that wags the dog, having well over half the faculty and students on campus. Clearly, Chancellor Chalmers was guilty of the fallacy of *suppressed evidence*.

In early 1971, Democrat John Connally, ex-governor of oil-rich Texas, testified before the United States Senate Finance Committee concerning his nomination as Secretary of the Treasury. He testified that the allegations of his "vast wealth" in oil and gas were false and that his total wealth in oil and gas was $7240. But when the *New York Times* then revealed that Connally had received money from the Richardson Foundation (set up by the late Texas oil millionaire Sid Richardson), Connally admitted he had been paid $750,000 by the Richardson Foundation for services rendered to Richardson's estate.[5]

This example illustrates how a man may attempt to conceal evidence while not quite actually lying. Connally's original testimony conveyed the impression that he had not profited from his proximity to vast oil wealth. And he managed to convey that impression without committing what is

[5] For more details, see the *New Republic*, February 13, 1971.

politely called an "error of commission" (that is, he did not actually lie). But his suppression of the very kind of information that he knew his questioners were looking for did amount to an "error of *omission*" (that is, he did mislead by omitting the kind of information he knew the Committee was seeking).

Finally here is H. R. Haldeman, Assistant to President Nixon,[6] arguing that President Nixon was *not* isolated from public opinion during the demonstrations in Washington against the 1970 American "incursion" into Cambodia:

> . . . *President Nixon himself went to the Lincoln Memorial at Sunrise on Saturday, May 9, to talk with young people who had come to Washington for that day's demonstrations.*

Haldeman conveyed the impression that the President and the "young people" had a heart-to-heart talk about Cambodia, Vietnam, foreign policy, etc. But no. The (suppressed) fact is that the President (in what might be called his "Lincoln Memorial Caper") talked about football and surfing.

2. Doubtful evidence

Another fallacy committed very frequently in conjunction with valid arguments consists simply in accepting an argument whose premises are both questionable and inadequately supported. Let's call this the fallacy of **doubtful evidence**.

In a July 1970 speech, President Nixon tried to leave the listener with the conclusion that the May–June 1970 American venture into Cambodia was both necessary and successful. One of his reasons was this:

> *Our screening of more than six tons of documents captured in the Cambodian operations has provided conclusive proof of Communist reliance on Cambodia as a logistic and infiltration corridor.*

---

[6] At UCLA, September 9, 1970. Quoted in UCLA *Benchmarks,* Summer 1970.

But it is extremely doubtful that so much material could have been screened
in so short a time. One observer's entire comment on the matter consisted
of a single question: "How did the CIA go through more than six tons of
documents so quickly, with steam shovels?" [7]

There are at least three important species of the genus *doubtful evidence*.

a. Unknown fact

The first is the fallacy of the **unknown fact**. This species breaks down
even further into those "facts" which are more or less *unknowable by anyone* (such as the number of snowflakes that fell in the blizzard of '88) and
those which might be known by someone at some time or other but in fact
are not known by the person committing the fallacy. Naturally, it is the
second category, dealing with things knowable in principle (and perhaps
known by others) but in fact not known by *us*, which is of major interest
here.

Here is an example from a political column by John Chamberlain: [8]

> But the Moscow imperialists—and they remain just that—have cer-
> tain fish to fry, and the continued blockage of the Suez Canal does not
> consort with **the number one Soviet priority, which is to prepare for a
> possible mortal struggle with the Red Chinese.** [9]

Ignoring the likelihood that the Soviets had many other reasons for un-
blocking the Suez Canal, how could Mr. Chamberlain know the number-
one Soviet priority at that time, even supposing the Russians *had* a
number-one priority? We have here a clearcut case of the fallacy of the
unknown fact.

Sometimes the unknown fact is *implied,* but not quite stated. Here is a
typical example, from a column by Rowland Evans and Robert Novak: [10]

---

[7] *I. F. Stone's Bi-Weekly,* July 13, 1970. Reprinted by permission.

[8] *New Haven Register,* August 24, 1970.

[9] Throughout this book, *boldface type* used in quotations signifies emphasis and
does not occur in the originals.

[10] *Lawrence* [Kansas] *Daily Journal World,* August 24, 1970.

. . . Law enforcement authorities have lost the scent of ex-UCLA professor Angela Davis, charged with murder in the San Rafael shootout. Like most of the Weathermen terrorists now being sought, Miss Davis **could be** *almost anywhere,* **shielded by the hippie subculture***.*

Although Evans and Novak didn't quite assert that Miss Davis was "shielded by the hippie subculture," their implication that this was the case is clear enough. Yet at the time no one who was talking seemed to have any idea where Miss Davis was; and Evans and Novak provided no evidence that she was being "shielded by the hippie subculture." [11]

Another example of *unknown fact* is furnished by Tom Hayden: [12]

*Nixon's promise to withdraw from Cambodia did have a temporary cooling effect, but it also blew away many lingering illusions about peace in Asia. The government had served notice to all but the most blind that its intention was to win the war through escalation—***even with nuclear weapons, if necessary***.*

Obviously Mr. Hayden, of all people, was not privy to one of the most intimate secrets of the Nixon administration (whether that administration would or wouldn't use nuclear weapons). He thus stated something as a fact which he could not possibly have known and hence was guilty of the fallacy of the *unknown fact*.

b. Doubtful evaluation

A perhaps even more insidious species of *doubtful evidence* is that of **doubtful evaluation**. We are guilty of this fallacy if we insert an unsupported controversial *value judgment* (as distinguished from an unsupported controversial fact) into an argument as a premise. [13]

---

[11] Subsequent to her capture, it became evident that Miss Davis had not sought refuge in the hippie subculture.

[12] In his article "All For Vietnam," *Ramparts* magazine, September 1970.

[13] Of course, real-life arguments are often so vague and ambiguous that it isn't clear whether a questionable value judgment is intended as a premise or as the conclusion of an argument. (If it is intended as a conclusion, then the fallacy is that of *begging the question,* discussed in the next chapter.) Extended discourse, where the conclusion of one argument is commonly used later as a premise anyway, tends to be particularly messy. Often, a writer simply intends the reader to adopt a general attitude for or against a particular group. Marquis Childs' newspaper column from which the remark quoted below about hippies is taken may be an example. Mr. Childs may simply have intended the reader to adopt an anti-hippie attitude.

Time magazine was guilty of the fallacy of *doubtful evaluation* in its report of a charge made by the National Association for the Advancement of Colored People (N.A.A.C.P.) that the Nixon administration had adopted a ". . . calculated policy to work against the needs and aspirations of the largest minority of its citizens":[14]

> *One* **accurate** *assessment of the controversy was offered by former Attorney General Ramsey Clark, who told the N.A.A.C.P. convention that he "hated to believe" that the Administration was anti-black. "It's not that they are aginners," he said, "but rather they are do-nothingers. They are guilty of neglect, not malice."*

Time furnished no evidence for its judgment that Mr. Clark's evaluation was "accurate." Yet the question of its accuracy was of great importance at the time in evaluating the Nixon administration on crucial racial issues.

This quotation is interesting because it illustrates how one word (the word "accurate") can be used to slant the viewpoint of a whole article and put the reader into a frame of mind receptive to the writer's message. The fact that only one word was used to do the job makes it all the harder to detect the fallacy.

In the above example, *Time* at least used an out-and-out evaluative term, the term "accurate." But more frequently the key words express both *facts and values,* thus tending to hide the fact that a value judgment has been made.

Marquis Childs does this in an interesting column in which he writes:[15]

> . . . *university* [of California] *officials estimate that 4,500* [nonstudent hippies] *are* **holed up in the warrens** *along Telegraph Avenue.*

The *fact,* shorn of all value tinge, is that university officials estimated that 4,500 nonstudents *resided* along Telegraph Avenue. But written this way, the line loses its power to conjure up an image of students living like rabbits in foul nests along Telegraph Avenue (an image for which Mr. Childs presents no supporting evidence) and thus loses its power to prejudice the reader against the 4,500 nonstudents.

[14] *Time* magazine, July 13, 1970, p. 11.
[15] Marquis Childs, "Student Revolution Brings a Counter Revolution," *New Britain* [Connecticut] *Herald,* Aug. 17, 1970, p. 14.

Incidentally, in the next paragraph Mr. Childs makes use of the fallacy of the *unknown fact:*

> *Living . . . partly as remittance men and women given an allowance by their parents* **on condition they do not come home**, *they are an unfailing potential for violence and upheaval.*

Again, evidence for the alleged fact is not forthcoming; indeed one suspects that it is the sort of matter about which a newspaper columnist could not possibly have had accurate information.

Advertising, of course, is full of doubtful and unsupported evaluations. Every advertiser wants the consumer to believe that *his* product is best. Most so-called "combative" advertisements (those which try to get the reader to switch from one brand to another of the same kind of product) implicitly amount to the argument: My product is best (*premise*); so you ought to buy my product rather than my competitor's (*conclusion*). If an ad of this kind fails to support the claim of superiority, it is guilty of the fallacy of *doubtful evaluation.*
For some mysterious reason, ads for alcoholic beverages seem to be guilty of this fallacy more frequently than others. An example is a magazine ad showing a picture of the product with the following inscription underneath:

> *For Memorable Moments . . .*
> *MOËT CHAMPAGNE*
> *. . . The Great Champagne of France.*

The argument implicit in this ad is that Moët Champagne is *the sole great* champagne of France (which produces the *best* champagne), and *therefore* for memorable moments you ought to drink it. In the same magazine, we find an ad which states:

> *BOLLINGER*
> *The aristocrat of French Champagne.*

But it doesn't say *why* it merits that title, any more than we're told why Moët is *the great* champagne of France.

c. Inconsistency

The fallacy of **inconsistency** consists in arguing from premises that are *contradictory*. Obviously, if two premises contradict each other, one of them must be false. So even if the argument in which they occur is *valid,* we commit a fallacy in accepting its conclusion.[16]

Politicians are famous for being inconsistent, but their inconsistency rarely is overt, explicit, or even exact. Perhaps this is true because politicians rarely speak with enough precision to be one-hundred-percent inconsistent.

At any rate, politicians frequently are more or less inconsistent in three general ways. One way is to say one thing at a particular time and place and something quite different at another time and place (without either explaining the change or retracting the former statement).

The following two statements by President Nixon on American Vietnam policy beautifully illustrate this version of the fallacy of *inconsistency.* He made the first statement on September 13, 1966, while he was out of office and campaigning for Republican candidates prior to the 1966 congressional elections:

> *He* [President Johnson] *owes it to the people to come clean and tell them exactly what the plans are; the people should be told now, and not after the elections.*

But on March 10, 1968, now himself a candidate for President of the United States, Mr. Nixon stated:

> *No one with this responsibility who is seeking office should give away any of his bargaining position in advance. . . . Under no circumstances should a man say what he would do next January.*

And then on May 8, 1968:

---

[16] Although it may seem odd, the fallacy of *inconsistency* can be committed only with respect to *valid* arguments. This is true because every argument with contradictory premises is valid (since contradictory premises imply any and every conclusion). And since anyone who is not a fool would doubt the truth of a pair of inconsistent premises, the fallacy of *inconsistency* turns out to be a species of the genus *doubtful evidence.*

Let's not destroy the chances for peace with a mouthful of words from some irresponsible candidate for President of the United States.

The Vietnam War also furnishes another famous (and disputed) example of this version of the fallacy of *inconsistency,* this time by President Johnson. During the election year 1964, President Johnson implied, and even appeared to say directly, that if elected he would neither enlarge the scope of the war nor send large numbers of American soldiers to Vietnam to fight. He repeatedly used expressions such as the following (uttered on June 23, 1964):

The United States . . . seeks no wider war.

(But notice the "weasel word": the United States *seeks* no wider war.)

One statement in particular (made on August 29, 1964) became quite famous, and was used over and over in the 1964 presidential campaign:

*I have had advice to load our planes with bombs and to drop them on certain areas that I think would enlarge the war and escalate the war, and result in committing a good many American boys to **fighting a war that I think ought to be fought by the boys of Asia to help protect their own land**. And for that reason I haven't chosen to enlarge the war.*

But, of course, the Johnson administration did commit a good many American "boys" to fighting in that war. So occasionally it was necessary for the White House to make announcements which in general were *inconsistent* with the above statement. Here is one issued by the White House on February 12, 1965:

On February 11 United States air elements joined with the South Vietnamese air force in attacks against military facilities in North Vietnam used by Hanoi for the training and infiltration of Vietcong into South Vietnam.

These actions by the South Vietnamese and United States governments were in response to further direct provocations by the Hanoi regime.

While maintaining their desire to avoid spreading the conflict, the

two governments felt compelled to take the action described above
[air strikes on North Vietnam].

The President may also have committed the fallacy of *suppressed evidence*, since he did not mention the provocations by our side which had led to the North Vietnamese provocations. But of course in such cases the problem is always where to stop. The series of escalations on both sides goes back at least to 1954, and probably to 1945. Obviously, the whole series cannot be enumerated every time Vietnam is discussed, nor is it practical every time even to ask which side committed the first provocative act, although this very controversial fact is important in assigning ultimate responsibility for the Vietnam War.

A second way in which politicians can be inconsistent and (usually) get away with it results from the fact that large organizations such as governments are composed of many men. Thus the President of the United States can say one thing, while eminent and responsible officials in his administration say the contrary.

At about the time President Johnson was stressing his policy against enlarging the Vietnam War, his Assistant Secretary of State, William P. Bundy, stated (on June 18, 1964):

> *We are going to drive the Communists out of South Vietnam even if that eventually involves a choice of attacking countries to the north.*
>
> *If Communist forces get the upper hand in Laos, the only response we would have would be to put our own forces in there.*

But, of course, the Democrats have no monopoly on inconsistency with regard to Vietnam. On April 30, 1970, Republican President Richard Nixon made interesting use of a third common variety of *inconsistency*, which is to *say* one thing while *doing* another. Here are excerpts from his April 30, 1970, announcement that the United States was sending ground troops into Cambodia:

> *In cooperation with the armed forces of South Vietnam, attacks are being launched this week to clean out major enemy sanctuaries on the Cambodian-Vietnam border. . . .*

He then went on in the same announcement to virtually contradict himself by saying:

We shall avoid a wider war. . . .

A more striking example of this fallacy was furnished by Vice President Spiro T. Agnew after a trip to Asia: [17]

> *. . . I have told the Cambodian government that the United States is interested in a continued non-aligned status for Cambodia, that we would continue to be of help in the military assistance program, that we would attempt to help them with the free nations of Asia in any way we could economically,* **but that we want them to understand that we aren't going to become militarily involved in Cambodia.**

This was spoken at a time when the American government "unofficially" admitted it was bombing in Cambodia in support of Cambodian ground forces, as well as for other reasons. It was spoken only two months after the American ground troops' military incursion into Cambodia.

Politicians often are forced by circumstances to commit the fallacy of *inconsistency* when, by rising in office, they come to represent different constituencies with different viewpoints. Similarly, they often commit this fallacy in order to "keep up with the times"; what is popular at one time often is unpopular at another.

One of the classic examples of *inconsistency* in an effort to keep up with the times is Lyndon Johnson's changing stance on the Negro and civil rights. As a congressman and for a while as a senator from Texas, he consistently voted and spoke *against* civil rights legislation. But when he became a power in the Senate his tune modified, and as President it changed completely. Here are two quotes which illustrate Johnson's fundamental *inconsistency over time* on the question of race and civil rights legislation. The first statement was made in 1948 at Austin, Texas, when he was running for the Senate:

> *This civil rights program* [part of President Truman's "Fair Deal"], *about which you have heard so much, is a farce and a sham—an effort*

---

[17] The *Boston Record American* used this excerpt from an Agnew speech as a "guest editorial" on August 31, 1970.

to set up a police state in the guise of liberty. I am opposed to that program. I have fought it in Congress. **It is the province of the state to run its own elections.** *I am opposed to the antilynching bill because the federal government has no more business enacting a law against one form of murder than another. I am against the FEPC* [Fair Employment Practices Commission] *because if a man can tell you whom you must hire, he can tell you whom you cannot employ.*

But in 1964 Johnson was President of the United States. He had a larger constituency, and, more importantly, the average American's views on race and civil rights had changed. In that year Congress passed an extremely important civil rights act *at his great urging.* And in 1965 he delivered a famous speech at the predominantly black Howard University, in which he said in part:

> . . . *nothing in any country touches us more profoundly, and nothing is more freighted with meaning for our own destiny than the revolution of the Negro American.*
>
> *In far too many ways American Negroes have been another nation; deprived of freedom, crippled by hatred, the doors of opportunity closed to hope.*
>
> *In our time change has come to this nation, too. The American Negro, acting with impressive restraint, has peacefully protested and marched, entered the courtrooms and the seats of government, demanding a justice that has long been denied. The voice of the Negro was the call to action. But it is a tribute to America that, once aroused, the courts and the Congress, the President and most of the people, have been the allies of progress. . . . we have seen in 1957 and 1960, and again in 1964, the first civil rights legislation in this nation in almost an entire century.*
>
> *As majority leader of the United States Senate, I helped to guide two of these bills through the Senate. And as your President, I was proud to sign the third. And now, very soon* **we will have the fourth— a new law guaranteeing every American the right to vote.**
>
> *No act of my entire administration will give me greater satisfaction than the day when my signature makes this bill, too, the law of this land.*

And on August 6, 1965, he did sign the Voting Rights Act into law. But he did not explain why it was no longer ". . . the province of the state to run its own elections." He did not explain his about-face on questions of race and civil rights legislation.

President Nixon apparently felt forced to do the same sort of thing. Compare some of his typical remarks on Vietnam prior to the 1968 election with those made after he had been elected President.

Prior to the 1968 election:

> The United States cannot afford any more compromises with the Communists, whether called neutralization or something else. [April 2, 1964]

> When you buy peace at any price it is always on the installment plan for another war. [January 29, 1966]

> There is **no reasonable possibility of a negotiated settlement** . . . further discussion of a negotiated settlement delays the end of the war by simply encouraging the enemy that we are begging for peace. [August 7, 1966]

> The North Vietnamese and the Vietcong are not going to change their attitude by virtue of the U.S. protesting for peace . . . the only effective way . . . is to prosecute the war more effectively. [February 5, 1968]

> We have to stop it with victory, or it will start all over again in a few years. [July 1968]

After becoming President of the United States:

> We must recognize that peace in Vietnam cannot be achieved overnight. A war which has raged for so many years will require **detailed negotiations** and cannot be settled at a single stroke.
> . . . I reaffirm now our willingness to withdraw our forces on a specified timetable. We ask only that North Vietnam withdraw its forces from South Vietnam, Cambodia and Laos into North Vietnam, also in accordance with a timetable. [May 14, 1969]

> We will be conciliatory at the conference table, but we will not be humiliated. [April 30, 1970]

E. Laurence Chalmers, Jr., Chancellor of the University of Kansas, was guilty of *inconsistency* in relating two conflicting versions of a particularly important event that occurred on the university's campus in the spring of 1970, after the United States sent ground troops into Cambodia. In an article about nineteen turbulent days on the University of Kansas campus, he wrote:[18]

> *All Thursday afternoon, Thursday evening and early Friday morning the Senate Executive Council met to consider what our actions should be. A group of 200–300 students and non-students waited outside Strong Hall until I went out at 2:00 a.m. to inform them that there would be a convocation at 2:00 p.m. in the Stadium on Friday and that* **a proposal would be brought before all students and faculty members for their consideration**. . . . *Approximately 15,000 students, faculty members, and staff members attended. At least whatever would happen would not occur as a result of a small vociferous minority. I presented the proposal with further clarification. Bill Ebert endorsed it and I called for a standing "Aye" vote.*
>
> *Almost as one, the assembled throng rose and shouted a single word of endorsement, and it was over.*

But two pages later in the same publication we are given the chancellor's account to an alumni group away from the campus:

> Question: . . . *with regard to the other universities mentioned that used the same plan* [the proposal mentioned in the above passage]. *Was the decision to use the plan made by students or administration in each of these schools?*
>
> Chalmers: *It varied.* . . . *At KU, SenEx* [Senate Executive Council—composed of nine members] *is empowered to act for the students and faculty in emergency situations, and that's it.*
>
> *So, in effect, at 2:00 a.m. Friday, we had already determined what the University of Kansas was going to do.*

So much for a proposal that "would be brought before all students and faculty for their consideration."

---

[18] On page 3 of the *Kansas Alumni* (May 30, 1970).

3. False charge of inconsistency

At this point, let's digress for a moment in order to clear up an important point that may be bothering many readers. When a person says one thing at one time and then says it's contradictory later, he is not automatically guilty of the fallacy of *inconsistency;* he may have rational grounds for changing his mind.

Take the person who argues, "I used to believe that women are not as creative as men, because most intellectually productive people have been men; but I've changed my mind because I believe now (as I didn't then) that *environment* (culture, etc.), and not native ability, has been responsible for the preponderance of intellectual men." Surely, he (or she!) cannot be accused of inconsistency, since he (or she) has presented new evidence to explain the change in opinion.

The trouble in the above Johnson and Nixon examples is that neither man ever explained *why* his statements changed from one time to another or even admitted that they *had changed.*

In contrast, consider the charge that the famous philosopher Bertrand Russell was guilty of the fallacy of *inconsistency.* Soon after World War II, he advocated attacking the Soviet Union if the Russians failed to conform to certain standards, and yet in the fifties he supported the "better Red than dead" position.

Russell *would* have been guilty of *inconsistency,* were it not for the fact that he attempted to provide good reasons for his change of mind as to how to deal with the Russians. He felt, and stated, that Russian acquisition of the atomic bomb made all the difference in the world. Before they had the bomb, he believed it to be rational to deal with them in ways that became irrational after they had acquired such great power. Hence, Russell was not guilty of the fallacy of *inconsistency.*

On the contrary, it is his critics who are guilty of employing a fallacy that might as well be called the **false charge of inconsistency**. For it is fallacious to charge an opponent with inconsistency *merely* because he has changed his position.

More recently, Hy Gardner was guilty of a *false charge of inconsistency* in his Sunday magazine question-and-answer column: [19]

[19] "Glad You Asked That," by Hy Gardner, Copyright 1970, Field Enterprises, Inc. Reprinted by permission.

Q. *New York's Mayor Lindsay recently said, "I have unending admiration for the guys who say, 'I simply will not serve in the Army of the U.S. in Vietnam and I am willing to take the consequences for it.'" Wasn't he a conscientious objector during WW II?*

A. *No.* **Lindsay did not practice what he now preaches.** *In WW II as a Navy reserve officer, he won five battle stars in destroyer action in the Mediterranean and the South Pacific.*

But Lindsay was not inconsistent, because he believes (and has given reasons for believing) that the Vietnam war and World War II are very different. On the other hand, Hy Gardner was guilty of a *false charge of inconsistency,* because he criticized Lindsay for not being consistent in his position on two situations which Lindsay has given reasons for believing are not comparable.

(It will become apparent in the next chapter that *false charge of inconsistency* is a subspecies of the fallacy called *straw man* [see p. 33], and in Chapter 3 it will become apparent that Hy Gardner's fallacy might be an example of *questionable classification* [see p. 64].)

Finally, before leaving the topic of consistency and inconsistency, let's dwell for a moment on the fact mentioned above that the fallacy of *inconsistency* is rarely encountered in its purest form. There are many degrees of inconsistency, and many ways in which its occurrence is veiled. Everyday talk is usually not sufficiently precise to enable the listener to say positively that the fallacy has been employed.

In discussing the American effort to put a man on the moon, President Kennedy addressed himself to the question *why* we should engage in such an effort. One of his answers was this:

We have vowed that we shall not see it [space] *governed by a hostile flag of conquest, but by a banner of freedom and peace.*

But in that same speech, as I. F. Stone pointed out, President Kennedy also said:[20]

. . . there is no strife, no prejudice, no national conflict in outer space. . . .

[20] *I. F. Stone's Weekly,* September 24, 1962.

This is *not quite* inconsistent with his first remark. But it comes so close that the two remarks can be considered to be inconsistent for all practical purposes.

Now, how about this one on starvation in Biafra following the Biafran defeat by Nigeria:[21]

> *Doubt is expressed by several experts involved in relief work that the new government of East Central State* [in the region formerly Biafra] *can take on the job* [feeding and medical care of three million war-weakened Ibos—the Ibos being the largest ethnic group in Biafra]. . . .
>
> *Although Biafra's secession came to an end in January and starvation no longer is a serious threat, hardships prevail because many people lack money to feed themselves, the experts say.*

As it stands, there is no inconsistency. But when we add the simple fact that free food was generally unavailable (there were almost no reserves, and, as suggested in the article, relief agencies were not able to feed all of those in need) one does arrive at what is at least close to a contradiction, namely that "starvation no longer is a serious threat" although *sufficient conditions* for starvation existed. A typical messy example from everyday life.

Summary of fallacies discussed in Chapter One

1. **Suppressed evidence**. The omission from an argument of known relevant evidence (or the failure to realize that relevant evidence is being suppressed).

    Example: The failure of Shell Platformate commercials to indicate that all other standard brands of gasoline contain Platformate.

2. **Doubtful evidence**. The use of doubtful or unsupported evidence to reach a conclusion.

    Example: President Nixon's statement that government intelligence had screened more than six tons of captured documents in a few weeks.

[21] *Kansas City Star*, June 28, 1970.

a. **Unknown fact**. The use or acceptance of doubtful evidence about matters of fact.

    Example: Tom Hayden's statement that President Nixon would use nuclear weapons in Vietnam if all else failed to win the war.

b. **Doubtful evaluation**. The use or acceptance of doubtful statements about values.

    Example: Time magazine's unsupported statement that Ramsey Clark's assessment of a racial controversy was "accurate."

c. **Inconsistency.** The use or acceptance of contradictory evidence to support a conclusion. Such evidence may be presented (1) by one person at one time, (2) by one person at different times (without explaining the contradiction as a change of mind and providing evidence to support the change), or (3) by different spokesmen for one institution.

    Example: Lyndon Johnson's stand on racial questions as a candidate for the U.S. Senate and his stand on racial questions as President of the United States.

3. **False charge of inconsistency**. Exactly what the name implies.

    Example: The charge that Bertrand Russell was inconsistent in advocating the use of force against the Russians at one time, while adopting a "better Red than dead" position at another; Russell explained this switch many times as being due to changing circumstances.

Exercise I for Chapter One

Determine which of the fallacies discussed in Chapter One occur in the following passages, and state the reasons for your answers. Although these exercises are taken from larger passages, in answering you are to assume that the larger passages contain no other relevant information. Starred items (*) are answered in Appendix B.

  *1. *President Lyndon Johnson:* The statement of the SEATO [Southeast Asia Treaty Organization] allies that Communist defeat is "essential" is a reality. To fail to respond . . . would reflect on our honor as a nation, would undermine worldwide confidence in our courage, would convince every nation in southeast Asia that it must bow to Communist terms to survive. . . . We seek the full and effective restoration of the international agreements signed in Geneva in 1954, with respect to South Vietnam. . . . We seek no more than a return to the essentials of the agreement of 1954. . . . In the long run there can be no military solution to the problems of Vietnam.

*2. *James J. Kilpatrick (in a political column, September, 1970, which used this statement in drawing further conclusions)*: The schools of his own state [Mississippi] have been subjected to Draconian edicts of the Fifth U.S. Circuit [Court].

*3. *Rowland Evans and Robert Novak (in a political column, August 1970, on Hanoi's opposition to Mideast ceasefire proposals and the Soviet–West Germany treaty; the statement was used later in drawing further conclusions)*: Apart from again revealing their ideological differences with Moscow, the North Vietnamese are venting the morbid premonition in Hanoi that the Kremlin may yet forcibly end the Vietnam war short of total victory.

4. Time *magazine, July 13, 1970 (in a story on President Nixon's white paper on the Cambodian invasion, in which* Time *agreed that Nixon was right to have invaded Cambodia)*: He claimed convincingly that U.S. and South Vietnamese troops had 1) conducted an effective military operation, 2) captured or destroyed a substantial amount of enemy supplies, 3) diminished any immediate threat of a major enemy assault on the Saigon area from sanctuaries in Cambodia and 4) complicated Hanoi's problem of resupplying its troops.

*5. *David Ogilvy in* Confessions of an Advertising Man, *p. 32:* I always showed prospective clients the dramatic improvement that followed when Ogilvy, Benson and Mather took accounts away from old agencies—"in every case we have blazed new trails, and in every case sales have gone up."

6. *David Sanford,* The New Republic, *October 31, 1970:* The Secretary of the Interior recently gave Edgar Speer, president of U.S. Steel, a special "clean-water award," saluting that company's "initiative in pollution abatement" at two of its facilities. . . . No one objects more to air pollution than the presidents of the major polluting companies, . . . Speer thinks in terms of cost/benefit; we ought not to be carried away by the "dictates of emotion." He'd weigh carefully the ratio of fish killed and the cost of cleaning up the fish's habitat in determining whether clean water is worth the price. . . . the U.S. sued U.S. Steel as one of the major polluters.

7. *Political comment:* Liberals have been consistent on Interior Secretary Walter Hickel. They disapproved of his appointment *and* his removal.

8. *Editorial,* Hartford Courant, *September 1, 1970:* The United States Senate is scheduled to vote today on the Hatfield-McGovern amendment that would set a timetable for closing out the war in Vietnam. . . . [The Senate is] being asked . . . to invade the rights and responsibilities of the executive branch of government. Whether the Senate enjoys it or not, the President is the Commander in Chief of armed forces and so designated in the Constitution.

*9. *William S. White in* The Professional: Lyndon B. Johnson, *p. 155 (arguing that Johnson had changed his mind on labor):* . . . in 1935, [Lyndon Johnson] had voted, without a qualm, for the Wagner Act, Labor's Magna Carta. In 1946, while his career in the House was drawing towards its close, he voted, again without a qualm, for the Taft-Hartley Act, sometimes called, though most unfairly so, "the slave labor bill".

10. *William F. Buckley, Jr.,* The Governor Listeth: The Beatles are not merely awful, . . . they are God-awful. They are so unbelievably horrible, so appallingly unmusical, so dogmatically insensitive to the magic of the art, that they qualify as the crowned heads of anti-music. . . .

    Suddenly . . . riding in the back of the car, you look up, startled. That was *music* you just heard, blaring out of the radio. . . . not long after, you hear it again . . . and you realize, finally, that indeed, rock is here to stay.

*11. *Nutrition expert Frederick Stare, answering the charge that dry cereals—Wheaties, Corn Flakes, etc.—are not sufficiently nutritious* (New York Daily News, *August 5, 1970*): Stare said cereals with milk "provide approximately the same amount of protein and calories as a bacon-and-eggs breakfast." And they also provide substantially more calcium, riboflavin, niacin, thiamin, and iron and substantially less saturated fat. . . . Popeye's spinach doesn't begin to compare with the over-all nutritional worth of breakfast cereal—any cereal. . . .

12. New Britain [*Connecticut*] Herald, *October 15, 1970:* Manchester Mayor Nathan Agostinelli . . . seized a demonstrator's flag Monday when President Nixon was in Hartford and stomped on it. Nixon, according to published reports, sought Agostinelli out and praised him for his actions.

13. *Editorial,* Hartford Times, *September 11, 1970, on the topic of an extra twenty minutes of school time for teachers; the extra*

time was objected to by the teacher's union: Insisting that teachers be in school [twenty minutes] longer than children may seem to some teachers like a factory time-clock operation, but it probably troubles the conscientious teacher far less than those who regularly leave school at the final bell.

*14. *AP report, October 24, 1970, of a Nixon speech before the United Nations:* "I invite the leaders of the Soviet Union to join us in taking that new road; to join in a peaceful competition, not in the accumulation of arms but in the dissemination of progress; not in the building of missiles but in waging a winning war against hunger and disease and human misery in our own countries and around the globe." . . . The President presumably had delivered a similar message to the Soviet foreign affairs chief. . . .

15. *Testimony before the Senate Foreign Relations Committee, November 24, 1970, and reported in* I. F. Stone's Bi-Weekly, *December 14, 1970:*

Senator Church: What do you expect the bombing will accomplish?

Secretary Laird: The bombing, I think, will stop the violation of these understandings [that the United States could fly unarmed reconnaissance planes over North Vietnam unmolested].

Church: Has the bombing in the past ever caused the enemy to acquiesce in our demands or to make concessions?

Laird: Yes it has.

Church: It has? When did it have that effect in the past?

Laird: Well, the last protective reaction flight [i.e., bombing] that was flown in the North was in May, and after that strike there was an indication by the other side that they would abide by those understandings, and they did until the month of November when they shot down an unarmed reconnaissance plane. . . .

Church: Was this the only attack upon a reconnaissance plane that occurred or were there a series of attacks on reconnaissance planes?

Laird: We had attacks upon our planes, Senator Church. But this was the first plane shot down.

16. *Joseph Alsop,* Hartford Courant, *September 24, 1970:* In Illinois, . . . Adlai Stevenson III . . . in 1968 . . . described the Chicago police as "Storm troopers in blue." . . . Stevenson named former U.S. attorney Thomas Foran, the prosecutor of the "Chicago Seven" as vice chairman of his campaign for the

Senate. . . . The Rev. Joseph Duffey [running for the Senate in Connecticut] . . . told the English reporters of "An American Melodrama" that "I guess you could call me a revisionist-Marxist." For Duffey, . . . civil disobedience was also a useful tool of social change.

17. *Editorial,* New Britain [*Connecticut*] Herald, *September 10, 1970:* [Highjackings] wouldn't be justified even though the cause might be the finest, the highest, the most moral. And that is because the hijackings are violence, the kind of violence that represents a throwback to barbarian behavior.

18. *Naval Investigative Service directive, reported by AP, January 3, 1971:* A Naval Investigative Service office will not initiate any investigation . . . when the prediction [predication? provocation?] for the investigation is mere expression of views in opposition to official U.S. policy. . . . Nothing herein is intended to inhibit or preclude normal reporting of information . . . on those individuals whose expressed controversial views may be adjudged to have a potential for embarrassment to the Department of the Navy.

Exercise II for Chapter One

Find examples in the mass media (newspapers, magazines, radio, and TV) of fallacies discussed in Chapter One, and explain why they are fallacious.

Chapter Two

Fallacious Because Invalid—I

It don't even make good nonsense.

Davy Crockett, *remarking on a statement by President Andrew Jackson*

We now turn to a discussion of arguments that are *fallacious because invalid*. This is a vast category; almost a hundred species are distinguished in recent literature on the subject. In this chapter and the next, sixteen of the more important of these will be considered.[1]

1. Ad hominem
(argument to the man)

The fallacy of **ad hominem** argument, often called the **genetic fallacy**, consists in an attack on the man argued against, rather than on his argument.

Senator Jennings Randolph, in a United States Senate debate on a proposed constitutional amendment requiring equal protection of the law without regard to sex (August 26, 1970), committed this fallacy when he dismissed women's liberationists, and thus their arguments, with the remark that women's liberationists constituted a "small band of bra-less bubbleheads." This line may have been good for a laugh in the almost all-male Senate, but it was irrelevant to arguments the women's lib representatives had presented. Randolph attacked *them* (through ridicule) rather than their arguments.

---

[1] Most of those omitted are just minor variations or occur only infrequently in everyday life. Their omission thus constitutes no great loss.

Al Capp, the creator of Li'l Abner, is a frequent user of ridicule, and thus of *ad hominem* argument. Students leaving in protest during one of his addresses once prompted Capp to remark:[2]

> *Hey! Don't go! I need an animal act! You with the beard! Why don't you walk on water?*

In ridiculing women's liberationists as "bra-less bubbleheads," Senator Randolph resorted to namecalling, on a rather low level. But *ad hominem* namecalling need not be so crude. Here is an example with a good deal of literary merit, representing Vice President Spiro T. Agnew at his very best:[3]

> *A spirit of national masochism prevails, encouraged by an* **effete corps of impudent snobs** *who characterize themselves as intellectuals.*

The examples of *ad hominem* argument given so far are clearly fallacious. But *ad hominem* arguments are not always fallacious. In a courtroom, faced with conflicting testimony from witnesses *A* and *B,* convincing testimony that *A* is a liar often does constitute good grounds for rejecting *A*'s testimony in favor of *B*'s.

It often is quite hard to decide whether an attack on a man is fallacious or not. In particular, we need to assess the *relevance* of the attack to the issue at hand.

In the courtroom example, a man's being a liar is a relevant character defect because it bears directly on the reliability of his testimony. But evidence that a witness is a miserly millionaire who refuses to aid his starving mother, while equally derogatory, is not relevant to the veracity of his testimony. In the former case, we may be justified in rejecting a man's testimony; in the latter we probably are not.

But the problem is even more complex than this. A man who is known to be a liar is not thereby completely untrustworthy. Rare indeed is the man who cannot be counted on to tell the truth in some cases. So sometimes the evidence that a man frequently lies is overruled by more specific evidence indicating that his testimony *in this case* is likely to be reliable.

A known liar testifying in a particularly gruesome and horrible murder case may well be a reliable witness, because the crime no doubt horrifies

---

[2] Reported in the *Hartford Courant,* September 6, 1970.

[3] From a speech delivered in New Orleans, October 19, 1969.

him as much as it does anyone else. Similarly, most petty liars would be reliable testifying, say, about an attempt to assassinate a president of the United States, if for no other reason than the awe in which that office is held. But a pathological liar, for instance one who seeks notoriety, would probably not be a reliable witness even in an assassination trial.

Nevertheless, in the vast majority of cases, attacks on a man rather than on what he says are fallacious. And such attacks can be rather subtle. Here is *Time* magazine on Yale Chaplain William Sloan Coffin, Jr., and the New Haven Black Panther murder trial:[4]

> *The climate was such that Yale Chaplain William Sloan Coffin, Jr., saw no unreason in characterizing the murder trial as "legally right but morally wrong." . . . How to explain such logic? The answer is that the New Haven Panthers have ample white guilt going for them at Yale.*

Time's argument was *ad hominem* because it attacked Coffin himself, through his motives, and not his argument. *Time* gave a *psychological motive* (white guilt) for Coffin's alleged error in reasoning, rather than an argument to demonstrate that he in fact reasoned incorrectly. Even supposing *Time* was correct in saying that a motive of white guilt was at work, what is wrong with Coffin's idea that the murder trial was "legally right but morally wrong"? *Time* erred in failing to answer that question, thus failing to support its implication that the statement is illogical.

One of the more important variations on *ad hominem* argument is **guilt by association**. Many people believe that a man is to be judged by the company he keeps. But many also hold that you shouldn't judge a man by his associates, any more than you judge a book by its cover. Which view is correct?

The answer is that it *is* rational under certain circumstances to judge a man by his associates. However, only rarely will such a judgment have a *high degree of probability* attached to it.[5] In the absence of other evidence, a man frequently seen in the company of different women known to be prostitutes is rightly suspected of being connected with their occupation in a way which casts doubt on his moral character. Similarly, a man who is discovered to associate frequently and closely with several men known

---

[4] *Time,* May 4, 1970, p. 59.
[5] Degrees of probability are discussed further in Appendix A.

to be agents of a foreign government is rightly *suspected* of being an agent of that government himself.

But we always must be cautious in the use of evidence of this kind. For it is *indirect;* it is *circumstantial.* Its best use is as evidence leading to further investigation, not as evidence leading to firm conviction. *Direct* evidence almost always is preferable and almost always takes precedence. The man who frequently associates with prostitutes *may* on investigation turn out to be conducting a sociological investigation or even to be a minister shepherding his flock. The close associate of spies may be a counterspy or an innocent cover being taken advantage of by his "friends."

Nevertheless, when judgments must be made solely on the basis of indirect evidence, as they sometimes must, it may be reasonable to judge on the basis of a man's associates.[6]

The trouble is that indirect evidence of this kind is misused much more often than it is used correctly. We all are familiar, if we will think for a moment, with cases in which the indirect evidence of a person's associates and habits has been used to damn him, although contradictory direct evidence was either already in hand or was easily obtainable.

This is true in particular in politics, where the "guilty" association can be quite remote. An example is the tactic employed by Connecticut Republican State Chairman Howard E. Hausman against the 1970 Democratic candidate for the United States Senate, Rev. Joseph Duffey.[7] Hausman questioned Duffey's patriotism on the grounds that Duffey associated with Georgia State Representative Julian Bond, who was quoted as saying that patriotism is a "stupid idea." What Bond had said was this:

We must reject this stupid idea of patriotism that has made us first in war, last in peace and last in the hearts of our countrymen.

[6] This fact generates important moral and political problems. It often is true that in the absence of direct evidence a man's qualifications for obtaining insurance, being hired for a job, etc., are most rationally judged on the basis of indirect statistical evidence. Thus, insurance companies may refuse to insure Negroes who live in the black ghettos of large cities, or they may charge them much higher rates, on the grounds that statistically the risk is higher in such cases. The same is true with respect to auto insurance for single males under twenty-five years of age. But, although it is *rational* to assume the risk is higher, there is a question as to the *morality,* or at least the political advisability, of permitting actions on the basis of such rational assumptions. For actions based on gross statistical classifications of this kind inevitably are unfair to those who most deserve fair treatment. An example is the Negro who is denied insurance simply because he resides in a certain area, but who happens to be a reliable person trying desperately to overcome environmental and social handicaps. By acting on indirect statistical evidence, the insurer does him an injustice and helps to perpetuate the conditions which produced the statistics in the first place.

[7] Reported in the *New Britain* [Connecticut] *Herald,* September 10, 1970, p. 4.

Said Hausman:

> *I can't believe that the people of Connecticut want as their next U.S. Senator a man who is associated with the view that patriotism is stupid.*

Overlooking the fact that Bond's statement is *ambiguous* and could be interpreted to mean that *certain kinds* of patriotism are stupid but that others perhaps are not, Hausman still is guilty of the fallacy of falsely charging *guilt by association*.

First, such *indirect* evidence carries little weight in cases where direct evidence is available, and much direct evidence was available indicating candidate Duffey was as patriotic as the next man.

And second, the charge constituted a particularly nasty form of *guilt by association* in which the opinion of a man's *casual* associate was judged to be his opinion. Duffey's reply to Hausman, although exaggerated, had a kernel of truth in it:

> *He's holding me responsible for everything said by anybody I ever associated with.*

2. Two wrongs make a right

Just as it is almost second nature for politicians to attack their opponents by means of *ad hominem* argument, so also it is natural for them to defend themselves against the charges of others by use of the fallacious idea that **two wrongs make a right**. The erroneous rationale behind this fallacy is that if the "other side" does it, or some other evil, then it's all right if I do it.

Here is a rather mild though otherwise typical example. It concerns the apparent difficulty the two major political parties had in finding qualified black lawyers to serve as judges in the South:[8]

> *Georgia Republicans say they don't know of a single black Republican lawyer who could be appointed to a judgeship. They add smugly that*

[8] Reported in the *New Republic* article "Picking Judges in Georgia," August 15, 1970.

if the Democrats couldn't find a Negro judge in all those years, how can anybody expect the Republicans to find one now?

The fallacy here is setting up the Democrats as a standard of conduct. Past Democratic errors in no way justify current Republican errors. Two wrongs simply do *not* make a right.

An Associated Press dispatch which attempted to explain the atmosphere in Vietnam prior to the American massacre of civilians at My Lai 4 contained a more subtle version of *two wrongs make a right:*[9]

In Vietnam the killing of civilians was a practice established by the Viet Cong as a major part of the war long before the first U.S. ground troops were committed in March, 1965.

distortion! - used above example possibly out of context.

The implication is that if *they* do it, then it's all right if we do it.

When we stop and *think,* the fallacious nature of such an implication is clear. But in daily life it often doesn't strike us as fallacious, in particular when we seem to be giving "them" back nothing but a taste of their own medicine.

But the taste-of-their-own-medicine attitude in these cases is misguided. This would be true even if there were something to the "eye for an eye and tooth for a tooth" version of justice, a conception of justice many rational men reject. The babies killed at My Lai, for example, could not have been the Viet Cong who murdered civilian Vietnamese. The fact that some Viet Cong have engaged in civilian murder cannot possibly justify our doing the same thing. We are not less evil by being copycats.

Ladislow Dobor, leader of the Brazilian Popular Revolutionary Vanguard was guilty of the fallacy of *two wrongs make a right* in his statement concerning the Vanguard's kidnapping of foreign diplomats in Brazil to barter for the release of political prisoners from jail:[10]

We see nothing "unfair" in kidnapping an "innocent person," since the authorities arrest not only revolutionaries but many ordinary people as well.

[9] Quoted in *My Lai 4: a Report on the Massacre and Its Aftermath,* by Seymour M. Hersh, Random House, New York, 1970.

[10] Reported in *Ramparts* magazine, October 1970.

But the fact that the Brazilian government has engaged in immoral acts does not justify their revolutionary opponents in doing so. This is a typical example of *two wrongs make a right*.

One of the more interesting varieties of the fallacy *two wrongs make a right* is called **common practice**. This fallacy occurs when the appeal is not just to the practice of one's opponents but to the practice of large numbers of people.

Big businessmen are guilty of this fallacy when they attempt to justify salaries of over $100,000 per year on the grounds that almost all top executives of large firms are paid such princely sums. So are college professors when they attempt to justify their use of departmental secretaries for private correspondence by pointing out that their colleagues do the same thing.[11]

Common practice was appealed to by Shell Oil executives when Shell was charged with misleading advertising in its Platformate advertisements (discussed in Chapter One). Said a Shell spokesman:[12]

> *That same comment could be made about most good advertising of most products. All our campaign is saying is that Super Shell is designed to give you good mileage. . . . Of course, Platformate is nothing new. . . . We never claimed that Platformate was an exclusive ingredient.*

True, they just misleadingly implied it. But you can't justify littering the airwaves with misleading implications by appeal to *common practice* any more than you could so justify littering the highways.

3. Straw man

The fallacy of the **straw man** consists in attacking (or defending) a position similar to but different from the one your opponent holds (or attacks).

---

[11] This demonstrates that college professors and businessmen are guilty of the same kind of fallacy but obviously not that their "crimes" are equally serious, any more than a workman's theft of a hammer would rival the theft of millions by General Electric executives in the famous price-fixing conspiracy.

[12] Quoted in the excellent book on advertising, *The Permissible Lie,* by Sam Sinclair Baker, World Publishing Co., Cleveland and New York, 1968, p. 39.

Here is an example from a speech by Vice President Spiro Agnew (on a Western congressional campaign trip during 1970) in which the *straw man* was manufactured out of thin air:[13]

> *The issue* [in the November elections] *is whether a free people operating under a free and representative system of government will continue to govern the United States, or whether they will cede that power to some of the people—the irresponsible people, the lawbreakers on the streets and campuses and their followers, their sycophants, and the people who subscribe to their activities behind the scenes, the radical liberals.*

The issue Agnew raised was a straw one. There was not the slightest chance that Agnew's "radical liberals" would be ceded power via the 1970 elections for the United States Senate and House.

Now, let's hear Al Capp on Mayor John Lindsay's remark about serving in the Army. Capp quotes Lindsay as saying:[14]

> *The Americans I have unending admiration for are the guys who say, I simply will not serve in the Army of the United States and I am willing to take the consequences. Those are the guys who are heroic.*

Capp then remarks:

> *And so, if Lindsay is elected, his first act as commander-in-chief will, no doubt, be to withdraw the Army from everywhere. . . .*

This illustrates the fallacy of the *straw man* because, as Capp knew very well, Lindsay was referring to service in *Vietnam;* he was not advocating pacifism in general. (Incidentally, compare Al Capp's version of what Lindsay said with the one from Hy Gardner's column cited in Chapter One. Notice the crucial words "in Vietnam" that do not appear in Capp's version.)

[13] The *New York Daily News* used this speech as a "Guest Editorial" on September 12, 1970.

[14] See his column, "Al Capp Here," *New York Sunday News,* August 30, 1970, p. C23.

Finally, here is an example of the perpetration of *straw man* whose success was very quickly and visibly evident. After President Nixon sent ground troops into Cambodia in June 1970, touching off a great deal of unrest throughout the country, Princeton University adopted a plan whereby the university would schedule no classes for a short period prior to the November 1970 elections, thus enabling students to campaign for political candidates if they wished. For a while it looked as though the Princeton plan would spread to many other campuses around the country.

But then Senator Strom Thurmond of South Carolina entered the picture. He attacked the plan and asked the Internal Revenue Service to determine how the plan would affect the tax-exempt status of educational institutions which adopted it.

The result was much agitation and, finally, a report by the American Council of Education which was sent to member institutions around the country warning colleges to be careful about campus political activity which might lose them their tax-exempt status. The report warned colleges against any ". . . political campaign on behalf of any candidate for public office" and stated that a person making a gift to a college would not be allowed a tax deduction if the college violated I.R.S. rules.[15]

All of this made college administrators think twice; very few colleges adopted the Princeton plan. The University of Kansas was one of the schools that did not adopt it (although the plan had quite a bit of support on the K.U. campus), and Thurmond's *straw man* seems to have played an important role. The *Lawrence* [Kansas] *Daily Journal World,* June 22, 1970, after quoting K.U.'s Chancellor E. Laurence Chalmers, Jr., to the effect that K.U. would not give time off for political campaigning in the fall, reported that the Kansas Board of Regents had adopted "with the unanimous approval of the chief administrators of the schools" a policy requiring Board approval of all state college calendar changes. This policy, said the *Journal World,* ". . . is designed to protect the tax-exempt status of the institutions, and that status would be jeopardized by partisan political activity."

This incident illustrates an extremely common use of *straw man* in political infighting. Internal Revenue Service regulations prohibit tax-exempt institutions from engaging in *partisan political activity*. But Senator Thurmond knew, or should have known, that adoption of the Princeton plan could in no sense be considered *partisan* political activity by a college or university. Nevertheless, as he characterized the plan (his *straw* plan), there *was* danger of loss of tax-exemption. This fact came out in the AP

---

[15] The American Council on Education report received wide press coverage. See, for example, the AP story printed in the *Kansas City Star* on June 21, 1970.

article titled "Warning to Colleges" which appeared in the *Kansas City Star* on June 21, 1970:

> *A project linked with Princeton University* **to help elect doves and defeat hawks in Congress** *was attacked last month by Senator Strom Thurmond (R.-S.C.). The senator said he would ask the Treasury to investigate.*

The result was that colleges across the country reacted to the Princeton plan as though it really were a college project "to help elect doves and defeat hawks" and thus really did constitute a threat to their tax-exempt status.[16] They reacted to Thurmond's *straw man,* not to the true Princeton plan.

4. Distortion

The fallacy of the *straw man* often is perpetrated by distorting the argument of one's opponent and then attacking that *distorted* version. But **distortion** is used in other ways and so deserves to be classified as a separate fallacy.

Of course, *distortion* itself is not necessarily bad or fallacious. In the form of *exaggeration,* for instance, it is a time-honored literary device used by most great writers at some time or other with great satirical or poetic effect.

Great satirists, such as Jonathan Swift, have used exaggeration in order to shock people into seeing what they take to be man's true nature. Similarly, they have used these devices in an attempt to reduce that strange gap in most of us between mere belief and belief which serves as an impetus to action.

But devices that can be put to good uses can generally be put to bad ones as well; thus we have the fallacy of *distortion.*

Let's start with a rather obvious (once it is pointed out) and fairly innocuous example:[17]

---

[16] The more cynically inclined suspected at the time that worried administrators seized on Thurmond's straw as a welcome excuse for not adopting a plan which was sure to further anger already quite angry taxpayers and alumni.

[17] From *New Republic* article, by Les L. Gapay, September 12, 1970, p. 10.

> [Congressman] *William H. Natcher of Kentucky, highwayman of the District of Columbia,* **who wants to cover all of Washington with pavement,** . . .

In other words, he wanted to build more highways in the nation's capital than did the writer.

Distortion can be accomplished quite easily, with just a single word or perhaps a short phrase. That is one reason why it often slips by unnoticed. Here is an example:[18]

> *Since the beginning of a* **massive** *airlift on January 23, the United States has flown 113 jeeps and trucks to Nigeria.*

The airlift was intended to aid in overcoming what truly was *massive* starvation following the collapse of the Biafran attempt to gain independence from Nigeria. Those threatened with starvation numbered in the *millions.* So the 113 airlifted jeeps and trucks could hardly be said to represent a *massive* airlift in comparison, for instance, with the amount of material flown into Berlin *every day for months* during the Russian blockade of Berlin in 1948. The word "massive" was used to exaggerate the importance of what was in fact a miniscule effort to reduce Biafran deaths by starvation.[19]

Here is another example of *exaggeration* doing its work by means of one word:[20]

---

[18] From the *New York Times,* February 15, 1970, p. 10.

[19] This example also beautifully illustrates the fallacy of *inconsistency* (between words and actions) discussed in Chapter One. On September 10, 1968, prior to his election, the then presidential candidate Richard Nixon issued a statement on the Biafran war which contained the following remarks: "This is not the time to stand on ceremony or to 'go through channels' or to observe the diplomatic niceties. . . . The time is long past for the wringing of hands about what is going on." Compare this with his *actions* after becoming president in January 1969, and during the long year in which hundreds of thousands starved to death prior to Biafran defeat in January 1970. Compare it also with the "massive" aid President Nixon sent to Nigeria after the Biafran capitulation, when he did "go through channels" and did "observe the diplomatic niceties" to the point that our aid was relatively ineffective.

[20] Quoted from *News and Views,* a publication of the Capital Federal Savings and Loan Assn., Summer 1970, from the column, "Across the Chairman's Desk," by Henry A. Bubb.

For several years a small percentage of our population [the context makes it clear that the writer has in mind chiefly campus dissidents] *has tried to persuade us that* **everything** *we believe in,* **everything** *we have done in the past, and* **everything** *we plan to do in the future is wrong.*

It is true that many students at the time did in fact believe that a great deal of what Americans believe in, have done, and plan to do in the future is wrong. But by using the word "everything" the writer of this passage falsified by *exaggeration* (something he ought to have been aware of, since he is a Regent of the University of Kansas).

Finally, an example using just two words to accomplish its deception. Here is Tom Hayden on Vietnam:[21]

The U.S. government already has demonstrated its willingness to attempt **subtle genocide** *in Vietnam under the pretense of waging a "war of attrition."*

This must be a gross distortion; otherwise the United States soldiers then in Vietnam must have been the worst bunglers in history. How could we have been engaged in genocide in Vietnam, subtle or otherwise, during a period in which the total Vietnamese population increased?

5. False dilemma

The fallacy of **false dilemma** occurs when the number of possible positions or alternatives with respect to some question is erroneously reduced. Usually the improper reduction is to just two alternatives (which accounts for the name **black and white** often given to this fallacy).

Here is a newspaper editorial which manages to be guilty of *false dilemma* and one other fallacy in near-record time:[22]

---

[21] In his article "All for Vietnam," *Ramparts,* September 1970, p. 27.

[22] *Lawrence* [Kansas] *Daily Journal World,* June 25, 1970. Reprinted with permission.

Alternative?

One suggestion to those who don't care much for policemen is that the next time they get in trouble, call a hippie!

The writer of this editorial is guilty of the fallacy of the *false dilemma,* because he implies that those who don't care much for policemen (exactly which policemen is left vague) have as their alternative *no policemen whatever* (that is the implication of the phrase "call a hippie"). Clearly, there are many other alternatives, many other police models. London bobbies, who ordinarily carry no weapons, are an example.

False dilemma frequently occurs in conjunction with other fallacies which help set up the false alternative. The hippie-policeman editorial is an example since it also argues against a *straw man.* Lawrence residents who didn't care much for local policemen certainly did not advocate having *no* police whatever; they simply wanted a different kind of policeman (less likely to shoot to kill, for instance). Hence the "no police" position constitutes a *straw man.*

In an interesting article Frank Baldwin argued against a "Korean"-type "solution" to the Vietnam problem. (By a Korean-type solution he meant roughly one in which the division between North and South would be retained and the border between the two guarded on the south by South Vietnamese and a few American troops.) But he then went on to conclude:[23]

The Korean experience indicates that there is no "Korean Solution" for Indochina, **only an American solution: swift and irrevocable curtailment of American involvement.**

This is fallacious because he offered no arguments in favor of "swift . . . curtailment of American involvement," [24] and (what is to the point here) he never tried to prove that his "American solution" was the only alternative to a "Korean solution."

---

[23] "A 'Korean Solution' for Vietnam?," *New Republic,* July 18, 1970.

[24] Thus making him guilty of the fallacy of *begging the question,* to be discussed shortly.

The oversimplification inherent in *false dilemma* is a stock-in-trade of most politicians. One of the recent masters of the art is Richard Nixon. His tendency to think in terms of opposites, a natural for *false dilemma,* has been pointed out many times. Here is an example from a Nixon speech on welfare:[25]

> *After a third of a century of power floating from the people and from the states to Washington it is time for a new federalism in which power, funds and responsibility will flow from Washington to the states and to the people.*

Nixon thus overlooked the vast middle ground between the two extremes in which it is overwhelmingly likely the best solution lies. Commented Hinds and Smith: "A reasonable position would suggest that any brand of federalism demands that power, money and responsibility be shared. The situation simply cannot be totally one way or the other." Some power should flow one way, and some the other way, with the balance differing from case to case. (Incidentally, Nixon's characterization of the past third of a century is so oversimplified that it amounts to nothing better than a caricature of the truth. In addition, he failed to mention that for almost one fourth of that third of a century, he was vice president under Eisenhower, a president with whom he professed to agree on all basic issues.)

6.   Tokenism

When action is clearly called for but is politically inexpedient, politicians frequently turn to **tokenism**. That is, they make a token gesture (do a very little of what is required) and then shout about it as loudly as they can.

On May 31, 1970, an earthquake in Peru killed about 50,000 people, and left an emergency in its wake of major proportions. (It is unlikely that that many people have been killed in the United States in all the earthquakes, hurricanes, and tornadoes combined over the last 100 years.) Relief aid was desperately needed by the Peruvians. The American response was a trip to Peru by Mrs. Nixon (widely publicized—a picture of Mrs. Nixon hugging a little earthquake victim appeared on page one in many newspapers around the country). But very little effective aid ever

[25] See the article "Nixspeak: Rhetoric of Opposites," *The Nation,* February 16, 1970, by Lynn Hinds and Carolyn Smith.

reached Peru from the United States.[26] Clearly, our hearts weren't really in the relief venture; the American efforts were only a *token gesture,* designed to pacify the few in the United States who wanted to aid the Peruvians.

The American relief efforts in Biafra, both during and after the Nigerian war, also exhibited this kind of *tokenism.*[27] In this case, the American government, under both Johnson and Nixon, seemed perfectly willing to relieve the mass starvation in Biafra, but was unwilling to do so against Nigerian objections and unwilling to exert the pressure necessary to change the Nigerian government's position on relief aid. So the government did the "natural" thing, and gave token aid to the church groups, UNICEF, and the Red Cross, the agencies attempting to get food into blockaded Biafra.[28] After the war, the American government channelled its "massive" aid (recall the fallacy of *exaggeration*) of 113 jeeps and trucks through the Nigerian government itself, even though there was little reason to think that very many of these vehicles would ever reach the eastern part of Nigeria (the former Biafra) and actually be used in the crucial relief efforts in the first month or so after the war ended. (Very few ever were so used.)

The fallacy involved in *tokenism* is this: if you mistake the token gesture for the genuine article, you commit a fallacy. Judging from the lack of complaints from Americans after Mrs. Nixon's visit to Peru, for example, it is reasonable to assume that a great many Americans committed this fallacy at that time.

Professional politicians are not the only ones who attempt to mislead via *tokenism.* Ralph Nader has pointed out that Consolidated Edison of New York paid its board chairman more in one year than it spent on pollution control in five (this was roughly during the period 1965–1970). At the same time, General Motors spent about ten times more on advertising per year than it did on air pollution research. Its pollution research budget was around 0.1% of its gross annual sales.

---

[26] See, for instance, the article by Roger Glass in the *New Republic,* September 19, 1970.

[27] To get an idea of the size of this catastrophe, consider the estimates by most experts who were there during the worst starvation that *at least* a million of the thirteen million or so Biafrans starved to death in a two-to-three-year span.

[28] The fact that this token American aid did save thousands of lives, even if only temporarily, is irrelevant to the charge of *tokenism,* in view of the grisly grand total of over a million deaths by starvation.

The token nature of big business and government actions frequently is masked in large-sounding figures. The average American cannot hope to earn a million dollars in an entire lifetime. So when he hears that a large corporation will spend $20,000,000 on anti-pollution efforts, he is impressed with the apparent size of the venture. He may not notice that the amount is to be spent over a period of years. And he forgets, if he ever knew, that the corporation has yearly sales in the billions, and spends millions per year just on the corporate image. (Indeed, much spending on pollution during the period 1968–70 looked suspiciously like image-building, given the immense fanfare which accompanied each project and the widespread use of anti-pollution as a theme in institutional advertising.) The average American forgets also that the federal government's budget now is measured in the hundreds of billions of dollars per year.

7. Begging the question

When arguing, it is impossible to provide reasons for every assertion. Some of what we say or do must go unjustified, at least for the moment. But if, in the course of an argument, we endorse without proof some form of the very question at issue, we are guilty of the fallacy generally called **begging the question**. This fallacy is much more common than might be supposed; in particular the radical left and right seem prone to it. Here is an example from the left:[29]

> [Richard Pough, President of the Open Space Institute] . . . *was asked what he would have said to a British scientist who pooh-poohed concern over DDT in a recent TV debate* [by saying] *"Why should we care about the state of penguin fat?"*
>
> *With soft anger, Pough said he would have reminded the scientist that DDT is in us too.*
>
> *In contrast, ... a young marine biologist from Columbia, a student participant in the DDT debate, . . . [said of] the British scientist [, . . . he] "shouldn't be in a position of power and influence."*
> *Another generation. Another answer.*

True. But which answer exhibits better logic? Mr. Pough's, because his answer does not *beg the question*.

[29] From an article in the *Village Voice*, July 30, 1970, by Anna Mayo.

Question-begging occurs frequently in disputes between partisans of extremely different positions. Thus, the rejoinder "But that amounts to socialism!" often is heard in disputes over public medical care, even though the other side is perfectly aware of this fact and may even be attracted to the proposal precisely because it *is* socialistic.

Similarly, so-called "black militants" frequently speak (without proof) of the "oppression" of blacks when arguing with whites who deny that blacks still are oppressed in the United States.

To avoid *begging the question,* the anti-socialist must present *reasons* for rejecting anything that smacks of socialism, and the black militant must present evidence of actual cases of current oppression of blacks in the United States. Otherwise, they beg the underlying issues in their disputes and are less likely to convince their opponents.

The DDT example illustrates question-begging on the left. But "establishment" types argue by means of begged questions too. Almost every political speaker, of whatever stripe, is guilty of at least minor instances of question-begging. Spiro Agnew's speeches are a case in point. Here is an example from a speech on radicals and violence given on May 2, 1969, a time of great campus unrest and some violence over civil rights, Vietnam, and other problems of the times:

> . . . *Aside from self-claimed romantic charisma, the radicals' appeal is highly suspect* **in a democracy which responds to the electorate's demands**.

But his radical opponents were vehement in denying that *our* democracy at that time responded to the electorate's demands, exactly the justification they gave for their radical actions.

Summary of fallacies discussed in Chapter Two

1. **Ad hominem**. Attacking the arguer rather than the argument.
    Example: Senator Randolph's dismissing women's liberationists as "a small band of bra-less bubbleheads."

    a. **Guilt by association**. Unfairly judging a man by the company he keeps.

Example: Judging senatorial candidate Duffey to be unpatriotic because of something a casual political acquaintance said about patriotism.

2. **Two wrongs make a right**. Just what the name implies.
    Example: The AP report which implied that, since the Viet Cong killed civilians in South Vietnam, it wasn't so bad that we did too.

    a. **Common practice**. It's not wrong, or at least it's excusable, because it is commonly done.
        Example: Justification of huge salaries on the grounds that just about all top business executives are paid a great deal of money.

3. **Straw man**. Attacking a position similar to but significantly different from your opponent's position.
    Example: Senator Thurmond's attack on the so-called Princeton plan as a project "to help elect doves and defeat hawks in Congress."

4. **Distortion**. Distorting an opponent's position.
    Example: Tom Hayden's claim that the United States was engaged in subtle genocide in Vietnam.

    a. **Exaggeration**. Distortion by exaggeration.
        Example: Characterizing the sending of 113 jeeps and trucks to Nigeria as a "massive airlift."

5. **False dilemma**. Erroneous reduction of alternatives or possibilities, usually a reduction to just two.
    Example: The editorial which implied that the public had a choice between only two alternatives: police as they are and hippies (that is, no police whatever).

6. **Tokenism**. Mistaking a token gesture, usually ineffective, for an adequate effort.
    Example: General Motors' spending 0.1% of its gross annual sales on air pollution research.

7. **Begging the question**. Failure to support the very question at issue.
    Example: The student's response to the scientist's lack of worry about the harmful effects of DDT: "[He] shouldn't be in a position of power and influence."

Exercise I for Chapter Two

Determine which fallacies occur in the following passages, and state the reasons for your answers.

*1. *New Jersey State Attorney George F. Kugler, Jr.* (New York Times, *August 17, 1970*): "I'm not saying there are no abuses." . . . but [he] added that the problem of obtaining justice for poor persons was a problem everywhere in the U.S.

*2. *Evans & Novak column:* More serious, however, was [University of Michigan President Robben] Fleming's acceptance of a 10 per cent Negro enrollment goal, the major demand of the March student strike. Substantive arguments against the 10 per cent quota . . . are formidable. To raise black enrollment from the present 3.5 per cent would leave precious little in scholarship funds for poor white students.

*3. *Les L. Gapay, The* New Republic, *September 12, 1970 (in an article unfriendly to McCormack):* [U.S. House of Representatives] Speaker John McCormack, who retires at the end of this session, slouched in a seat on the floor. He will be the last Speaker of the House who did not attend high school.

4. People who live in glass houses shouldn't throw stones.

*5. *Column by James J. Kilpatrick, September 1970:* . . . A revulsion against the temporary may create a vast market for things that endure. A society gorged upon sex may rediscover love.

6. a. *Spiro Agnew, Cleveland, Ohio, June 20, 1970*: We are not going to heed the counsel of the Harrimans and Vances and Cliffords, whom history has branded as failures. . . .

   b. *Lawrence O'Brien, Democratic National Chairman, Washington, D.C., reply to the above:* You'd think that of all people, Mr. Agnew would know the difference between a donkey and an ass.

*7. *AP story,* New Haven Register, *August 21, 1970:* He [Senator Sam Ervin, Democrat of North Carolina] said the . . . [constitutional amendment guaranteeing equal rights for women] approved in the House 350–15 last week could abolish all federal and state laws making distinctions between men and women —even if it meant ending necessary legal protection.

8. *TV interviewer:* What makes you think 18-year-olds are
qualified to vote?

    Eighteen-year-old: Have you looked lately at the hacks
adults have voted into office? How could we do worse than that?

9. *Oliver Wendell Holmes:* The life of the law has not been logic;
it has been experience.

10. *House Appropriations hearings on the 1971 supplemental, pp.*
609–610, released December 8, 1970. Reported in I. F. Stone's
Bi-Weekly, *December 28, 1970:*

    Congressman Frank T. Bow, Republican, Ohio: How did
this so-called leak get out with regard to Kent State?

    FBI Director, J. Edgar Hoover: That did not come from
the FBI. But it did cause me great concern. The first time I
knew of it was when the *Akron Beacon-Journal* had a great
headline—it is part of the Knight chain of newspapers—saying
"FBI: No Reason for Guard to Shoot at Kent State." I knew
this was untrue. We never make any conclusions. . . . There
were certainly extenuating circumstances which caused the
guard to resort to the use of firearms. Perhaps they were not as
completely trained as they should have been, but certainly some
stated they feared for their lives and then fired; some of the
students were throwing bricks and rocks and taunting the National Guardsmen.

    Congressman Bow: Do you mind this being on the record?

    Hoover: Not at all.

11. Hartford Courant, *January 3, 1971, story on the 1970 income*
tax: Perhaps it was the influence of inflation, but the old familiar
$600 has been raised to $625 for 1970. A dependent is now
worth $625.

12. Hartford Courant, *December 21, 1970, AP story on Soviet ef-*
forts to crush political dissent in Russia: Minister of Culture
Yekaterina Furtseva publicly berated an American correspondent for "poking his nose into our internal affairs" when he asked
a question related to the case of disgraced novelist Alexander
Solzhenitsyn.

    "If you cannot punish the killers of your government leaders,
you have no right to be interested in such questions," the
[Soviet] culture minister retorted.

13. *Al Capp, in his column,* New York Daily News, *September 13,*
1970: Mayor Lindsay of New York and Senator Ribicoff of

Connecticut are usually in perfect agreement on such issues [as] that college students are forced to blow up buildings and people because Spiro Agnew is so mean to them, and that looters and arsonists are blameless: it's the police who are sent in to save the community from them who cause all the trouble.

*14. *George Meany, American Federation of Labor President, quoted in the* New York Times, *August 31, 1970:* To these people who constantly say you have got to listen to these younger people, they have got something to say, I just don't buy that at all. They smoke more pot than we do and if the younger generation are the hundred thousand kids that lay around a field up in Woodstock, N.Y., I am not going to trust the destiny of the country to that group.

15. *Article critical of President Nixon by Robert W. Dietsch, The* New Republic, *September 12, 1970:* Suggestions are piling up on White House desks (not the President's of course, he keeps his neat).

*16. *Lionel Tiger, Rutgers University, replying to critics in the* New York Times Magazine, *November 15, 1970 (his article argued for a genetic basis for male dominance in many fields):* [My critics] have the responsibility to provide a better scientific explanation for the observable data about sex differences in behavior before objecting to the one offered in my article.

*17. *Judith Milgrom Carnoy,* Ramparts *magazine, November 1970 (an article on the Kaiser-Permanente health system, in which she argues that the Kaiser plan dispenses second rate health care):* The real answer to America's medical problems . . . is not in Kaiser; it lies, rather, in decentralized medical care, organized not for profit but for humanity.

18. *Thomas A. Porter, Dean, School of Arts and Sciences, Central Connecticut State College, in a November 1970 report titled "School of Arts and Sciences: 1970–1980":* Each department of the school should begin at once to plan how to utilize various instructional patterns and/or new instructional techniques so as to make quality instruction available to all students who seek it. The problem of closing students out of classes which they want and need can only become more serious as our enrollments increase. Efforts in this direction by departments may include the creation of large lecture classes (not always at the lower division level) and utilization of T.V., auto-instructional labs, and other technological aids. It can be argued, of course, that this

approach sacrifices individual communication between faculty and student and dehumanizes education. On the other hand, nothing sacrifices communication so much as being closed out of a class entirely.

Exercise II for Chapter Two

Find examples in the mass media of fallacies discussed in Chapter Two, and explain why they are fallacious.

Chapter Three

Fallacious Because Invalid—II

The task of logic is to serve as a spiritual hygiene, cautioning
men against the disease of intellectual confusion.

Rudolf Carnap

Let's continue our discussion of the more important fallacies in the category *fallacious because invalid*.

1. Appeal to authority

No one knows everything. So we often have to consult experts before making decisions. But there are good and bad ways to do this; improper appeals to experts constitute the fallacy of **appeal to authority**.

The problem is to distinguish proper from improper appeals to authority, a problem about which the relevant authorities (logicians and writers on rhetoric) have had relatively little to say. There are, however, a few rules of thumb which are of some practical use:

a. An authority in one field is not necessarily worth listening to in another. The opinions of famous athletes who endorse Gillette blades in TV commercials are a case in point; there is no reason to suppose that athletes know any more about razor blades than anyone else. Similarly, to cite an example from politics, a man who is expert in making and selling automobiles (whether his name is Charles Wilson or Robert McNamara) is not thereby qualified to oversee the defense of the nation.

b. It is generally fallacious to accept the *opinion* of an authority (as opposed to his arguments) on topics about which experts disagree. The same is true of opinions in fields about which relatively little is known.

Judges and juries often violate this principle, and thus commit the fallacy

49

of *appeal to authority,* when they decide about a defendant's sanity or competence *solely* on the basis of one psychiatric *opinion.* Judges, of all people, ought to know how easy it is to obtain contrary expert testimony on most psychological matters.

c. When experts disagree, the layman must become his own expert, turning to acknowledged experts for *evidence, reasons,* and *arguments,* but not for conclusions or opinions. This is especially true with respect to political matters because of the tremendous controversy they arouse. But it applies elsewhere too. The judge who merely accepts a psychologist's opinion ought instead to ask for the *reasons* which led the psychologist to his opinion. Similarly American presidents need to go into the complex details which lie behind the opinions of their economic advisors, rather than confining themselves, as President Eisenhower is said to have done, to whatever could be typed onto one side of one page.

d. Finally, anyone who feels that he must appeal to an expert in a way which violates any of the above rules should at least consult the past record of that authority. Experts who have been right in the past are more likely to be reliable than those who have been wrong.

It is surprising how often even this rule of last resort is violated. Think of the many senators and congressmen who accepted expert military opinion that the war in Vietnam would end in 1969 or 1970, even after having heard military experts testify incorrectly so often over the years about the end of that longest war in American history. Or recall President Nixon's economics advisors, who remained in favor with the president even though their predictions for 1970 on inflation and unemployment proved to be way off the mark. If you have to rely on expert opinion, at least choose experts with a good track record.

The danger of the fallacy of *appeal to authority* results largely from the tendency to trust in the authority of all pronouncements by high officials and other famous people. Senator Joseph R. McCarthy's charges in the early 1950s that Communists infested the Department of State ("I have here in my hand the names of . . .") were taken seriously, and caused so much trouble for our country, precisely because he was a *United States Senator.*

There are two important variations of the fallacy of *appeal to authority.* They result from the fact that the "authority" need not be a single person, or even a group of persons. The first variation is **popularity**.

Everyone knows how difficult it is to force oneself to speak out in a group against the general sentiment of that group. The power of human cowardice, wedded to the desire to be on the winning side, is the basis for the fallacy of **popularity**, which is simply the human tendency to go along with the crowd, to believe what others believe. (Sometimes this is called the fallacy of **de-**

mocracy, or of **numbers**.) In other words, for many the crowd is the authority. For many, the mere fact that a view is widely held, and thus "representative," is sufficient to make that view respectable; the mere fact that a view is *not* widely held is sufficient to make it suspect.

Here is an argument which has these two assumptions as implicit premises.[1]

> *The freedom and flexibility afforded the broadcaster under the 'fairness doctrine' to select in good faith the spokesman for the* **representative** *viewpoints seems the best means yet devised for insuring that the public is exposed to all* **significant** *points of view on important public issues.*

In other words, only popular viewpoints are significant, an utterly foolish idea, especially in light of the history of great ideas, which have so often been initially unpopular.

A more clearcut case of the *popularity* version of *appeal to authority* was employed by Spiro Agnew at a Republican dinner in Jackson, Mississippi:[2]

> *Before I came down here, one* [political pundit] *told me that Southern voters wouldn't listen to Republicans, Southern voters won't support Republicans, and Southerners won't vote Republican. He told me he was* never *wrong. And then he drove off in his Edsel.*

And since Edsels were a big sales flop, they obviously were the wrong car to buy. A humorous example, but human beings, especially in large groups, are manipulated by such trivia.

Politicians know that it's good practice when attacked to defend themselves not by answering the charge against them but by attacking the person who leveled it. Florida's former senator George Smathers used the fallacy of *appeal to authority* in his "defense" against an accusation of wrongdoing raised by the late columnist Drew Pearson. Pearson, of course, specialized in investigations of political wrongdoing, and over the years enjoyed the

---

[1] A remark by Leonard H. Goldenson of ABC, reported in his newspaper column by John S. Knight, August 14, 1970.

[2] Mississippi Republican Dinner, Jackson, Mississippi, October 20, 1969.

wrath of countless political figures. Said Senator Smathers in his defense
against Pearson's accusation:

*I join two Presidents, 27 Senators, and 83 Congressmen in describing
Drew Pearson as an unmitigated liar.*

All of which was somewhat irrelevant to the truth of Pearson's accusation.

Finally, let's take an example from the law. In the 1970 New Haven
Black Panther trial, the jury first reported to the judge that they were dead-
locked. The judge then read a part of an old Connecticut charge called the
"Chip Smith charge," which is used to prod the minority on a jury to go
along with the majority verdict. It asks the minority to reconsider their position in view of the verdict of the majority of jury members who "have heard
the same evidence with the same attention and with equal desire to arrive
at the truth and under sanction of the same oath."
The legitimacy of the Chip Smith charge rests on the assumption that the
majority is more likely to be right than the minority. But if a juror is convinced by the Chip Smith charge that the majority view is correct "beyond
a reasonable doubt" *because* it is the majority view, then he commits the
fallacy of *appeal to authority,* the majority being his authority. For he places
the indirect evidence of the majority verdict ahead of the direct evidence of
courtroom testimony.

The second interesting variety of *appeal to authority* is **traditional wisdom**.
The past, and the familiar, have as secure a hold on us as the opinions of
others.
Although the old have perhaps had more experiences to draw on than
the young, so that their view of a problem often carries special weight, it is
fallacious to suppose that the opinions of older *generations* are based on
more experience than those of the current generation. Just the reverse is
true; those alive today have more experiences to draw on than did past generations, for knowledge tends to be handed down from generation to generation and thus on the whole to increase. (A lot that is false gets handed down
too, but no one ever said thinking correctly is easy.)
Nevertheless, the fact that something has always been done a certain way
seems to be a sufficient reason for many people to continue doing it that way.
Here is Senator Sam Ervin, of North Carolina, telling how he replied to
women who were in favor of the equality-for-women amendment to the
Constitution:[3]

---

[3] Quoted in the *New York Times Magazine,* September 20, 1970.

I tell them, "Why ladies, any bill that lies around here for 47 years without getting any more support than this one has got in the past **obviously** *shouldn't be passed at all. Why, I think* **that affords most conclusive proof that it's unworthy of consideration.**"

It's hard to imagine a more clearcut case of the *traditional wisdom* variety of *appeal to authority*.

Most cases of *traditional wisdom* are not so clearcut. The appeal to tradition often is concealed or halfhearted. Here is an example from an article on judicial abuse of migrant laborers in New Jersey.[4] Richard A. Walsh, deputy state public defender, in reply to the charge that migrants were being deprived of due process of law, is quoted as saying:

It's not right, it's unjust and we know it, **but that's the way the system works down there.**

This was a halfhearted use of *traditional wisdom* because Mr. Walsh never quite said that past practice constituted an excuse, but, in the absence of any great effort to correct the admitted injustice, the last clause simply functions to excuse that injustice.

Another example of *traditional wisdom* is furnished by John S. Knight in a column which dealt with a complaint by Senator J. William Fulbright of Arkansas that President Nixon was getting too much TV exposure. Senator Fulbright wanted Congress to get equal time. Said Mr. Knight:

The Senator . . . must recall Franklin D. Roosevelt's famous "fireside chats" over radio which did so much to influence the nation's thinking during his years in the White House. **No one protested then that FDR was being unduly favored.** . . .

Perhaps someone should have. In any event, the dispute is not settled by appeal to past practice as the authority on the matter.

---

[4] *New York Times,* August 17, 1970, p. 34.

2. Provincialism

The fallacy of **provincialism** is similar to that of *appeal to authority*. It stems from the natural tendency to identify strongly with a particular group, and to perceive experience largely in terms of in-group versus out-group.

This tendency, on the whole, has some good things to be said for it, since a person's well-being often depends on that of his group. But when in-group loyalties begin to intrude on the process of determining truth, the result is often fallacy. The tendency toward provincialism results, for one thing, in normally enlightened people displaying shocking ignorance or prejudice. Here is an example from an American newspaper series on Japan:[5]

> *The* [Japanese] *empire supposedly was founded about 600 B.C., but for the next 24 centuries the Japanese people lived in almost complete isolation from* **the rest of the world.**

"The rest of the world," of course, meant the Western world. The writer ignored the great influence of China on Japan during much of that 24-century period.

Henry J. Taylor was guilty of this fallacy in one of his political columns:[6]

> . . . *the great Declaration* [of Independence] *begins:*
>   *'When in the course of human events . . .'*
> *and* **for the first time in man's history** *announced that all rights came from a sovereign, not from a government, but from God. . . .*

But as every schoolboy ought to know, that idea goes back a good deal further than 1776.

Provincialism often results in a false conception of the importance and moral quality of one's own group. The "space race" between the Soviet Union and the United States furnishes a good example.

From 1957 until some time in the 1960s, the Soviet Union was ahead of the United States in space by a very small margin, chiefly due to our

---

[5] *Lawrence* [Kansas] *Daily Journal World,* August 8, 1970.
[6] *Topeka* [Kansas] *Daily Capital,* July 1970.

lack of a powerful propellant. During this time, although we were behind, American exploits received bigger headlines and greater coverage in this country than did those of the Russians. But the Russians did receive good coverage. When the United States forged ahead, coverage of American space shots greatly increased, while coverage of the Russians declined. Compare, for instance, the coverage of the *second* American manned moon flight with that of the Russians' *first* unmanned soft landing and return from the moon. (It hardly need be said that Russian coverage of the space race has been much more provincial than ours.)

Yet throughout this period, the achievements of both space efforts were very close; both accomplished important and similar tasks. The average American, however, relying on news reporting which played on the already provincial nature of its audience, received the impression that by 1968 our achievement had become far superior to that of the Russians. This helped confirm many Americans in their conviction that our system (capitalism) is superior to theirs ("atheistic socialistic communism"). Thus, our human tendency to think we are the smartest, strongest, and best, and our tendency to overlook the accomplishments of the rest of the world was intensified.

In its extreme form, the fallacy of *provincialism* turns into a worse vice, the fallacy of **loyalty**. This is the fallacy of believing (or disbelieving) in the face of great contrary evidence *because* of provincial loyalty.

The reactions of many Americans to the My Lai massacre constitute a good example.[7] On reading about My Lai, a teletype inspector in Philadelphia is reported to have said he didn't think it happened: "I can't believe our boys' hearts are that rotten." This response was typical, as was that of the person who informed the *Cleveland Plain Dealer,* which had printed photos of the massacre, "Your paper is rotten and anti-American." Surveys taken after wide circulation of news about the massacre revealed that large numbers of Americans refused to believe "American boys" had done such a thing. The myth of American moral superiority seems to have been a better source of truth for them than evidence at hand. One wonders if any amount of evidence would be sufficient to convince those people who set loyalty above the truth. They are like the clerics who refused to look through Galileo's telescope to see the moons of Jupiter because they *knew* Jupiter could not possibly have moons.

Let's end our discussion of *loyalty* and *provincialism* on a lighter note. The *New York Times* (September 17, 1970) carried a photo of a smiling

---

[7] The reactions described here are from Seymour M. Hersh's book *My Lai 4: A Report on the Massacre and Its Aftermath,* Random House, New York, 1970, pp. 151–152.

President Nixon addressing a pleased-looking audience at Kansas State University. Underneath the photo, the *Times* reported that the President had just noted to the audience that he was wearing a tie with the K.S.U. school colors, purple and white. Having thus made the provincial appeal, the President then had a more receptive audience for serious subjects. Wearing a particular tie is so simple a matter; yet human minds are often controlled by such simple gestures.

3. Irrelevant reason

In the standard account of fallacies in traditional textbooks, a fallacy called *non sequitur* (it does not follow) is often included. Some texts describe *non sequitur* as a fallacy in which the conclusion does not follow from the given premises. But in this sense, any fallacy in the broad category *fallacious because invalid* could be said to be a *non sequitur*.

More careful writers use *non sequitur* to describe those arguments in which the "evidence" in the premises is *irrelevant* to the conclusion, and not, as is usually the case with such fallacies as *ad hominem* and *appeal to authority,* relevant but insufficient to establish the conclusion.

It is the more carefully defined version of *non sequitur* which fits our basic classification. However, let's drop the ambiguous term *non sequitur* and talk instead of the fallacy of the **irrelevant reason**.

An example is the newspaper columnist who argued that prices had gone much too high by pointing out that the average housewife spends at a rate of $20 per hour at the supermarket, while her husband earns only $2.95 per hour. The *rate of speed* at which a housewife spends money is completely irrelevant to the charge that prices are too high. A man may spend a third of his yearly salary in half an hour when he buys a new automobile, or an entire year's salary merely as down payment on a house. But this tells us nothing whatever about whether auto or house prices are rising too rapidly, or even rising at all.

The fallacy of *irrelevant reason* was committed on a wholesale basis by the Democrats during the Johnson administration. In reply to charges that the United States had no business in Vietnam, either morally or to satisfy our national interests, Johnson administration officials frequently replied that such talk only prolonged the war by making the enemy believe that America's will to fight was declining. This reply in all likelihood was true; but it was utterly irrelevant to the question of our justification for being in

Vietnam. (Needless to say, the Republicans committed the same fallacy after winning the presidency in 1968.)

Irrelevant reason and several other fallacies tend to blend into one another. *Ad hominem* reasoning is the best example of this, because in the extreme case an attack on a man is completely irrelevant to his argument. Here is a good example from an article critical of a recent best selling book:[8]

> *James Simon Kunen, a* **young heavily haired dissident,** *has become a* **wealthy post adolescent** *as author of the best selling "The Strawberry Statement," a report on* . . .

The emphasized phrases are designed to prejudice the reader against Mr. Kunen's book, and against its point of view on student political activities, by attacking the book's author. So the passage clearly is an example of *ad hominem* argument. But it also illustrates the fallacy of *irrelevant reason,* because the attack on the book's author comes very close to being completely irrelevant to the question of the book's quality. (A person who argued that it is relevant would have to present evidence that young "heavily haired" dissidents are incapable of writing good books.)

Of course, it doesn't matter much how we classify the passage; the important point is to understand that the passage contains a fallacious attempt to prejudice the reader against Mr. Kunen's book.

This example is interesting because it illustrates the power of a few carefully chosen irrelevant adjectives to completely change the tone of a passage, even though they provide little if any pertinent factual evidence. All the passage really says, once the irrelevant flavoring is removed, is something like this:

> *James Simon Kunen, the author of the best-selling* The Strawberry Statement, *a report on* . . .

4. Ambiguity

A term or phrase is **ambiguous** when it has more than one meaning. Most English words are ambiguous, but their ambiguity usually is fairly harmless.

---

[8] Milton Gross, *Chicago Sun Times,* August 2, 1970.

The English word *snow,* for instance, can be used to refer to the quite harmless flaked H_2O or to the extremely dangerous drug heroin. But in most cases in which this word is used, it is clear from the context which meaning is intended.

However, some uses of ambiguous terms are far from harmless. When the ambiguity of a word or phrase leads to a mistaken conclusion, we have the fallacy of **ambiguity**. (A person who tries to trade on ambiguity to confuse his listeners *argues* fallaciously; but typically he doesn't *commit* the fallacy of ambiguity because he isn't convinced by his own argument.)

On the occasion of the visit of Israeli Premier Golda Meir to Washington, D.C., on September 18, 1970, a U.S. State Department spokesman was quoted as saying:[9]

> *Our objective continues to be to have the negotiations resume. We are encouraging both sides to* **continue** *observing the cease-fire.*

This was said at a time when Egypt, while not engaged in actual fighting, was moving SAM-2 and SAM-3 antiaircraft weapons into the ceasefire zone. This was a violation of the cease-fire agreement, and hence the Egyptians could not have *continued* to do something they had not already been doing. The spokesman presumably meant that the United States was encouraging both sides to refrain from actual fighting. But his use of the word *continue* could easily have been taken to mean *continue to live up to the cease-fire agreement.* Anyone who concluded from the spokesman's statement that Egypt had been living up to the cease-fire agreement committed the fallacy of *ambiguity.*

Evans and Novak furnish us with another example of this fallacy:[10]

> *His* [Nixon's] *claim that his new Administration really intends to fulfill* [William] *Scranton's* **evenhanded policy** *between Israel and the Arab states. . . .*

The expression "evenhanded policy" here could mean either a policy halfway between the Arab and Israeli positions or a fair policy. By describing

---

[9] In the *Hartford Courant,* September 19, 1970, p. 1.
[10] From their column of June 30, 1970.

the Scranton policy as "evenhanded," Evans and Novak entice support for it from those who favor a "halfway" policy as well as from those who will endorse any policy they consider "fair." And along the way the columnists mask the fact that labelling a policy "evenhanded," even if accurate in one or another sense of that term, provides no good grounds for adoption of the policy. (In defense of Evans and Novak, it should be pointed out that the Scranton policy was widely referred to as "evenhanded." They were just passing on the ambiguous label.)

Finally, here is another portion of the May 2, 1969, speech by Spiro Agnew. Notice that the *ambiguity* occurs in an aside, which makes it just that much harder to detect:

> *Aside from the small point that our primary and secondary schools should strengthen their curricula in civics . . . so that even our youngest children learn that civil rights* **are** *balanced by civil responsibilities. . .*

The word *are* in this passage is ambiguous. So the passage can be taken to say either that we should teach children the moral truth that there is a responsibility (duty) corresponding to every right or that in fact in the United States our civil rights are upheld and balanced by our civil responsibilities. Since Agnew in this and other speeches has hinted at both of those interpretations, the passage could be taken either way, or even both ways. But taken in the second way it surely is something many minority groups (Negroes, American Indians, Puerto Ricans, etc.) would vehemently deny. (Construed in this way, the passage is guilty of *begging the question*.) But if opponents attack this sentence, Agnew supporters can always win the argument simply by switching to the first meaning—that civil rights and civil responsibilities *ought to* balance.

Studied ambiguity is a perfect device for protecting yourself from legitimate attack; all you do to defend yourself is shift meaning at the opportune moment.

5. Slippery slope

The fallacy of **slippery slope** consists in objecting to a particular action on the grounds that once such an action is taken it will lead inevitably to a similar but less desirable action, which will lead in turn to an even less desirable action, and so on down the "slippery slope" until the horror lurking at the bottom is reached.

There is a slightly different version of *slippery slope,* according to which if we are *justified* in taking the first step over the edge, every other step is justified also. But in this version of *slippery slope* it is clear that the last step is not justified. So the first step isn't either.

People frequently argued against medicare in the late 1960s on the grounds that it was socialized medicine for the aged and would lead to socialized medicine for all, and then to socialized insurance of all kinds, socialized railroads, airlines, steel mills, etc. It was also argued that whatever justified socialized medicine for the aged justified it for everyone, and justified as well socialized railroads, etc., "down the slope" all the way to a completely socialistic system.

The fallacy of the *slippery slope* is committed in this example if you accept *without further argument* the idea that once the first step over the edge is taken the slide all the way down is inevitable. The fact is that in cases similar to that of medicare the first step sometimes does and sometimes doesn't lead to more steps. Even in Great Britain under Socialist governments, the economy has not been fully socialized. Some industries are nationalized and some are not. So it would take further argument to determine the facts in the particular case of medicare.

The variations on *slippery slope* are almost limitless. Two, the **Balkanization theory** and the **domino theory**, have been employed quite frequently in recent years.

The Balkanization theory was employed during the Nigeria-Biafra civil war. People argued then that we could not permit Biafra to break away from Nigeria because such a break would produce a chain reaction in which every tribal group in Africa would attempt to gain independence, thus "Balkanizing" Africa.

But there was little or no evidence to support such conjecture. In the first place, an independent Biafra would have been larger in population than over half the nations in the world, so it would hardly have exemplified "Balkanization." And secondly, civil wars of independence gain their impetus primarily from factors internal to the nation in question, not from the success of attempts in other nations. The Biafran attempt to gain independence is itself a case in point, since it came after secessionist attempts elsewhere in Africa (as in the Congo) had failed.

The classic case of the use of the *domino theory* is, of course, Vietnam. Everyone seems to have used it at one time or another, starting with the French:[11]

> *Once Tongking* [Northern Indo-China] *is lost, there is really no barrier before Suez,* . . .

The Americans then joined in, one of the first being John Foster Dulles:[12]

> *If Indo-China should be lost, there would be a chain reaction throughout the Far East and South Asia.*

Here is William P. Bundy:[13]

> *If South Vietnam falls, the rest of Southeast Asia will be in grave danger of progressively disappearing behind the Bamboo Curtain, and other Asian countries like India and even in time Australia and your own* [country—Japan] *will in turn be threatened.*

Even Bob Hope got into the act:[14]

> *Everybody I talked to there* [Vietnam] *wants to know why they can't go in and finish it, and don't let anybody kid you about why we're there. If we weren't, those Commies would have the whole thing, and it wouldn't be long until we'd be looking off the coast of Santa Monica* [California].

[11] General Jean de Lattre de Tassiguy, General in charge of French forces in the Far East, September 20, 1951. This, and several of the examples which follow, are quoted in the book *Quotations Vietnam: 1945–1970,* compiled by William G. Effros, Random House, New York, 1970, Chapter Three.

[12] Secretary of State under Eisenhower, April 5, 1954.

[13] Assistant Secretary of State for Far Eastern Affairs under Johnson, September 29, 1964, in Tokyo, Japan.

[14] Quoted in the *New York Times Magazine* article, "This is Bob (Politician-Patriot-Publicist) Hope," by Anthony J. Lukas, October 4, 1970, p. 86.

All of these versions of the *domino theory* reveal the simplistic attitude that is characteristic of *slippery slope* in any of its variations. But sometimes that first step will lead to all the rest; sometimes it won't. We must examine every given case for the details which make all the difference. If we fail to do so, we reason fallaciously.

6. Hasty conclusion – *not enough evidence.*

In many textbooks, the fallacies about to be discussed are set apart from those just presented and are characterized as *inductive fallacies.* (See Appendix A for a discussion of the difference between induction and deduction.)

But this standard division is not very useful. Almost all of the fallacies discussed in this text, including *slippery slope, ad hominem,* and *false dilemma,* are primarily inductive fallacies, for the simple reason that it is rare in daily life to claim deductive certitude for the conclusion of an argument. (This is an *extremely* important point which most textbooks on fallacies overlook.)

The fallacy of **hasty conclusion** is generally described as the use of an argument which presents evidence relevant to its conclusion, but insufficient by itself to warrant acceptance of that conclusion.

In a sense, a great many of the fallacies so far considered satisfy this criterion. *Ad hominem* and *appeal to authority* are good examples. But the trouble with *ad hominem* arguments and fallacious appeals to authority is that their evidence is insufficient because a *better kind* of evidence (generally more direct) is available or required. More of the same kind (such as another attack on the man rather than on his argument) wouldn't make the argument any better. Let's restrict the term *hasty conclusion* to fallacies in which it is not the type of evidence but the lack of sufficient evidence that is at fault.

A news story on a local flurry of flag-stealing (*New Britain* [Connecticut] *Herald,* October 1970) quoted a local citizen:

> *They took both the flag and the pole. This just thoroughly demonstrates the lack of law and order.*

But all by itself, it just doesn't. In the best of times there will always be some lawbreaking, especially of this minor variety. The evidence *is* relevant, and more evidence like it might establish the conclusion. But taken alone, it can't possibly do so.

Another example of *hasty conclusion* comes from an article which argued that medical treatment is less and less worth the money.[15]

> . . . *increased treatment by . . . doctors . . . has shown steadily declining results. Medical expenses concentrated on those above forty-five have doubled several times over a period of forty years with a resulting 3 percent increase in life expectancy in men.*

Does this prove the point? No, because the conclusion that we're not getting our money's worth is a bit too hasty. There are all sorts of reasons why life spans might have *decreased* over the last forty years had it not been for improvements in medical care which have cost so much money. Cigarette smoking, pollution, less exercise, and poorer diets are several such reasons. So it may be that doctors have had to fight a battle just to keep us as healthy as we used to be, much less make us healthier. (The argument is a poor one for other reasons also. It fails to take account of the fact that in the last forty years prices have more than doubled. And it overlooks the likelihood that beyond a certain point it will take extremely complicated devices and sophisticated drugs to increase a man's life span even by a small amount. But a small increase, and 3 percent isn't all that small, may well be worth the added expense and effort.)

In 1970, Senator Mike Mansfield, Democrat from Montana, tried to pin the label "recession" onto the economic troubles the United States had suffered during most of the first two years of the Republican Nixon administration:

> . . . *the country is mired in inflation, unemployment, and war, and . . . whether the term is used or not, these words spell recession.*

What he meant was that these conditions *prove* the existence of a recession. But they don't, although rising unemployment is very good evidence of a recession. Mansfield appealed to the right kind of evidence, but the conditions he listed don't in themselves add up to a recession (and some of his

[15] *New York Review of Books,* July 2, 1970.

evidence, though relevant to his conclusion, would normally tend to help disprove it: war and recession are not commonly associated in the twentieth century; war is usually associated with *expansion*).

It is interesting to note that the Nixon administration had deliberately manipulated the economy to slow down business expansion in order to try to slow down inflation. If this slowdown amounted to a business downturn in 1970, it was very slight. But the word *recession* has negative overtones. So the Nixon administration didn't want the label *recession* attached to the slowdown, although the administration had itself deliberately induced it. Naturally, the Democrats tried to pin the label *recession* on the slowdown, whether it fitted exactly or not.

7. Questionable classification

Hasty conclusion is a special variety of a wider species we might call **questionable classification**, or **false classification**. The fallacy of **questionable classification** occurs when we classify something incorrectly, given the evidence we have or could have. For instance, Senator Mansfield's classification of the 1969–1970 business slowdown as a recession was a questionable one, since the evidence he presented didn't prove the slowdown warranted that label.

But there are many instances of *questionable classification* which don't quite fit the category *hasty conclusion*. Robert Waters reported in one of his newspaper columns that the United States Chamber of Commerce had classified 152 United States congressmen as "big spenders," because each of them had voted to override President Nixon's vetoes of four bills he had labelled "excessive spending bills." [16] The four bills, for domestic matters, appropriated a total of about 2½ billion dollars more than the 40½ billion Nixon had asked for.

But labelling these congressmen "big spenders" involved a bit of *questionable classification*. Many of them had attempted to reduce expenditures for other matters, such as the outer space program, the SST, and ABM, as well as many other military programs. So they weren't necessarily big spenders. They might have been more correctly classified as people who wanted to spend money *differently* than did the Nixon administration. But it would have been politically unproductive to brand them as *spend-it-differently* men, while it was politically expedient to brand them as *big spenders*.

The program of NOW (National Organization of Women—a women's liberation group) once included in its list of recommendations for securing

[16] "Washington Scene," *Hartford Courant,* September 3, 1970.

equality of the sexes the proposal that facilities be established to rehabilitate and train divorced *women*. They further recommended that the ex-husbands in question, if financially able, should pay for the education of divorced *women*.

But stated this way, their recommendation exhibited *questionable classification* (to say nothing of female chauvinism). The group in need of rehabilitation clearly was not divorced women, but divorced *persons,* or better yet divorced *homemakers*. For if a man happened to be the partner who took care of the home while his wife earned the bread, surely he would be entitled to aid in the event of a divorce just as much as would a woman in the same situation. A divorced female wage-earner should have the same financial obligations to her ex-spouse that a divorced male in the same situation would have. Of all groups, NOW, with its concern for *equality* between the sexes, should not have classified the needy group as divorced *women*.

This last example of *questionable classification* is particularly interesting because the correct and incorrect classes (divorced homemakers and divorced women) are close to being identical in membership. There are relatively few divorced males in the United States who fit the classification divorced homemaker. Close overlap of this kind is frequent when the fallacy of *questionable classification* occurs, and it is a major reason why this fallacy is so common.

But it also is a major reason why it is very important to avoid making questionable classifications. In some areas of the United States, the overwhelming majority of "deprived children" (whatever exactly that means) are nonwhite (whatever *that* means). Deprived children, as a group, do less well in school than nondeprived children. Hence, nonwhites do less well than whites. But to classify backward students as nonwhites leads naturally to the conclusion (for which there is no good evidence—see Chapter Four) that their being nonwhite is the *cause* of their backwardness. And we are all familiar with the way in which this conclusion has been used to defend racially segregated schools in the United States.

8. Questionable cause

You are guilty of the fallacy of the **questionable cause** (or **false cause**) if you label a given thing as the cause of something else on insufficient evidence.

The fallacy of *questionable classification* frequently entails *questionable cause*. This is true because we classify partly in order to determine causes.

Once we classify slow learners as mostly nonwhite, it is easy to take the next step and conclude that their being nonwhite is the *cause* of their being slow learners.

But even in cases where the *classification* is correct, it doesn't follow that we have discovered a causal connection; the connection we have discovered may be *accidental.*

Here is an example, from the logic-textbook-writer's best friend, Spiro Agnew. He was speaking of Lawrence O'Brien, Democratic Party Chairman who had been Postmaster General under Lyndon Johnson and who became president of a Wall Street brokerage firm after Johnson left office:[17]

> *Under his [O'Brien's] adroit management, the firm collapsed, and it is presently being liquidated. Isn't that a splendid credential for a man who would advise the President of his country on economics?*

The implication of Agnew's comment is that O'Brien's lack of ability *caused* the brokerage firm to collapse. Now there is no doubt that the *classification* is correct; O'Brien does belong in the unenviable class of people who have presided over a business firm as it went under. The question is whether this proves that he was unreliable on economic theory or even as a businessman. In other words, the question is whether the firm went under *because* he lacked ability.

And put this way, the answer is obvious; the conclusion is much too hasty. There are many cases of financial disaster presided over by first-rate businessmen who at some earlier or later time proved their business acumen. The Edsel was one of the biggest financial disasters in American business history. But it would be foolish to conclude from its failure that Henry Ford II, the man who rescued the Ford Motor Company from the brink of disaster after World War II and who increased Ford's share of the highly competitive auto market during his presidency of the firm, didn't know how to run a business.

In addition, Agnew's argument is guilty of the fallacy of *suppressed evidence.* O'Brien's firm went under at a time when brokerage firms as a group suffered great losses. His was by no means the only firm that was forced to liquidate. Indeed, it is ironic that Agnew should even have mentioned the matter, since it was commonly charged at the time that Wall Street's losses were the result of President Nixon's economic measures intended to cure the inflation problem. O'Brien himself is said to have

[17] Reported in *Newsweek* magazine, August 31, 1970.

characterized his company as ". . . one of many firms that was victim of the Nixon administration's disastrous economic policies."

Another *Newsweek* story (August 31, 1970) quotes Charles Morgan, Jr., of the American Civil Liberties Union:

> *The Uniform Code of Military Justice is uniform, is a code and is military—and* **therefore** *has nothing to do with justice.*

But even if it is true that "justice" is not what results from actual applications of the Uniform Code of Military Justice, it does not follow that the particular features of this code that Morgan cites are the cause of that condition. Those features alone are not sufficient to *cause* injustice. There have been other social systems in which enforcement of uniform military codes resulted in a brand of justice at least as good as any other generally available in that culture. In considering the possibility of such a causal connection, Morgan might better have argued for a different conclusion, namely that *at the present time in the United States* a uniform military code will miss the mark of justice. This suggests that injustice stemming from use of the United States Uniform Code of Military Justice could well result, at least in part, from cultural factors, and not merely from the uniformity of a military code.

The same article in *Newsweek* contains still another example of the fallacy of the *questionable cause*. It asks concerning the My Lai massacre:

> *. . . should the G.I.'s be punished for, in effect,* **trying too hard**—*by gunning down civilians in a village long sympathetic to the Viet Cong?*

Overlooking the question of what might justify the commission of such a massacre, is it reasonable to say that the *cause* of the massacre was too great effort on the part of the soldiers in question? Even a cursory reading of firsthand accounts of the massacre will correct such a simplified view.[18] Furthermore, *Newsweek* failed to provide sufficient evidence to support its view of what caused the slaughter.

---

[18] Those who have read no firsthand accounts of the incident will have to rely on the word of this book's author. Whether in doing so the reader commits the fallacy of *appeal to authority,* given the availability in book form of such testimony, is a question best left to the reader.

9. Questionable analogy

We reason by analogy for much the same reason that we classify and assign causes, namely to understand and control ourselves and our environment. In fact, analogical reasoning is a common way in which we reason to causes.

But analogical reasoning can go wrong in pretty much the same ways as general reasoning about causes. And when it does, the result is the fallacy of **questionable analogy** or **false analogy**.

It is very difficult to say precisely when analogical reasoning is fallacious, just as it is difficult to determine exactly when any kind of generalization is fallacious. The subject is one of extreme controversy, unlikely to be resolved in the near future. Nevertheless, this doesn't prevent our being able to spot fairly clearcut cases of questionable analogy.

Here is a letter to the editor of the *New York Times Magazine*:[19]

> *Milton Friedman's defense of pure Adam Smith is like Billy Graham's defense of the literal truth of Genesis. To believe that a laissez-faire economic theory offers any hope of promoting a viable society, is as naive as the belief that Adam and Eve were the first man and woman.*

If a reader responded to this analogy by reexamining his beliefs as to the validity of Adam Smith-Milton Friedman economic theory, then the analogy served a useful purpose and no fallacy was committed. The same is true if the analogy led to an insight into laissez-faire economic theory, or if the reader was moved from mere passive rejection or acceptance of this kind of theory to a belief having the potential to affect actions (such as voting).

But if the analogy *convinced* a reader that Friedman's defense of Adam Smith is not cogent (as it might have if, for instance, the reader had just recently given up literal belief in the Garden of Eden), then the reader reasoned fallaciously. The analogy as printed [20] contains no *evidence* that belief in Adam Smith is like belief in Adam and Eve. (Let's pass over what religious fundamentalists might say on the matter.) So the analogy

---

[19] By C. W. Griffin, Denville, New Jersey, published October 4, 1970, and reprinted by permission.

[20] Mr. Griffin's arguments for his analogy were cut by the *Times*. See pp. 167–168 for the complete letter.

failed as a complete *argument*. It stated that two things are alike, but failed to state how, or why.

But it is quite difficult in actual practice to decide when an analogy is a good one and when it isn't. Good analogies frequently are rejected on spurious grounds. Here is an example from an article discussing the refusal of a father to reveal the whereabouts of his hippie daughter on grounds that the parent-child relationship should be legally privileged, just as is the husband-wife relationship:[21]

> *But should there be such a privilege* [contrary to present law]? *. . . There is, of course, a counter-argument. As Mr. Schaefer says* [Philip Schaefer, New York lawyer who helped draft domestic relations legislation], **"What if the child the parent is protecting is Jack the Ripper?"**

But Mr. Schaefer argued fallaciously. The argument for a special parent-child relationship is an analogical one based on the resemblance between the parent-child and husband-wife relationships. Presumably, Mr. Schaefer favors the special privilege (of not having to testify against one's spouse) granted in the husband-wife relationship. Yet a husband is as likely as a child to turn out to be a Jack the Ripper. So Mr. Schaefer has failed to describe a relevant difference between the two relationships; he thus has failed to show what is wrong with the analogy, which on its face (and in view of other material in the article) has much plausibility. His fallacy might be said to be that of incorrectly rejecting a plausible analogy.

Perhaps in a spirit of anti-dogmatism it would be a good idea to end this chapter with an example that presents a bit of a dilemma. Here are two letters to the editor on the same topic. Since they take diametrically opposed positions, at least one must be fallacious.[22] The dispute is over violence in America, the radical left, hippies, law and order, and all that:[23]

[21] *New York Times,* January 3, 1971, p. 6E.

[22] Of course, they both may be fallacious.

[23] Written by Hazel Teichmann, this letter appeared in the *Lawrence* [Kansas] *Daily Journal World,* May 22, 1970. The answering letter by Steve Phelps appeared a few days later. Both letters are reprinted by permission.

Editor, Journal World:

So, my young friends, and those over 30, now that you have read St. Mark, suppose you go on and read the other Bible books—all of them. You will learn a lot.

But do it now, for if my little parable should come true, this book, along with all the rest, will be gone as it was in Germany.

I'll also suggest that you go back to your history books, while you can, and read about Hitler's Youth Brigade, the Brown Shirts.

And, oh-yes! Read about England's Chamberlain who backed down and let the Nazis overrun Europe. Then do some retracting in your thinking.

The reply:

I read with interest Hazel Teichmann's letter of May 22, in which she admonished our youth to read about England's Chamberlain who backed down and let the Nazis overrun Europe.

I agree that is one side of the coin to be considered, but may I suggest that in order to get a complete picture of both sides, they also consider that it was only with the acquiescence of its "great silent majority," those flag waving patriots who shouted "My country— right or wrong" as they were led down the path to war, that Germany was able to create the war machine that it did.

I don't know if Germany had bumper-stickers in the 1930's, but if it did I'll bet they read something like "Germany—love it or leave it!"

Two analogies. At best, only one is correct. But which one? Analogies are where you find them. And they can be found almost anywhere.

**Summary of fallacies
discussed in Chapter Three**

1. **Appeal to authority**. Improper appeal to authority.
   Example: Senator Smather's defense against Drew Pearson by appeal to the authority of two presidents, 27 senators, and 83 congressmen.
   a. **Popularity**. Appeal to the crowd as the authority.
      Example: Spiro Agnew's characterization of a man as wrong in buying an Edsel because Edsels were a *sales* flop.

b. **Traditional wisdom.** Appealing to the past as an authority.
Example: Senator Ervin's statement that failure of the Congress for 47 years to act on a proposed equal-rights-for-women amendment constituted conclusive reason for rejecting the amendment.

2. **Provincialism.** Assuming that the familiar, the close, or what is one's own is *therefore* the better or more important.
Example: The far greater coverage in the United States of American space efforts than of those of the Russians.
   a. **Loyalty.** Deciding the truth of an assertion on the basis of loyalty.
   Example: Refusal to believe the evidence that United States soldiers had shot and killed defenseless women, children, and tiny babies at My Lai 4 in South Vietnam.

3. **Irrelevant reason.** Use of evidence entirely irrelevant to a conclusion.
Example: Arguing that prices are too high on the grounds that the average housewife spends at a rate of $20 per hour at the supermarket.

4. **Ambiguity.** Use of ambiguous terms to mislead (or which in fact mislead).
Example: The State Department spokesman's statement that both sides in the 1970 Israeli-Egyptian disputes should *continue* observing the cease-fire, although Egypt had already broken the cease-fire agreement by moving missiles into the cease-fire zone. So there was misleading ambiguity in the suggestion that the Egyptians should *continue* to observe what they had already violated.

5. **Slippery slope.** Failure to see that the first step in a possible series of steps doesn't inevitably bind one to the rest, or inevitably lead to the rest.
Example: Claims—unargued for—that medicare would *inevitably* lead to complete socialism.
   a. **Balkanization theory.** The conclusion that the breakup of one nation into parts will inevitably result in the breakup of others.
   Example: The belief that if Biafra successfully broke away from Nigeria, all sorts of tribal groups in Africa would try to establish independent nations.
   b. **Domino theory.** The conclusion that if *A* falls, so will *B*, then *C*, and so on.
   Example: The belief that if South Vietnam goes Communist, so will Laos, Cambodia, Thailand, the rest of the Far East, etc.

6. **Hasty conclusion.** Use of relevant but insufficient evidence to reach a conclusion.
Example: A newspaper's claim that the theft of a flag *and a flagpole* "thoroughly" demonstrated a lack of law and order.

7. **Questionable classification.** The incorrect classification of something, given available evidence.

   Example: The classification as "big spenders" of those congressmen who voted to override the president's veto of some domestic spending programs, although many of these same congressmen had sought to *reduce* military expenditures.

8. **Questionable cause.** Labelling something as the cause of something else on insufficient evidence.

   Example: A magazine's suggestion that Vietnamese civilians were massacred by American soldiers *because* the soldiers were "trying too hard," although available evidence suggested a more complex cause of the massacre.

9. **Questionable analogy.** Use of analogy alone, with no further evidence, to argue that a likeness exists.

   Example: The statement, intended as a sufficient argument against belief in laissez-faire economic theory, that such belief is "as naive as" belief in the literal truth of Genesis.

Exercise I for Chapter Three

Determine which fallacies (if any) occur in the following passages, and state the reasons for your answers.

   *1. *John Corry in* Harper's *magazine, November 1970:* "We will have our manhood even if we have to level the face of the earth," Huey Newton told the Panther convention, and this is not so much inflammatory as it is sad, a confession that the Panthers do not have something that the other boys in town take for granted.

   *2. *UPI story:* Mrs. Martha Mitchell (Attorney General Mitchell's wife) blames American educators for destroying the country. "They are totally responsible for the sins of our children."

    3. *Jack Newfield,* The Village Voice, *October 1, 1970:* I agree it was unfair the way [Richard] Ottinger was able to outspend Paul O'Dwyer in the primary, but it strikes me as a hollow issue. Any politician who has money will spend it. . . . And I didn't hear too many complaints about Lindsay out-spending Procaccino in 1969.

    4. Ad for Masterpiece pipe tobacco:
   Eva Gabor: "Darling, have you discovered Masterpiece? The most exciting men I know are smoking it!"

5. *John P. Roche, political column, October 1970:* Every society is, of course, repressive to some extent—as Sigmund Freud pointed out, repression is the price we pay for civilization.

6. *Newspaper story:* Thor Heyerdahl has done it again, crossing the Atlantic in a papyrus raft designed after ancient Egyptian tomb carvings. Landing in the Western Hemisphere on the island of Barbados, he was greeted by the Barbados Prime Minister, Errol Barrow, who declared, "This has established Barbados was the first landing place for man in the Western world."

7. New York Times Magazine, *August 30, 1970:* The new constitution foisted on Japan by the U.S. after WWII contained a "no war" clause, forbidding Japan to rearm. But [General Douglas] MacArthur, himself a principal architect of the Constitution, restored the Japanese army, calling it first a "National Police Reserve," and then "Self Defense force."

*8. *Column by Joseph Alsop, January 4, 1971:* You can argue about the exact moment when . . . after World War I [the world passed from a postwar to prewar period]—about whether it was when Hitler reoccupied the Rhineland without resistance or when the harsh resulting challenge met with no adequate response from Britain or France or anyone else.

9. *Letter from a father to his college daughter:* Dear Helen,
   Gladys tells me that Fred has invited you out for New Year's Eve. She says you're just going out with him because you need a date for a New Year's Eve party. But if your old man means anything to you now that you're so grown up and in college, *don't* go to that party with Fred. Before you know it, you'll be going steady with the guy, and according to Gladys he's on marijuana. If you go steady with him, you're going to try the awful stuff, and God forbid end up one of those—what do you call it—speed freaks, or maybe when that wears out a dope addict. Don't go out with that boy Fred—or forget about Europe next summer.

10. *Article in college newspaper:* A committee on teaching evaluation in colleges is the coming thing.
    John Cunniff, June 30, 1970, in a column titled "College Degree Not Necessary," which attempted to refute the statement that "No youngster will have a chance in the future without a college degree": More than two-thirds of the job openings arising from occupational growth and replacement needs through the 1970s will be in clerical, sales, service, blue collar and farm jobs that usually do not require a college degree.

12. New York Sunday News, *column by Jerry Greene, September 6, 1970:* . . . the violations [of the Israeli-Arab ceasefire agreements] aren't all that serious. President Nasser's troops haven't yet done any Sam-3 missile movement or emplacement that could not have been done in any 12-hour period, before or after the Aug. 7 ceasefire deadline. . . . In about 79 days of . . . highly effective air strikes, the Israelis hammered at everything that looked like a missile site in the stretches west of the Suez. . . . the Israelis knocked out or damaged at least half the missiles emplaced by the Arabs in the months preceding Aug. 7. But the Egyptians kept doggedly at it. . . .

*13. *Dr. Max E. Eisenring, on the occasion of his election to the Insurance Hall of Fame:* I started my insurance career as an actuary. But it needs no actuary to know that there is no insurance without statistics. Yet there are no statistics, in the sense used and necessary for insurance operations, without the recurrence of similar events. Even life insurance, in the classic form, would become obsolete if, say, some wonder drug were all of a sudden to produce a longevity of hundreds of years. While such a thing is fortunately rather unlikely to happen in the foreseeable future, the idea of perhaps revolutionary changes is by no means far-fetched in regard to the non-life [insurance] lines.

14. Hartford Courant, *October 19, 1970:* . . . Lowell Weicker, the Republican candidate, [was charged] with illegally using public funds to mail campaign material. . . .

   "My staff has definite orders not to send out campaign material on Weicker's frank," [Henry Price, assistant to Weicker,] said.

   He admitted that mistakes have been made by "inexperienced staff members," and said that if Mrs. Wexler sent him the four letters she is using as evidence, he will make sure "the post office has a check for 24 cents tomorrow morning."

15. Let him who is without sin cast the first stone.

*16. *John F. Kennedy:* Why, some say, the moon? Why choose this as our goal? They may [as] well ask why climb the highest mountain? Why thirty-five years ago fly the Atlantic? Why does Rice play Texas?

17. *Robert Reinhold, the* New York Times, *August 17, 1970, in a story on a battle between Regents and faculty at the University of Texas, in which Silber was fired:* The chief antagonists are Dr. John Silber, the charismatic and ambitious dean of the College of Arts and Sciences, and Frank C. Erwin, Jr., chair-

man of the Board of Regents and a political friend of former President Lyndon B. Johnson. . . .

*18. *Senator Robert C. Byrd, Democrat from West Virginia, in a statement to the President's Commission on Campus Unrest, September 9, 1970:* It is high time that professors who distort the perspective of young minds, who advocate the overthrow of our system of government, who corrupt and pervert the educational process, be purged from our educational institutions. . . .

The social studies in particular are dominated by the high priests of radicalism, and it is little wonder that many American young people get a badly distorted picture of their country, its present and its past. . . .

There is something dreadfully wrong with college governing boards and administrations which allow faculties . . . to become overloaded with fuzzy-minded, phony liberals whose heroes are Che Guevara, Fidel Castro, Ho Chi Minh, and Mao Tse-tung.

19. *William F. Buckley, Jr.,* The Governor Listeth, *p. 226, explaining how American soldiers could have murdered at My Lai after only a few months in uniform:* [A] society deprived of the strength of religious sanctions . . . hugely devoted to hedonism . . . to an indifference to authority and the law . . . I would contend that [an] . . . explanation for what happened, according to this analysis, is—not Vietnam, but, to reach for a symbol—Berkeley.

20. *Column by John Cunniff, July 1970:* Do Americans eat well in comparison with other nations? Millions of Americans still have poor diets, but generally speaking most Americans can afford to eat well. In the U.S. and Canada less than 20% of all "personal consumption expenditures" are for food. In less developed countries, the figures are much higher.

21. *Kerner Commission Report (Report of the National Advisory Commission on Civil Disorders), p. 236:* The hostility of Negro parents and students toward the school system is generating increasing conflict and causing disruption within many school districts.

But the most dramatic evidence of the relationship between educational practices and civil disorder lies in the high incidence of riot participation by ghetto youth who have not completed high school. Our survey of the riot cities found that the typical riot participant was a high school dropout.

22. *Presidential Press Conference, July 1, 1970:* Questioner: Do you feel that in the modern world there are situations when a president must respond against a very tight deadline when he cannot consult with the legislative branch? [The question was general, but in context had specific reference to the incursion into Cambodia which was taken without prior consultation with the Congress.]

President Nixon: Well, another good example, of course, is the Cuban missile crisis. President Kennedy had a very difficult decision there and two hours and a quarter before he ordered the use of American men to blockade Cuba, he told the Senate and Congressional leaders.

I can assure the American people that this President is going to bend over backwards to consult the Senate and consult the House whenever he feels it can be done without jeopardizing the lives of American men. But when it's a question of the lives of American men, or the attitudes of people in the Senate, I'm coming down hard on the side of defending the lives of American men.

*23. *Spiro Agnew, Cleveland, Ohio, June 20, 1970:* When we took office, there were close to 550,000 American troops in Vietnam; we have brought 115,000 home. . . . We will bring another 150,000 home by next Spring. . . . The enemy has paid and will continue to pay a heavy price for having misread the people and the president of the United States.

24. *Lyndon B. Johnson, quoted by his brother Sam Houston Johnson in his book* My Brother Lyndon: "That's the trouble, Sam Houston—it's always my move. And damn it, I sometimes can't tell whether I'm making the right move or not. Now take this Vietnam mess: How in the hell can anyone know for sure what's right and what's wrong, Sam? I got some of the finest brains in this country—people like Dean Rusk, Walt Rostow and Dean Acheson—making some awful strong and convincing arguments for us to stay in there and not pull out. Then I've got some people like George Ball and Fulbright, also intelligent men, whose motives I can't rightly distrust—and them telling me we've got to de-escalate or run the risk of a total war. And Sam, I've got to listen to both sides. . . . I've just got to choose between my opposing experts. No way of avoiding it. But I sure as hell wish I could *really* know what's right."

*25. *Column by Evans & Novak, August 1970:* . . . charged with murder in the San Rafael shootout. Like most of the Weathermen terrorists now being sought, Miss Davis could be almost anywhere. . . .

Exercise II for Chapter Three

Do the following passages contain fallacies? If so, which ones? State the reasons for your answers.

1. *President Nixon on the uproar over plans to use only men waiters at the Hotel del Coronado, Coronado, California, September 1970:* They claim we're not letting women be waitresses. . . . Why did they want to do that kind of work? Let the men be waiters.

   After the story was blown up by the press, Presidential Press Secretary Ziegler stated, "Whenever you have women writing stories, there's a certain emotionalism involved."

2. *Young Marxist movie director who declared himself against everything the Cannes Film Festival represented, yet still permitted his film to be shown at the Festival (when accused of inconsistency),* Harper's, *September 1970:* I'm against the state, and the state owns the Metro, and the railroads and the airlines, but that does not mean that I must refuse to travel.

3. *Column by John Chamberlain, September 1970:* If [Senator] Proxmire has his way, the technological distance between Western Europe and America is destined to be whittled down by American defaults on "R and D" [research and development]. The edge of American air development will be blunted by slowdowns or cancellations of supersonic experimentation; the space program will have fewer spinoffs; . . . the Pentagon will be starved, . . . as sums are wasted in constructing more and more of that ugly cement-block housing that is destined to be the slums of tomorrow.

4. *New Britain, Connecticut, Mayor Manafort, quoted in* New Britain Herald, *October 23, 1970, in a story about a court's permitting anti-Vietnam War demonstrators to display the Viet Cong flag:* I am appalled and terrified that anyone would condone such a slap in the face to the heroes of the greatest country on the face of the globe. . . . The next thing we know the lovers of North Vietnamese and Viet Cong will open recruiting centers here. . . . how long [would] these people last in Hanoi marching up the street with an American flag in their hand?

5. *Ted Dillon, President, Dow Chemical Co.,* Wall Street Journal, *December 1967:* Why do we produce napalm? In simplest form, we produce it because we feel our company should produce those items which our fighting men need in time of war when we have the ability to do so.

    A quarter of a century ago this answer would have satisfied just about everyone who asked this question. Today, however, it doesn't. Today we find ourselves accused of being immoral because we produce this product for use in what some people consider an unjust war. We are told that to make a weapon because you're asked to do so by your government puts you in precisely the same position as the German industrialists who pleaded at their Nürnberg trials that they were "only following orders."

    . . . we reject the validity of comparing our present form of government with Hitler's Nazi Germany. In our mind our government is still representative of and responsive to the will of the people.

6. *Don Whitehead in his book,* The Dow Story, *1968:* Our position on the manufacture of napalm is that we are a supplier of goods to the Defense Department, and not a policy maker. We do not and should not try to decide military strategy or policy.

    Simple good citizenship requires that we supply our Government and our military with those goods which they feel they need whenever we have the technology and capability and have been chosen by the Government as a supplier.

Exercise III for Chapter Three

Find examples in the mass media of fallacies discussed in Chapter Three, and explain why they are fallacious.

Chapter Four

Statistical Fallacies

There are lies, damn lies, and statistics.

Benjamin Disraeli

By and large, statistical fallacies are just variations on the fallacies already considered. But they're such important variations that they warrant separate treatment.

1. Some examples

The statistical fallacy that politicians and others are most frequently guilty of is simply the suppression of known and relevant data (a variation on the fallacy of *suppressed evidence*).

Republican victory claims in the nationwide 1970 U.S. Senate races furnish a typical example. These claims were based on the fact that in off-year elections (years when no president is being elected), the party of the incumbent president almost always loses Senate seats. In the 1970 elections, the Republicans *gained* two Senate seats.

In this case, the suppressed evidence is quite simple. In the first place, Republicans ignored the fact that a victorious presidential candidate usually carries a comfortable majority of senators of his own party along with him and that the larger the majority, the greater the loss two years hence (on the average). But in 1968, President Nixon, elected by the tiniest of margins, failed to carry a Republican Senate in with him. So only a very small Republican loss would be expected, in any case.

Even more important is the suppressed fact that 25 Democrats and only ten Republicans were up for reelection, due to the Johnson landslide of

1964. Such an imbalance of risk is almost unprecedented. Once we take it into account, the Democratic showing begins to look quite respectable, and Republican claims of victory out of order. Having risked fifteen more seats, it is not surprising the Democrats lost two more races than did the Republicans.

And, finally, the two-seat improvement looks even less like a victory when it is noticed that two of the Democratic losses (those in New York and Connecticut) may have resulted from unusual three-way races which hurt the Democrats more than they did their opponents.

Notice again that this fallacy could not be detected by the uninformed; they always are fair game for the slick operator. The political professionals who crowed victory for the Republicans were in a position to know that pertinent information was being suppressed; it was the uninformed man in the street who was misled.

The battles surrounding the Massachusetts no-fault insurance law provides another case in which the man in the street should have known (but generally didn't) that information was being suppressed. One of these battles centered on attempts to lower auto insurance premiums by 15 percent. The response of the insurance industry was a vast campaign in which they claimed that bankruptcy was possible. Typical was the article in the *New Britain Herald* (October 12, 1970, by David L. Walter) on the problems of the insurance industry, and their need to raise rates:

> *Over the past ten years, the insurance industry has paid out $2 billion more in claims than it has collected in premiums, says a spokesman for the Insurance Information Institute . . .*

The impression given is that without a rate increase, insurance companies would soon be unable to pay insurance claims.

But this conclusion was not warranted by the facts, as the spokesman for the I.I.I. and the writer of the article ought to have known. Insurance companies don't just put premiums in a vault; they *invest* them, and use investment profits along with premiums to meet insurance claims. So the pertinent figures were *total* income and total outgo, which yield total profits. During the ten years in question, the insurance industry took in comfortably more in premiums and investment profits than it paid out in claims and operating expenses.

The average person tends to see issues in simple terms. He doesn't want to get down to the nitty-gritty details or read the fine-print arguments. This usually results in his being taken, no matter what the field. But in the case of *business politics,* where statistics are king, it results in deceit on a grand scale.

One of the classic ploys of this type was detailed in an article by *Ramparts* magazine.[1] American Telephone and Telegraph Co. (A.T. & T., the Bell Telephone system) is one of America's largest military contractors, its particular baby being the ABM. In one case, its subsidiary, Western Electric Company, took a profit of $113 million on an Army ABM contract of $1.6 billion. This amounts to "only" 7.9 percent, and those satisfied with outward appearances no doubt looked no further, satisfied that 7.9 percent is not very far out of line.

But in fact, the profits to Western Electric and thus to Bell Telephone were immense and grossly out of line. The above figures served only to conceal suppressed data, which *Ramparts* magazine brought to the surface. For Western Electric itself did only $359 million of the work, including $82 million for administrative expenses. So its profits at the very least were 31.3 percent, a tremendously exorbitant profit rate.

Here is roughly how it worked so that everyone profited but the federal government (and thus you and me). Western Electric subcontracted $645 million of the contract to Douglas Aircraft, which took a profit of $46 million (7.6 percent). Douglas then subcontracted all but $103 million, so that its profit on actual work done was 44.3 percent. Of course, the subsubcontractors, Consolidated Western (a division of U.S. Steel) and Fruehoff Trailer Corporation, also took their profits.

So the government ended up paying profits to Consolidated and Fruehoff, profits on profits to Douglas, and profits on profits on profits to Western Electric.

The details of a particularly flagrant overcharge on part of this contract illustrate the care that must be exhibited in handling profit and loss statements.

Here is the *Ramparts* account of this detail:

> *Probably the greatest chutzpah shown by Western, however, was in the scrupulous insistence on paying rent of $3 million to the government for the use of two surplus plants where much of the Nike production work was done. Ordinarily the government would have simply donated the use of the plants, but Western insisted on paying. Then again, Western has to make a buck too, so it added the $3 million to its "costs." The government had to turn around and give the rent*

[1] November, 1969. Notice that it is a *non*mass media magazine which ran this exposé.

*money back as a reimbursement, plus $209,000 profit on it. Nothing
excessive, just about seven percent. A reasonable profit.*

Finally, it ought to be pointed out that military contracts are different
from many others only in degree. Bell, for instance, uses the same profit
on profit system in its purchases of telephones from—surprise—Western
Electric. First, Western Electric takes a profit on the "sale" of the telephones to Bell, and then Bell takes a profit on the "cost" of telephones purchased from its own subsidiary, Western Electric.

Statistics always seem precise and *authoritative.* But statistical facts can
be just as unknowable as any others. My favorite example of unknowable
statistics comes from a letter received several years ago:

*Dear Friend: In the past 5000 years men have fought in 14,523 wars.
One out of four persons living during this time have been war casualties. A nuclear war would add 1,245,000,000 men, women, and children to this tragic list.*

But it is ludicrous to present such precise figures as facts. No one knows
(or could know) the exact number of wars fought up to the present time,
to say nothing of the number of war casualties. As for the number of casualties in some future nuclear war, it would depend on what kind of war,
and in any event is a matter on which even so-called "experts" can only
speculate.

But it is not just oddball statistics which are at present unknown. Some
of the most important statistics of all, those published by the federal government on business conditions in the United States, have their doubters.
Oskar Morgenstern is one expert who put his doubts into words, in an article in *Fortune* magazine[2] which reveals the problems of the statistics
gatherers.

One of the major problems with government statistics is that their margin
of error (not usually reported) is greater than the "significant" differences
they often report. We read in the newspapers that the economy grew in a
given month at a rate amounting to 5 percent a year, perhaps an increase
of one percent over the previous year. Everyone is pleased at this increase

[2] *Qui Numerare Incipit Errare Incipit* (roughly: "He who begins to count begins to
err"), *Fortune,* October, 1963.

in the growth rate of the economy. But the *margin of error* on government growth rate statistics very likely is much greater than one percent, as Morgenstern indicated, citing one of the government's own revisions:

> *If the rate for the change* [in growth] *from 1947 to 1948 was determined in February, 1949, when the first figures became available, it was 10.8 percent. In July, 1950, using officially corrected figures, it became 12.5 percent; in July, 1956, it fell to 11.8 percent—a full percentage point. All this for the growth rate from 1947 to 1948!*

Add to this the fact that even the officially corrected figures cannot take account of the deliberately misleading or false figures businessmen sometimes provide the government (to cover their tracks or to mislead rival companies) and it becomes clear that the margin of error on figures for the gross national product has to be fairly large. In addition, there is the problem arising from the need to use a base year (because of price fluctuations):

> *If a year with a high (or low) gross national product is chosen as base year, this will depress (or raise) the growth rate of subsequent years. . . . An unscrupulous or politically oriented* [!] *writer will choose that base year which produces the sequence of (alleged) growth rates best suited to his aims and programs. . . . These are, of course, standard tricks, used, undoubtedly, ever since index numbers were invented.*

In other words, if you want to show that a given year had a high rate of growth, choose a low base year, and vice versa for a low growth rate. Meanwhile, the true rate of growth remains unknown, except for broad, long-term trends.

Government statistics may report confidently on things that are not *known* with such precision, but at least they bear some resemblance to the truth. Many statistics, however, don't even have that virtue. An example is the statistical evidence obtained from surveys which ask "loaded" or biased questions. In general, the technique is to ask a question in such a way that you are more likely to get the desired answer. Thus, Congressman Larry Winn, of Kansas, annoyed perhaps by letter-writing campaigns asking for relief aid to Biafra, may have desired to provide himself with an excuse for doing nothing about Biafran starvation by asking his constituents the following loaded question:

> *Do you favor direct United States military intervention to provide aid to Biafra?*

Not unexpectedly, given the military intervention in Vietnam at that time, only 8 percent said "yes"; 92 percent said no.

Had he wanted a large "yes" vote, he could have framed the question differently and been assured of an overwhelming vote in favor of aid to Biafra:

> *Do you favor sending aid to Biafra to stem the tide of horrible starvation which has taken over a million lives, mostly infants, children, and the aged, and which will take the lives of more millions of Biafrans if we don't send aid soon?*

This does not mean it is impossible to ask a *neutral* question, although topics such as the Nigeria-Biafra war make objective questioning difficult. In this case, if Congressman Winn had read his mail more carefully he would have noticed that most of his constituents were asking for greater U.S. government aid to church relief groups that were airlifting food into Biafra, and not for military intervention. So his question should have read something like this:

> *Do you favor greatly increased aid (food and relief planes) to church groups currently flying food into Biafra?*

But Congressman Winn was a piker at the loaded question gambit when compared to Henry A. Bubb, president of Capital Federal Savings and Loan Association. In his column in Capital Federal's *News and Views,* mailed to all depositors, he occasionally asked his readers to respond to questions about political issues. Here is one of his gems:

> *Do you think that we should continue to lose precious lives and spend $26 billion a year for the war in Vietnam while we only spend $1.9 billion a year to relieve poverty and riots at home?*

The response, in case you're in doubt, was "yes"—18 percent, "no"—82 percent, a figure he could have more or less reversed simply by asking the question this way:

> *Do you think we should stop wasting $1.9 billion per year on slackers in the U.S. who won't work and can't support themselves adequately while at the same time we increase our $26 billion expenditure in Vietnam and thus strike a greater blow against the atheistic communists who threaten our Democracy?*

One final Bubb masterpiece from the same survey:

> *Should the government's program for aid to dependent children, which has skyrocketed from $1.6 million to $3.7 million per year in the last decade, continue unchecked?*

The vote? "Yes"—27 percent, "no"—73 percent. It takes a strong person to vote for a program which has "skyrocketed unchecked," even if it's for the kiddies.

Polls also are used to determine consumer preferences and habits. Of course, statistics compiled from such surveys need not be worthless; it is possible to construct reliable surveys, although it is generally expensive and takes trained personnel. But all too frequently, surveys of this kind are worthless. Here is an example which was intended to prove that exact point:[3]

> *A sidewalk researcher in New York City asked passers-by what books they preferred to read from a specified list of paperbacks. The winners were: Shakespeare, the Bible, and a few classics.*
>
> *After each interviewer answered, the researcher told him to select one of the listed books as a gift to be sent for cooperating. . . . The book most people selected was* Murder of a Burlesque Queen *by Gypsy Rose Lee. The researcher stated: "The biggest trap you can fall into is believing what people tell you they want."*

---

[3] Cited in *The Permissible Lie,* by Samm Sinclair Baker, World Publishing Co., Cleveland and New York, 1968, Chapter 10.

Yet, that is exactly what most surveys, including political surveys, report.

Statistics often seem more significant than they are, leading to commission of the fallacy of *hasty conclusion* in its statistical version. During the 1970 race for Governor of Connecticut, it was pointed out that Emilio Daddario missed 119 roll calls on bills before Congress in the previous session, whereas his opponent Thomas J. Meskill only missed 112. Daddario defended himself by claiming he didn't miss *important* roll calls, a defense objected to by Meskill on the grounds that Daddario had missed votes on a drug-control measure, on railroad legislation, and on organized crime.

While Meskill's statistics are pertinent to the charge that Daddario didn't do a good job in Congress, they don't come close to proving the point, even leaving aside the thought that voting on bills is only one of the important jobs of a congressman. For merely missing a roll call, even on an important bill, is not necessarily significant. The bill may have been doomed to failure or certain to pass without a particular congressman's vote. He may pass up a vote in such a case so as not to annoy certain power groups among his constituents by voting against their narrow interests. In addition, it is impossible to tell from the subject matter whether a bill is important. Some railroad legislation, for instance, can be fairly trivial in nature.

Finally, in assessing the 119 to 112 ratio, we have to bear in mind that committee votes often are much more important than those on the floor of the House; often, the import of a vote cannot be determined even by carefully reading a particular bill.

Prior to Senate defeat of a bill providing a $290 million subsidy for the proposed U.S. supersonic transport plane (SST), backers of the bill tried to line up support for it by blunting one of the main objections to the SST, namely sonic boom. They did this by passing a motion banning supersonic flights over land in the United States. As a result, some senators who felt that sonic boom was a greatly overplayed issue found themselves voting *for* the bill banning supersonic land flights, even though they were against the content of the bill: They did so hoping that as a result the $290 million SST appropriation would be passed by the Senate the next day.

The SST vote also illustrates the difficulty of assessing failure to vote on a measure. Senator Magnuson attached an amendment to the overall transportation budget bill (of which the SST appropriation was a part) which stipulated that the Portland, Oregon, international airport would get no funds until detailed and exhaustive environmental studies were completed. Oregon's Senator, Mark Hatfield, tried to get the amendment removed, but was told that Senator Magnuson might be willing to strike his amendment *after* the SST vote was taken. Senator Hatfield was thus in a bind. He was known to be opposed to the SST. Yet if he voted against the SST appropriation, Magnuson's amendment would not be withdrawn, and Portland would lose its airport funds. On the other hand, it would look bad to vote for the SST appropriation, since he was a well-known opponent of it. He did the only thing he could, under the circumstances, and announced he had a long-standing speaking engagement elsewhere. An Oregon voter who *merely* noted the missed vote simply failed to grasp the problem, and completely missed Hatfield's attempt to save Portland's airport money.[4]

There are a great number of statistical variations on the fallacy of *hasty conclusion*. But one, the fallacy of the **small sample**, is sufficiently important to warrant separate discussion. Statistics frequently are used to project from a sample to the "population" from which the sample was drawn. This is the basic technique behind all polling, from the Gallup Poll to the Nielsen TV ratings.

But if the sample is too small to be a reliable measure of the population, then to accept it is to commit the fallacy of the *small sample,* a variety of the fallacy of *hasty conclusion*. This fallacy is committed frequently at election time, because a sufficiently large representative sample generally is quite expensive and difficult to obtain. There is a great deal of controversy about how large a sample has to be, but there should be little argument about the following examples.

An Evans and Novak column (October 1970) contained the following on the 1970 Connecticut Senatorial race: "In the blue-collar neighborhoods of this old factory town, the Rev. Joseph Duffey is losing—and losing badly —his audacious bid to weld a neo-Rooseveltian coalition. . . ." Their statement was based on a poll of 67 Bridgeport voters in normally Democratic Italian-American working-class precincts, which showed Senator Thomas Dodd with 43 percent of the vote, Rep. Lowell Weicker with 27 percent,

---

[4] The SST story actually is even more complicated than that. In December 1970, the Senate voted against the $290 million appropriation for the SST. But anyone who rated his state's senators solely on their votes up to that time again was guilty of *hasty conclusion*. For the vote came late in the year and some senators may have known what was coming next on the issue: a beautiful squeeze play by the House. The House passed an amended Department of Transportation bill which included three months' additional funding for the SST, and then adjourned for the year. A Senate vote against this bill would have cut off all funds for air traffic controllers (thus grounding all commercial planes) and for DOT employees. So the Senate voted for the bill and thus to extend SST funding for three months more. So another "crucial" vote came up in March 1971. A citizen interested in the SST thus had to keep up with the topic for some time in order to determine how his representatives in Washington really affected the issue. (Senator Hatfield, incidentally, voted against continued funding for the SST in the March 1971 vote.)

and Duffey with only 11 percent. This obviously was too small a sample on which to base more than tentative conclusions.[5]

The *Hartford Times* (September 13, 1970), in a story on University of Connecticut "Hard Hats" (conservative faculty members), stated that "hardliners" tend to teach at the University of Connecticut in the physical sciences, while more liberal types tend to teach liberal arts. This conclusion was based on a study of the voting pattern on three resolutions concerning punishment for disruptive students. The trouble is that the three votes constitute too small a sample from which to draw more than a tentative conclusion.

This survey also was defective in lacking **instance variety**, thus being *unrepresentative*[6] of the population as a whole. In this case, the population was all relevant attitudes of University of Connecticut faculty members; the survey checked only those on punishment for disruptive students. A man who voted to punish disruptive students may not have been a "hardliner" on other issues.

And then there are the statistical variations on the fallacy of *questionable cause*. A *New York Times* article on marijuana which argued that marijuana is harmful to health cited a report that twelve American soldiers in Vietnam had been reported to have smoked marijuana and to have had acute psychotic reactions. The implication was that marijuana smoking *caused* the psychosis.

But the statistic cited is not significant by itself. Statistics linking one thing with another rarely are. In this case, we need to know at least the incidence of psychosis among U.S. soldiers in Vietnam who have not smoked marijuana. The horrors of war, after all, may well have been responsible for the psychosis, not marijuana.

Statistics have such an authoritative ring that it seems possible to do just about anything with them and get away with it. One trick is to juxtapose otherwise valid statistics in a way that *seems* to yield significant results, but actually does not, because the statistics are not of comparable types, or because a more important comparison has been overlooked.

---

[5] Duffey did lose the election, and he lost primarily because he failed to pile up margins in cities like Bridgeport. But the election figures for Bridgeport show that Duffey lost there to *Weicker,* not Dodd. The figures were Duffey 18,273, Weicker 21,674, and Dodd only 5,909, a far cry from the sample cited by Evans and Novak. (Of course, the actual results are irrelevant to the charge of *small sample*. The sample would have been too small even if, luckily, it exactly mirrored the election results.)

[6] See Appendix A for more on instance variety and representative samples.

In 1970, the Consolidated Edison Company of New York wanted to double the capacity of its power plant in Astoria (an area of Queens, a borough of New York City). Antipollutionists were against this expansion. In trying to combat the pollution charge, Con Ed's Jerry V. Halvorsen, Environmental Affairs Coordinator, argued that the expanded plant would actually reduce pollution:[7]

> *Let 5 stand for the existing capacity of the Astoria plant. Multiply by 1, the percentage of sulfur in the fuel we use now. And you get 5. Now let 10 stand for the proposed double capacity of the plant. Multiply by .37, the percentage of sulfur in the fuel we will use in the future. You get 3.7. And 3.7 is less than 5.*

The conclusion he wanted the reader to draw was that pollution would be reduced even though power capacity would be doubled. But he obtained this result by comparing "apples with oranges." (He also was guilty of a bit of *suppressed evidence.*) For if low-sulfur fuel was to be used in the new expanded plant, then it could be used in the plant already in existence. Doubling capacity would after all double pollution, as Miss Mayo was quick to point out.

Statistical comparisons of crime rates at different times or places frequently are fallacious because the *quality* of the statistics differs so much. In many parts of the country, apparent increases in the crime rate can be achieved simply by changing the recording habits of police officers, for instance, by recording minor crimes by blacks against blacks, Chicanos against Chicanos, or Indians against Indians. In New York City, police can increase the crime *total* simply by walking down almost any main street and arresting hot dog, pretzel, or ice cream vendors; if a decrease is desired, they simply become blinder than usual to these everyday violations of the law. The same is true of prostitution, gambling, and homosexual activity, areas of crime in which the police generally have a special interest.

Statistics on parking violations in many big cities suffer from this same fault. A New York City policeman who ticketed every illegally parked car he saw would have little time for anything else. Police statistics simply do not accurately reflect the actual incidence of lawbreaking. Hence, if we compare figures on lawbreaking for one place or time with those for another, the result is apt to be ludicrous.

[7] Quoted by Anna Mayo in the *Village Voice,* August 13, 1970.

Equally silly are many of the statistical comparisons which fail to take account of inflation or (occasionally) deflation. A piano ad touted Steinway pianos as a "growth investment," on the statistical grounds that many older Steinways were selling for as much or more than their original cost. Now this does prove that buying, say, a $3000 Steinway is less expensive in the long run than buying a $3000 Pontiac, since in ten years the Pontiac will be worth next to nothing. But it doesn't prove Steinways are a *growth* investment, since the dollars of twenty or thirty years ago, or even ten, were worth much more than those of today. Steinway should have tried to convert the figures to a neutral basis (a tricky business) before making a comparison.

Perhaps the classic inflation example is the one inadvertently furnished by Marvin Kitman in his book, *Washington's Expense Account*. Mr. Kitman was trying to prove that George Washington had lived relatively high on the hog during the Revolutionary War, which is true, and also that he padded expense accounts, which is possible but not proved by Kitman's figures.

Washington's accounts were kept primarily in Pennsylvania pounds. Mr. Kitman translated them into dollars via the Continental (Congress) dollar, equating 26 Continental dollars with one Pennsylvania pound. The trouble is that the value of the Continental dollar fluctuated widely, mostly downward, eventually becoming just about worthless (the origin of the phrase "not worth a Continental").

Kitman listed Washington's total expenses as $449,261.51 (note the aura of authority in that last 51¢!). An "expert" (who preferred to remain anonymous—perhaps because of the amount of guesswork involved) suggested $68,000 was a better figure.

In these examples, the comparisons themselves are faulty. Often, however, while the comparison is on the up and up, the *conclusion* is misleading. It is frequently stated that the American Indian has less to complain about than is usually supposed, that we can't have treated the Indian all *that* badly in the United States, since there are more Indians in the United States now than when Columbus "discovered" America. (This is disputed by some experts, who think the standard estimates on the Indian population in 1492 are too low. But in any event, the population then was probably not greatly different from what it is now.)

But even supposing the cited figures are correct, what do they prove? A more significant figure would be this (but still not terribly significant, given the immense amount of direct evidence that white men mistreated Indians). Take the number of whites and blacks in the U.S. in, say, 1783 (the end of the Revolutionary War), and compare that to the number of their descendants alive today (that is, don't count later immigrants and their progeny—a good trick because of interbreeding, but not impossible to estimate). Now compare this increase with that of the American Indian. What we would no doubt find is that the white and black populations doubled many times over, while the Indians' remained fairly stable.[8] If we had no direct evidence, then this comparison would be significant; but it would support the idea that the white man did, after all, mistreat the Indian.

Statistics would seem to be the last place in which to encounter the fallacy of *ambiguity;* numbers, after all, are so very precise. But what numbers are used to *count* may not be so precise.

In 1970, Attorney General John Mitchell stated before the International Association of Chiefs of Police that the federal government placed only 133 taps during the first seven months of 1970. But (as was pointed out in the *New Republic,* October 24, 1970) he must have had in mind only one kind of wiretap, for his figures did not include taps used in "internal security" cases, 48-hour "emergency" taps, or *bugs,* as opposed to wiretaps. The latter was especially deceptive, because Mr. Mitchell could expect police officers to know the difference between a wiretap and a bug, but not his wider audience, the general public, to which his statement ultimately was addressed. The public could be expected to assume that 133 was the total of electronic eavesdropping by the federal government. (If caught in the act, Mitchell could always have said he was speaking loosely, a defense that it is hard to counter, because life is short and in daily life we do tend to save time by speaking loosely.)

2. Statistical fallacies in context

It is relatively easy to spot statistical fallacies when they're extracted from surrounding material. But it's another matter when a batch of statistics are thrown at you in a whole article or column. Here is a political column which contains at least two statistical fallacies. The reader is invited to do his own analysis before reading this writer's opinion:[9]

---

[8] Actually, Indian population steadily declined until the Indians were completely conquered at the end of the nineteenth century. But in the past fifty years or so, their number has increased.

[9] The column is by John Cunniff. © 1970, the Associated Press. Reprinted by permission.

New York (AP)—Inflation Notes:
The cost of a college education is going to be higher again this fall.
Parents have become so accustomed to this statement that it no longer
has any shock effect. But the figures, nevertheless, are rather numbing.

The median charges for tuition, fees and room-board are expected
to total about $2,502 in private coeducational colleges, up $200 from
the 1969–1970 academic year.

Private women's colleges will be about $234 higher at $2,737, and
private men's schools higher by $211 at $2,840. But those are the
medians, meaning the figures half way between the highest and the
lowest.

And what are the extremes? Well, at Bennington College in Vermont
you must figure on total expenses of $4,325, which is $5 more than
the price at Sarah Lawrence. Radcliffe, Tufts, Monterey Institute of
Foreign Studies and several other schools will cost $4,000 or more.
But students at public schools, such as the New York city colleges,
may pay as little as $60.

The figures were compiled by the Life Insurance Agency Manage-
ment Association to convince the public that they need to save well
ahead to meet tuition costs—preferably through an insurance program.

At the rate prices are rising, however, the industry may find a good
many families borrowing the cash value of their policies.

Once upon a time inflation was at the rate of only a couple of per-
centage points a year and most people hardly noticed it at all. But now
it's 6 per cent or more and few families can ignore it.

In an effort to show how damaging this can be if permitted to con-
tinue, the U.S. Savings and Loan League figured out that 30 years
from now a man would have to earn $57,435 to equal his present
$10,000 salary.

A $20 bag of groceries, 1970 style, would cost $114.87 in the year
2000. A $500 color television set would sell for $2,871, and a $3,000
automobile would carry a price tag of $17,230. A $25,000 home
would be priced at $147,000.

Shocked? You should be. But don't forget either that these figures
are not likely to be approached. Most economists would tell you that
in all probability the economy would collapse long before 2000.

The statistics, some of them, are interesting and informative. But the
conclusions, stated or implied, are another matter. Let's start with the comparison between private school costs and those of public schools. In the
first place, we are given the *average* for private schools, as well as two of
the highest figures, but only the lowest figure for public schools. But sec-

ond, and more important, the figures for private schools cover room and board, while the $60 figure quoted for public schools does not; another example of comparing apples with oranges.

The column also quotes scare statistics on how damaging it would be if a 6 percent inflation rate continued into the future. A $25,000 home would cost $147,000, a $20 bag of groceries $114.87. But mere inflation proves nothing. The question is how *income* rises in comparison. If prices 30 years from now are six times higher than at present, then anyone making more than six times his present salary will be better off financially than now, and anyone making less than six times his present salary will be less well off. It's as simple as that.[10]

It is often supposed by laymen that scientific reasoning is on a very high level compared to political reasoning. But that is not always true of reasoning in the social sciences. And contrary to what many college students seem to believe, the writings of social scientists are *not* merely academic. Their conclusions often are used by politicians to justify pet positions, or to attack positions of their opponents.

Conclusions about racial differences in intelligence provide a perfect example of both the shoddy reasoning of some social scientists and, in particular, the political use of that shoddy reasoning.

In the late sixties and in 1970, the far right distributed a pamphlet by Henry E. Garrett titled *Children: Black and White,*[11] which attempted to prove that Negroes are inherently (genetically and biologically) inferior in intelligence to whites. Here is a summary of the pamphlet's major statistical points:

1. A 1963 Florida study discovered that only 6.1 percent of 1800 Negro public school children scored over 100 on the 1960 Stanford-Binet IQ test, compared to an average of about 50 percent for white students. Only 1.1 percent scored over 110, compared to 30 percent for white students. But 51.7 percent scored under 80, compared to only 8.2 percent of white students.

---

[10] Of course, the effect of inflation on economic activity is another matter, and one concerning which economists differ.

[11] The Patrick Henry Press, Inc., Virginia. Professor Garrett (Ph.D., Columbia University), was Chairman of the Columbia University Psychology Department for 16 years, and a past president of the American Psychological Association. His works were cited in a 1957 court case by parties opposing integration of the Louisiana public school system.

The parts of this pamphlet summarized here are similar to parts of the controversial 1969 *Harvard Educational Review* article by Arthur R. Jensen, "How Much Can We Boost IQ and Scholastic Achievement?" Jensen's article (it seems to me) suffered from the same general defects to be pointed out concerning the Garrett pamphlet.

2. A *national* study showed only 15 percent of the Negroes tested over 100, compared to about 50 percent for whites.

3. Army intelligence tests in 1966 show the following intelligence ratings of black and white draftees:

	Blacks	Whites
Superior	.3	7.6
High	3.3	32.1
Average	18.2	34.6
Low	38.2	16.0
Borderline	37.1	9.1

4. Well-known studies with twins (identical twins have identical genes) show that heredity is three times as important as environment in determining differences between individuals. Hence, only that much variation in performance can be attributed to environment. (This conclusion wasn't explicitly drawn in the pamphlet. But it generally is in works of this kind, so we've drawn it here.)

5. Army tests in WW I, WW II, and the Korean War show both whites and blacks improving their intelligence scores, but the percentage gap between the two groups remained about the same. Equal environmental improvement produced equal percentages of IQ improvement; the gap in performance did not close as it should have if intelligence potentials were the same.

6. A New Jersey-Pennsylvania test of 213 black and white students "matched for age, sex, courses of study and for 11 socio-economic factors," giving each student "a test of 74 items, 37 of which were identified as *cultural* and 37 as *non-cultural.*" The result was that the upper 25 percent of each racial group (53 of each) overlapped only 18 percent, not much more than the 15 percent found in random groups, and far less than would be expected in matched white groups of this kind.

7. Finally, crime statistics in the U.S. show the Negro crime rate per capita to be far higher than that of whites. For instance, an FBI report from the sixties shows that, per capita, Negroes have 10 times as many illegitimate children as white, commit 13 times as many murders, 6 times as many robberies, and 10 times as many rapes and assaults.

To assess statistical evidence of this kind, several questions should be raised.

1. *How accurate are the statistics?* In this case, we can discount reporting and calculating errors, since so many divergent sources all report

similar statistics. If these statistics are inaccurate, the error must be fairly systematic. So we begin to think of factors such as motivation (are white children on the average more highly motivated to score high by aspiring parents?), how the tests were administered (were black children frequently administered tests by hostile white teachers?), and physical condition of the test takers (were more blacks than whites malnourished?).

It turns out that there is evidence only on the second factor: in some tests, blacks in segregated schools with black teachers scored about the same as any other black students. So we can discount hostile test givers as a major source of error.[12] But the other two factors, motivation and physical condition, must be tested for before we can accept the exact statistics on IQ.

However, the statistics appealed to seem to indicate this much. American Negroes on the average have not been able to score as high as whites on IQ tests, even if the difference has not been as great as claimed in the pamphlet. In other words, we can assume that there is a statistical *correlation* between race (or cultural group? See page 100) and IQ scores. But we cannot yet assume a *casual connection* between these two factors.

2. *Is pertinent data being suppressed?* Every person will answer this question differently; it all depends on what a given person already knows. Experts on the topic are more likely to be aware of suppressed evidence than laymen. Those who are entirely ignorant on the matter, however intelligent, are out in the cold as usual.

In any event, here is evidence suppressed by the pamphlet in question that the author of this text happened to be aware of:

a. It is quite common for the same person to score significantly higher on IQ tests at one time than on another, in particular as a result of "compensatory education." [13]

b. Different studies of identical twins differ somewhat in results. But one study of 38 pairs of identical twins reared apart (notice how small the sample is—this is true for all identical twin studies yet conducted) indicated that the *average* IQ difference of such twins was 14 points, and that over 25 percent had IQ score differences larger than the average difference between blacks and whites in the United States.[14]

---

[12] But this doesn't rule out related possibilities. For instance, it is possible that white teachers primed white students better on the average than white *or* black teachers primed black students.

[13] See "A non-psychological approach to compensatory education," by Carl Bereiter, in *Social Class, Race, and Psychological Development,* edited by M. Deutsch, I. Katz, and (ironically) A. R. Jensen, Holt, Rinehart and Winston, New York, 1968.

[14] See I. I. Gottesman's article in the book *Social Class, Race, and Psychological Development* just referred to.

c. Studies show that lower-class *whites* do less well than middle- and upper-class *whites* on IQ tests,[15] thus casting doubt on race as the explanation of differences in IQ scores.

d. It is well known that American Jews score on the average a bit higher on IQ tests than do American white Christians. Yet Jews are as genetically white as anyone else, again casting doubt on (racial) heredity as the cause of black-white IQ test differences.

e. But perhaps the worst instance of *suppressed evidence* concerns the Army tests referred to by Professor Garrett in his pamphlet. For, as he ought to have known, Army test results from World War I provide stronger evidence *against* a racial explanation of IQ test score differences than the other way around.

The suppressed evidence is this. Although white recruits outperformed black on the Army's World War I alpha test (as Garrett indicated), Negroes from four Northern states (Ohio, Illinois, Indiana, and New York) had higher average scores than whites from most Southern states. The *Ohio* Negro median score of 45.35 was higher than that of whites from South Carolina (45.05), Tennessee (44.00), Texas (43.45), Oklahoma (43.00), Kentucky (41.50), Alabama (41.35), Louisiana (41.10), Georgia (39.35), North Carolina (38.20), Mississippi (37.65), and Arkansas (35.60).[16]

Northern whites, incidentally, did a great deal better than whites from Southern states. Whites from Illinois, for instance, averaged 61.6, while those of Arkansas averaged 35.6. The average difference between the two thus is 26 points, a much larger difference than the one between whites and blacks in most states. Yet no one has claimed that Northern whites are superior in *native* intelligence to Southern whites, or that Northern Negroes are superior to Southern whites.

f. Finally, there is the extremely interesting finding of Bruno Bettelheim and Benjamin Bloom that Oriental Jews from deprived families, when raised in Kibbutzim in Israel have higher IQs than those raised by their parents, a result which runs counter to the view that test-score differences are biologically determined.[17]

---

[15] One such study is mentioned in Gerome S. Kagan's reply to A. R. Jensen in *Harvard Educational Review*, Vol. 39 (1969), p. 275.

[16] See Ashley Montagu, "Intelligence of Northern Negroes and Southern Whites in the First World War," *American Journal of Psychology*, 1945, pp. 161–188, and his book *Man's Most Dangerous Myth: The Fallacy of Race*, Fourth Edition, 1964, World Publishing Co., Cleveland and New York, pp. 230–231, and 387–390.

[17] See the *New York Times Magazine*, August 31, 1969. This information is furnished in an article on A. R. Jensen and his view that American Negroes are genetically inferior in intelligence to American whites. Jensen's reply in that article also is quite interesting: "Bloom's and Bettelheim's argument would be more convincing if Negroes were to be raised in Kibbutzim . . . to see whether they improved greatly. . . . This is a study worth pursuing. But as it stands conclusions drawn from the Israeli work are rather wishful thinking." Why wishful thinking?

3. *Are there other plausible explanations of the evidence?* In this case, is it plausible to suspect that the higher test scores of whites are the result of environmental rather than genetic factors?

The answer to this question is obvious. It *is* plausible to assume that environmental factors are responsible, at least in large part, for test-score differences between Negroes and whites.

In the first place, the evidence just presented against a genetic explanation of the test-score differences is consistent with an environmental explanation. Presumably, whites in the North and South have roughly the same genetic inheritance; hence their difference in test performance must be due to environmental differences. The same is true of test-score differences of identical twins reared apart, since their genetic inheritances are identical.

But, equally important, we know from everyday experiences that Negroes are discriminated against in the United States in ways very few whites have ever experienced.[18] This means that their environment has been different in a way which *could be* the reason for the test-score differences between blacks and whites. (Whether it *is* the reason is another question.)

And there are other environmental possibilities. For instance, it is well known that a much larger percentage of blacks are malnourished than whites. It may be that malnourishment, not heredity, is the causal factor producing racial differences in test scores.

But the pamphlet we have been discussing anticipated the appeal to environmental differences, and argued against this possibility on two grounds.

First, it used the statistics on twins to bolster the other side of the argument, claiming that these statistics show heredity to be three times as important as environment in determining differences between individuals. But this argument is not very persuasive. First, once it is admitted that environment plays any role at all in IQ score differences, it must be admitted further that the degree to which it influences those scores may differ from person to person. (This follows because some people will have poorer—or better—environmental conditions than others.)

For instance, it is likely that poor education lowers IQ scores, and that the poorer the education the lower the scores. Thus, a given test of identical twins reared apart may reveal, not the *general* strength of environment compared to heredity, but rather its specific strength on the twins tested. In order to extrapolate from the results of a particular twin experiment, we

[18] Some whites would deny that significant racial discrimination still exists in the United States in more than isolated pockets. Rather than argue the fact, let's instead reason from what everyone must admit, which is that racial discrimination did exist for most Negroes until very recently. (This must be admitted because the discrimination was written into the law.) Thus, most adult Negroes grew up in a hostile environment foreign to all but a tiny handful of whites. And this alone is sufficient proof that there is a significant difference in the environments of black and white test takers.

would need to know that the twins tested had "average" environments, something it would be extremely hard to show for the experiments in question (especially given their small sample size).

This point is reinforced by a second one. For (as stated before) different twin experiments have yielded somewhat different results, as would be expected if the differences they revealed were determined by the specific differences in environment of the twins tested, and did not reflect the average effect of environment on test scores.

The second item used by the pamphlet to argue against environment as the reason for IQ test differences is the set of New Jersey-Pennsylvania "matched" scores. But we aren't told which eleven "socio-economic factors" students were matched for, and are given no evidence that the eleven used are the environmental factors most likely to affect IQ performance. There is a tremendous amount of controversy about the physiological, psychological, educational, and in particular *sociological* or *cultural* factors which might affect performance on IQ tests; we are given no assurance that the students were matched with respect to the controversial factors. And the role of culture in IQ scores is very controversial indeed. Many psychologists and educators claim that the standard IQ tests only score *cultural achievement* and not native intelligence, testing for the sort of thing that white middle- and upper-class Americans do best because their culture better prepares them for such activity. And some professionals would question the very possibility of constructing a culture-free intelligence test. (This is not to say that they are right. But their view is widely held, has evidence in its favor, and has not been positively refuted.)

4. *What other evidence would be useful in considering the issue?* Questions like this on race and intelligence rarely can be answered conclusively. But with the right evidence we ought to be able to settle the matter "beyond a reasonable doubt." What further evidence might be obtained without too great expense?

a. We might test IQ variability in societies more environmentally homogeneous (e.g., Sweden) than the United States. If environment is the crucial factor, societies that are more homogeneous ought to show smaller test-score differences than are shown in the white population in the United States.

b. We might investigate the effect of malnutrition on IQ scores. For instance, white migrant farm laborers frequently have malnourished children. Their scores later in life might be compared with other white scores. Similarly, many rural Negroes in some parts of the South, and some Negroes in large Northern cities have extremely malnourished children. Their scores later in life might be compared with those of better-fed Negroes.

c. American Indians are predominantly mongoloid (oriental) in racial makeup. Their test scores might be compared with those of Japanese-

Americans and Chinese-Americans. (Of course, we already know roughly what the answer will be on this test, because we know, in a rough way, that Japanese and Chinese-Americans do well on IQ tests, while American Indians do not.)

d. The status and customs of several immigrant groups have changed considerably since coming to the United States. The Irish and Italians are two such white groups. Test scores of Irish and Italian children fifty years ago and now might be compared with those of WASP children fifty years ago and now.

e. More work needs to be done on differences in IQ scores among different Negro cultural groups. We might compare the children of professionals with those of laborers, or children of families which have been middle class for more than two generations with children of lower-class families.

f. We might compare "privileged" black children with environmentally disadvantaged white and black children.

g. Finally, we might compare IQ scores of blacks and whites in societies where race prejudice is not as strong as it is in the U.S. (Brazil is a likely candidate.)

In arguing against Garrett's pamphlet, two powerful arguments were withheld. The first stems from everyday and historical knowledge, and is the kind of evidence many scientists are loath to accept. Yet such evidence may well be as significant as the shaky statistical evidence of the kind presented by Garrett (and other researchers as well).

Take history. Throughout history we see evidence that the elite of a society generally have considered lower classes to be intellectually inferior. And they have always had *evidence* with which to support this belief, namely the poor behavior of the lower classes. Pre-nineteenth-century England is a good example. Lower classes committed most of the (reported) crimes and were generally considered incapable of performing tasks requiring high intelligence. Yet many descendants of these lower-class Englishmen now are part of the WASP cultural elite in the United States, regularly score above-average on IQ tests, and rarely clutter up FBI statistics on crime.

Nonscientific reports from daily life also should lead to caution in accepting conclusions that downgrade environmental influences on intelligence. For instance, many books have been written recently by teachers in slum schools who report improvements in reading scores and in the general ability of slum children, resulting apparently from unusually effective teaching procedures which partially break through cultural barriers.[19]

[19] See, for instance, Jonathan Kozol, *Death at an Early Age,* Houghton Mifflin Co., Boston, 1967, and Herbert Kohl, *Thirty-Six Children,* New American Library, New York, 1967.

But we have saved for last the major objection to Garrett's arguments, as well as to all of the so-called "scientific" statistical studies done in the United States which conclude that Negroes are inherently inferior in intelligence to whites. The objection is simply that in the United States black (or Negro) and white are not *biological* concepts but rather *cultural* ones. The vast majority of those classified as black or Negro in the United States have significant caucasoid inheritance,[20] and a great many of those classified as white have some negroid inheritance. (There seem to be no professional estimates on the latter.) In addition, both of these groups have mild infusions of mongoloid (oriental) genes.

So, when researchers talk of lower IQ scores for *blacks* or *Negroes,* they are talking about lower scores for a *cultural* group heavily infused with white (caucasian) and oriental (mongoloid) genes. Similarly, when they speak of higher IQ scores for whites, they are speaking about higher scores for a cultural group very mildly infused with negroid and mongoloid genes. How, then, can such tests provide anywhere near sufficient evidence that one group (blacks) is *biologically* inferior in intelligence to another group (whites)?

In view of the above, two conclusions seem in order. First, Garrett's arguments need not be accepted. Indeed, his pamphlet can be taken as evidence of the thesis that some reasoning in the social sciences is just about as bad as typical reasoning in politics.

And second, we ought to conclude that the thesis that blacks are biologically inferior in intelligence to whites is unproved, to say the least. As yet we don't seem able to judge the relative importance of heredity and environment to intelligence, and thus are not yet able to decide the matter. We cannot now preclude the possibility that the average caucasoid (white) will turn out to be less intelligent than the average negroid (black), once neither has an environmental advantage over the other.

Summary of Chapter Four

Statistical fallacies tend to be just variations on the kinds of fallacies considered in earlier chapters, and in Chapter Four, we have examined these statistical variants, including:

---

[20] Remember that in most societies in which race prejudice exists, the offspring of mixed parents are classified as members of the disparaged race. In the U.S., anyone with *any* recognizably negroid inheritance automatically is classified as black, even if fifteen-sixteenths or more of his inheritance is caucasian.

1. **Suppressed evidence.**
   Example: The cited suppression of the fact that insurance companies *invest* premiums, and thus have income in addition to the premiums themselves with which to pay claims.

2. **Unknown fact.**
   Example: Government figures on the gross national product calculated down to tenths of a percent.

3. **Hasty conclusion.**
   Example: The Republican claim that Congressman Meskill had a better record in Congress than Congressman Daddario because Daddario missed several more House roll calls than Meskill.

4. **Questionable cause.**
   Example: The implication that marijuana caused American soldiers in Vietnam to have acute psychotic reactions.

5. **Ambiguity.**
   Example: Attorney General Mitchell's use of the word "tap" to mean only one kind of electronic eavesdropping (not covering so-called "bugs," for instance) in reporting statistics on government surveillance.

In Chapter Four, we also discussed the importance of knowing the margin of error of statistics.

Example: The federal government's figures for changes in the gross national product.

And we tried to show that statistics gathered by means of polls and the like are only as good as the techniques and questions they employ.

Example: The question on Vietnam asked in a survey by Henry Bubb.

A special variation on *hasty conclusion,* the fallacy of the *small sample,* was singled out for special discussion, as was that of the *unrepresentative sample.*

Examples: The Evans and Novak use of a sample of 67 Bridgeport voters, which illustrated the fallacy of the *small sample,* and the poll of University of Connecticut faculty on the punishment of disruptive students, which illustrated the fallacy of the *unrepresentative sample.*

Finally, it was pointed out that in comparing statistics, we must take account of their *quality.*

Example: In comparing statistics on crime in one time or place with that of another, we must take account of differences in the methods by which the statistics were compiled.

Exercise I for Chapter Four

Explain what (if anything) is wrong with the following uses of statistical evidence:

1. *Column by James J. Kilpatrick, August 1970, in which he argued for more action on the drug problem:* J. Edgar Hoover released his 1969 Crime Report a week ago. Last year, for the first time, there were more arrests in the U.S. for violations of drug laws than for violation of liquor laws—223,000 drug offenses against 213,000 liquor offenses.

2. *James J. Kilpatrick, in a September 1970 column in which he argued that Minneapolis schools were segregated, but were not being forced to integrate as were the schools of the South:* . . . some 68,000 pupils attended the 101 schools of Minneapolis. Of these, 5500 pupils, or 8.1% were black pupils. . . . The great bulk of these black pupils . . . were concentrated in a handful of schools [while] some elementary schools of Minneapolis are lily white.

3. Hartford Courant, *October 29, 1970, story by Jack Zaiman on a poll of 842 people, conducted by Research Associates for Senator Dodd. Weicker won the election, Duffey was second, and Dodd third:* Poll Question: Which candidate do you favor for election to the United States Senate? "Senator Dodd led with 30 percent . . . Duffey followed with 28 percent and Weicker trailed with 23 percent. . . ." 20 percent of the voter interviews were conducted in the home. The majority were conducted in shopping areas and work areas on a random basis.

*4. *AP story, July 1970, Lawrence [Kansas] Daily Journal World, in which the following figures on compacts are given: Chrysler's Plymouth Valiant Line (which includes the new Duster):* 123,386 (*177% increase over previous year*); *Ford Maverick:* 204,397 (*37% "daily sales rate percentage gain"—the Maverick was introduced on April 17, 1969*); *Chevrolet Nova:* 145,454 (*3.4% increase over previous year*): Chrysler Corp., sold 103,252 Dusters as it led the [compact car] industry in sales [in the first six months of 1970].

5. *Reported by Dan Nimmo in his book* The Political Persuaders. (*Mr. Nimmo presented this view and then argued against it*): . . . students of politics . . . point out that factors shaping voting choices are affected only marginally by campaign ap-

peals. The principal factor consistently related to voting decisions is the party loyalty of the voter. . . . So long as a substantial portion of the electorate is committed to a party (and studies indicate that proportion to be four out of five voters), campaigns will have little effect on voting patterns.

*6. An Evans and Novak political column rated as poor the chances of State Senator Sander Levin, Democratic nominee for governor of Michigan, on the basis of a poll of sixty-four blue collar suburban workers of Warren, Michigan. The poll showed 36% for Levin's opponent, 42% for Levin, and 22% undecided, in a normally very heavily Democratic stronghold. Later evidence showed that the poll correctly predicted the outcome of the election.

7. An ad for *Reader's Digest* claimed that 40% of their readers "seldom watch prime time TV," and implied that the best way to reach these people was by an ad in the *Reader's Digest*.

*8. *Private letter:* The concern for the Japanese killed by atomic weapons at Hiroshima and Nagasaki is misplaced. My brother was killed by the Japanese in the Bataan Death March of World War II, in which the Japanese inflicted terrible punishment on wounded and starving American soldiers. The Japanese are barbarians and don't deserve our concern.

9. *Story on Russian women by AP correspondent William L. Ryan, August 1970, arguing that women in Russia aren't treated very well:* The Soviet press points proudly to the number of Soviet women who are engineers, doctors, lawyers, and so forth, but—they are a small minority of the 130 million women in the Soviet Union.

10. New York Times Magazine, *August 31, 1969, article on Arthur Jensen and his theory that Negroes are on the average genetically inferior with respect to intelligence:* [Arthur] Jensen's most telling argument, he believes, and the easiest to grasp, proceeds from studies of identical twins—siblings whose genetic inheritance is precisely the same, since they have developed from a single fertilized egg. Psychologist Sir Cyril Burt and geneticist J. A. Shields studied 100 pairs of identical twins in England who were reared apart from each other. It was found that the separated twins were, on the average, only six points apart in IQ. By contrast, any two people in the total population, chosen at random, will be on the average 18 points apart. Non-identical siblings reared in the same household are on the average 12 IQ points apart.

*11. *1970 news story prior to Supreme Court decision on measure
      to give 18 year olds the vote in national elections. (The meas-
      ure also reduced the residency requirement to only 30 days)*:
      If 18 to 21 year olds get the vote in 1972, it won't make any
      significant difference, because younger voters have voted less
      frequently in the past than older ones anyway.

Exercise II for Chapter Four

Find two examples of misuses of statistics in the mass media and in each
case explain the error.

Chapter Five

Analyzing Extended Political Arguments

> The prejudice against careful analytic procedure is part of the
> human impatience with technique which arises from the fact
> that men are interested in results and would like to attain
> them without the painful toil which is the essence of our moral
> finitude.
>
> **Morris R. Cohen**

So far we have considered relatively short arguments, and these only to
illustrate fallacious reasoning. But in daily life we frequently encounter
much longer passages which in effect comprise arguments or series of related arguments. It takes more than just the ability to spot fallacies to deal
with such extended passages.

There are many methods for analyzing extended passages, and each
person will develop his own preference. The margin note-summary method
used here in analyzing an editorial and a political column is one which
many people find congenial, at least as a model to be more or less approached in daily life, as time permits and interest dictates.

The first step is simply to mark each important passage and, perhaps,
place an indication of its content next to it in the margin. The second step
is to use the margin notes to construct a summary of the article, which can
then be used in turn to evaluate the original work.

1. Editorials

Newspaper, magazine, radio, and TV editorials constitute an important
and interesting part of the political scene. Let's examine an editorial from
the *New York Times,* often said to be the best and most influential news-

paper in the United States. The flavor of their editorials reflects this august position.

Here is the *Times* editorial [1] with margin notes attached.

Astoria Compromise

As an interim answer to a difficult problem requiring immediate resolution, Mayor Lindsay's compromise decision on the proposed generating plant in Astoria has much to recommend it. Consolidated Edison has won permission to go ahead and build what it regards as urgently needed capacity to meet this community's electricity needs. But those who opposed the project because of understandable fear of additional pollution can console themselves that the expansion will be only half that originally requested.

Unfortunately, before the Mayor settled the issue, he fostered a bitter public debate that not only pitted some of his key subordinates against each other, but also inflamed the passions and fears of many. The angry reactions of some Astoria residents to the Lindsay compromise raise the unhappy possibility that the dispute has not ended, and that new and difficult roadblocks may appear to hamper those trying to build even the smaller generating plant the Mayor has approved.[2]

The future may show, however, that the real importance of Mayor

(1)   Conclusion: Lindsay compromise is good.

(2)   Permits Con Ed what it thinks is needed capacity.

(3)   But it's a true compromise: Con Ed permitted only ½ requested increase.

---

[1] Astoria Compromise, © 1970 by The New York Times Company. Reprinted by permission.

[2] No margin notes are needed for this paragraph because it contains no material pertinent to the main point at issue.

Lindsay's decision was its enuncia-tion of an important principle fun-damental to a rational anti-pollution policy. In effect, Mr. Lindsay has recognized that the city's supply of clean air is a limited resource whose availability must be protected by a comprehensive policy that takes ac-count of all sources of pollution, rather than merely dealing with in-dividual sources in isolation. "If some pollution is inevitable and the choice is between sufficient electrical power or streets congested with automobiles," the Mayor said, "I would choose electrical power."

Having articulated his correct un-derstanding that tradeoffs must be calculated and choices made, Mayor Lindsay has already appointed a five-member committee to work out a plan for limiting motor vehicle pollution here. The organization called Citizens for Clean Air has gone a step further and asked the Mayor to ban private automobile traffic from Manhattan south of 59th Street during business hours. This is the direction in which the city must move to protect its most pre-cious possession, the air its citizens breathe.

(4) Real import of L's decision: it voices idea that air is limited & all pollution sources must be considered.

(5) He advocates electric power over auto pollution when choice required.

(6) Believing tradeoffs necessary, he's appointed committee to plan.

(7) Lindsay asked to ban private cars from Manhattan at certain times & places.

(8) This will, eventually, have to be done.

And here is an itemized summary of what one person takes to be the main points of the editorial:

1. *Mayor Lindsay's compromise on Con Ed's Astoria plant expan-sion has much to recommend it.*

2. *It permits them to build what they believe is urgently needed capacity.*

3. *But it compromises with the other side, since Con Ed is permitted only half of the increase it asked for.*

4. *The real import of Lindsay's decision may rest in his voicing of the rational antipollution idea that clean air is limited and must be protected by policies that consider all sources of pollution.*
5. *Lindsay (rightly?) advocates choosing electric power over auto pollution when a choice is required.*
6. *Understanding that "tradeoffs must be calculated" and "choices made," Lindsay has appointed a committee to plan for limited auto pollution in N.Y.*
7. *Citizens for Clean Air has asked Lindsay to ban private autos from parts of Manhattan during business hours.*
8. *This is the direction N.Y. must move in to obtain clean air.*

At this point, two things should be said by way of caution in using the margin note-summary method. First, when you skip assertions in a passage, you make a value judgment that the skipped material is not important. It takes practice and skill to know what to include and what to omit, and "experts" will differ on such matters.

Second, margin notes and summaries are shorthand devices, and should be briefer than the passage analyzed (otherwise, why use them?). But any shortening runs the risk of falsification. When using margin notes or summaries to aid in reasoning, remember that you don't want to draw conclusions from the shortened version that would not be valid for the original.

Notice that the *Times* editorial contains very few, if any, unnecessary emotive or value-tinged terms, and was constructed in a fairly orderly way. (Compare this with the *Daily News* editorial used as an exercise at the end of the chapter.) Nevertheless, it is not a paragon of rationality. Let's take the important statements in the editorial one by one, and then append a general comment.

Assertion 1 simply presents the claim to be defended in the editorial, namely that Lindsay's compromise was, on the whole, good. Assertion 2 tells us what Con Ed believed, namely that the increase was needed. Was Con Ed right? A very technical question; the layman is forced to bow to Con Ed's view unless someone presents pertinent evidence to the contrary. Expert testimony of this kind frequently is refuted by other evidence. But in this case, apparently it was not; Con Ed did seem to need increased capacity to cover increases that were likely if unrestrained use of power continued to be permitted. (Whether they needed to *double* the Astoria plant capacity is another matter.)

Assertion 3 in effect comes close to saying that Lindsay's Solomon-like decision was right *because* it was a fifty-fifty compromise. The *Times* editorial thus seems to have committed what is often called the fallacy of the *golden mean,* since it nowhere *defends* Lindsay's decision *qua* its being a halfway measure. For instance, it doesn't argue that granting only one-quarter the requested increase would not be sufficient, or that granting it all would be too much. Assertion 4 is noncontroversial. Almost everyone pays lip service to it. (Living up to it is another matter.)

Assertion 5, while controversial, was not at issue between antipollution-ists, Con Ed, and the mayor. We have here a genuine value judgment of great importance concerning which all of us must make up our minds. If confronted (by the need to reduce air pollution) with a choice between re-stricting private auto travel or restricting electric power use (e.g., of air con-ditioners), which should we prefer? There are *facts* pertinent to the choice, such as the possibility of alternative modes of transportation. But they don't automatically determine the choice. It is human beings, using these facts, who must decide. Notice that the *Times* editorial neither presents these facts nor reasons from them. It simply presents its conclusion.

But it is assertion 6 which is the crux. (Let's skip 7 and 8 to shorten the discussion.) There are two important comments to make about 6:

a. Some opponents of Mayor Lindsay claimed that for a while at least, we could have both less powerplant pollution and less auto pollution with-out restricting the use of either, by (1) putting new power plants out of town in low-pollution areas; (2) requiring electric power producers such as Con Ed to use more expensive but also more efficient antipollution de-vices;[3] and (3) requiring more expensive but also more efficient auto pol-lution devices, ultimately requiring replacement of internal-combustion engines by something else, such as the gas-turbine engine.

b. Talk of "tradeoffs" and "compromises" masks the fact that while Con Ed was granted something tangible by Lindsay's decision (an increase in productive capacity), the other side was given talk and promises (a com-mission set up to *plan* for limiting pollution).

In other words, as opponents of Mayor Lindsay argued with some justi-fication, he granted an increase to Con Ed which inevitably would increase air pollution but only paid lip service to one of the antipollutionist arguments (that ultimately we must choose between power and autos, and power

[3] For example, Anna Mayo, in the *Village Voice,* August 13, 1970, states:
George Spitz, Upper East Side (of Manhattan) candidate for state senator and member of the IMREC environmental research firm, has discovered that controls exist but maintains that Con Ed does not want to pay for them. He recently in-formed the company's Robert O. Lehrman that the state of Kansas has sulfur con-trols, to which Lehrman retorted that Kansas had coal rather than oil-fired plants. Spitz says he fired back that Boston is using such controls in oil-fired plants.

should on the whole win). In addition, Lindsay ignored the other major antipollutionist proposals to expand power facilities out of town and to require more expensive but also more efficient emission devices and equipment.

The *New York Times,* it should be pointed out, seems to have been guilty along with Mayor Lindsay. In particular, the *Times* was guilty of suppressing evidence contrary to the conclusion it wanted to draw. This is one of the *Times'* chief devices for making its editorials seem plausible to its readers. Its position of prestige and authority does not permit open appeals to emotion or prejudice of the kind many other newspapers employ. (Again, see the *New York Daily News* editorial in the exercise section at the end of the chapter.) Omissions are much less obvious than the use of emotively charged phrases. They also are probably more effective with an educated but inadequately informed audience.

2.   Political columns

Let's get some more practice with the margin note-summary method of analysis. Here is a political column by the widely syndicated columnist Mary McGrory,[4] again with margin notes attached:[5]

Washington — Charles Reich's book, "The Greening of America," which caused a great stir in "radiclib" circles since excerpts appeared in the New Yorker *magazine, has nothing to do with the campaign— and everything.*

Focus: A book on what's wrong with America & how the young will right it.

Long after the last word has been mercifully spoken from the stump— and forgotten—it will be pondered and argued.   For it is a study of what is wrong with America and what the new generation is doing to make it right.

[4] © 1970, Washington Star Syndicate, Inc. Reprinted by permission.

[5] The numbers in the margin notes indicate where statements occur in the summary which follows.

Young Are An Issue

The young are an issue in this election, largely due to the exertions of the Vice President.

It also is a handbook of revolution, but before the Vice President dives for his dictionary, he should know it advocates a revolution by peaceful means, by the infectious sight of young Americans who love life and take literally the pursuit of happiness.

Reich, a professor of law at Yale, dismisses politics as a way of changing the system. It is not because the only political spokesman his generation has had, Senator Eugene McCarthy, was routed, or even because his young followers were beaten into the ground.

Reich thinks that political and legal reforms merely perpetuate a tyrannous corporate state, whose principal products are repression, dehumanization, war, pollution, injustice and pre-mixed peanut butter and jelly.

Change can be brought about only when the young revolutionaries can persuade their parents and the blue-collars to share their shattering assumption: "It doesn't have to be that way."

(4)¹ Politics won't change the system. . . .

(4)² Because internal reform just perpetuates the evils of the system.

(6) System change requires young to convince others that change is possible.

Consciousness III

This bold thesis sets Consciousness III people—Reich's designation for those smitten by the difference between the American Dream and its reality—apart from previous generations. Consciousness I worshippers of free enterprise and the

(3)¹ Type III: Smitten by difference between American ideals & actual practice.

(1) Type I: Believe in our system; are rigid, repressive, & think

"American way" are rigid and re-pressive, see themselves threatened by Communists, blacks and hippies.

Consciousness II, the bewildered parents of today, are the strivers, the status-seekers, failed idealists who accept the institutions and strive to reform the structure.

Reich coldly compares yester-day's stricken liberal giving a check or his name to a cause with today's youth who puts his body on the line to resist the draft, to shield the black or stay the bulldozer.

New Champions

The new generation has had other champions and defenders—George Wald and the authors of the Scran-ton Report, for example. Reich is the first to present the defiant in full profile, the whole culture with acid, rock, bell-bottoms, and an unshak-able belief that "man . . . is not a creature to be controlled, regulated, administered, trained, clipped, coated and anesthetized."

The Vietnam war, "a monster in-carnated out of the madness of the state," gave them unity and an audi-ence. In a reversal of roles still not assimilated, they led their elders in resistance to that madness. If it ever ends, they should be given a major share of the credit.

To Reich, they are bright, brave, questing, white-hot idealists, with a reverence for life and an acceptance of themselves and each other un-precedented in history. We must assume, in the light of that exploit, they can run a revolution.

While it is hard in this dark sea-

Communists, blacks, & hippies threaten them.

(2)   Type II: Parents, strivers, status-seekers, failed idealists who strive for internal reform of system.

(5)   Young who risk bodily harm are better than liberals who spend money in support of causes.

(3)[2]   Type III: Bright, brave, ideal-ists, revere life & accept each other more than have previous generations.

(3)[3]   Type III: Can run a revolution because of above [(3)[2]].

son to envision the world they might make in which affection and tolerance and individual worth will be the law, it is pleasant to contemplate.

Since Reich has gone so far to make them both admirable and lovable, and has done so much to enlighten their nervous elders about their nature and their goals, it is a pity that he did not express some reservations about the most unnerving aspect of their life style, their drug habits.

He is so evangelical about the awareness-sharpening qualities of marijuana, he almost forgets to indicate that their whole beautiful dream could go up in smoke.

(3)[4] Type III: Con: They use drugs.

Subsidized by Parents

He also neglects to mention that they are the first revolutionaries to be subsidized by Mom and Dad, who pay the bills while they float about looking for their "thing."

(3)[5] Type III: Con: Financially dependent on parents.

These are lapses which will be pounced upon by the people who would most profit from his provocative and potentially healing book— an eloquent plea for reconciliation at a moment when division is being pursued as a positive good by those in charge of our society.

(7) We need reconciliation, but those in power pursue division.

Having made margin notes on the copy, the next step is to construct a summary of the main ideas in her column:

1. *Reich distinguishes three types of people. Type I believe in the American system, are rigid and repressive, and think they're threatened by communists, blacks, and hippies.*

2. *Type II, parents (yesterday's liberals?), are strivers, status-seekers, idealists; they strive for internal reform.*

3. *Type III (the young? peaceful revolutionaries? hippies?) are disturbed by the difference between American ideals and actual practice. They use drugs (bad) and are financially dependent on their parents (bad), but they can run a (peaceful) revolution because they're bright, brave idealists who accept themselves and each other more than did any past generation.*

4. *Politics won't change the system, because reform from within just perpetuates the (in practice bad) system.*

5. *The young who risk bodily harm for their causes are better than yesterday's liberals who spend money in support of theirs.*

6. *To change the system, the young idealists must convince others that it can be changed ("doesn't have to be as it is").*

7. *We need reconciliation (which the young will bring?), but those in power pursue division.*

After a summary of this kind is made, we're in a better position to see how loose is the structure of the original, and how literary devices get in the way of clarity. Particularly loose is the variety of descriptions given for people of type II ("bewildered parents of today," "yesterday's stricken liberal") and type III ("today's youth," "young revolutionaries" "smitten by the difference between the American dream and its reality").

Of course, good literary devices need not reduce clarity. On the contrary, when properly used in the right context (what is right for a novel may not be right for political prose), they contribute to clarity. Anyone who has ever graded term papers knows that clarity and quality of style tend to go hand in hand. We must chalk up the lack of clarity and cogency in this case to the writer (or perhaps to two writers—Mary McGrory and Charles Reich).

Let's now turn to an evaluation of the McGrory column, and of Reich's position as it is given there.[6]

---

[6] One of the problems with political columns in newspapers is that they must be short, making adequate treatment of most issues quite difficult. For a better (and longer) account of Reich's theory, see his own account in the *New Yorker,* September 26, 1970, or " 'Greening of America'—Only on Weekends," by Joel Kramer, the *Village Voice,* November 19, 1970, or read Reich's book, *The Greening of America,* Random House, New York, 1970.

There seem to be two major defects in the column. First, the three-fold classification of political types is not a very good one. Many people, perhaps most, fall into two and sometimes all three of the categories described in this column. Aren't many who believe in the American system (type I) also parents, strivers, and status seekers (type II)? Aren't many of yesterday's (type II) stricken liberals also smitten (as are type IIIs) by the difference between the American dream and its reality? Don't some type Is and IIs also put their bodies on the line as do type III people?

In addition, the classification suffers from extreme vagueness, making it often difficult, or impossible, to know what empirical criteria to use in specific cases. What is it, after all, to be "worshippers of free enterprise and the American way"? How do we tell when people have "a reverence for life and an acceptance of themselves and each other"? How aware must we be of the disparity between ideals and practice before we can be said to be "smitten" with this knowledge? We all have some idea what these phrases mean; they aren't empty of meaning. So we can tell whether or not they apply in a few clear-cut cases. But in all too many cases their meaning is too murky to allow their application with any confidence.

One wonders, also, whether youth really is a cogent requirement for class III membership, since merely having passed the thirty, or even forty year mark seems to be no insurmountable bar to membership in the radical or hippie communities which presumably contain mostly type III people.

The three-fold classification suffers also from failure to cover all political types. In technical terms, it is not *exhaustive*. A great many people, from true conservatives (who aren't repressive) to socialists and communists (who aren't status seekers and who do want to change the system), are not members of any of the three classes.

But the main defect in this article is that it begs all the interesting questions. To see how large a defect this is, let's use the technique of bringing to bear opinions from other viewpoints. Since the column was written from the viewpoint of type III people, let's look at it from the viewpoints of typical members of the other two categories.

A typical type I person would challenge being characterized as repressive, claiming rather that he is for all the freedom and tolerance for a given person that is consistent with law and order and with freedom for everyone else. He would claim that the charge of repression results from his favoring harsh responses to those who refuse to work within the system, those who foment protests, riots, and violence which take freedom away from others.

He also would be inclined to wonder if perhaps the young radicals are not too impatient, expecting and demanding quick solutions to old problems, and failing to appreciate the slow improvements our system has yielded, particularly in material wealth. He would wonder if the young realize the great risks involved even in peaceful revolutions (although he would doubt that revolutions are likely to be peaceful).

Finally, he would ask whether the young, having lived their whole lives during the Cold War, have perhaps become so used to the threat from the Soviet Union and China that they treat it much too lightly.

These "right wing" conservative ideas may be wrong. But the McGrory column gave no indication that Reich seriously argued that they are wrong.

Most liberals (type II) would be inclined to agree with conservatives about the risks of working outside the system to effect change. While not satisfied with the reduced disparity between ideals and reality since World War II, and they would be more inclined than type IIIs to appreciate the progress that has been made on some of our basic problems since World War II. They would also be more aware of the repressive reaction which ill prepared action (bodies on the line) is likely to bring about.

In addition, they would doubt that all the brightness, self awareness, good will, and ideals in the world are sufficient to bring about major and lasting improvements without careful planning, organization, knowledge of history and sociological theory, long hard work, and cold cash—all of which they see lacking in what to them are the otherwise admirable young people of today. (Lack of knowledge of the past is perhaps the most frequently voiced liberal complaint against type III members of the younger generation.)

Finally, many liberals would be inclined to react strongly against the sentiment embodied in the fourth assertion (that you can't reform the system effectively from within by political means), on the grounds that meaningful although slow reform has occurred from time to time from within, especially in recent years.

It may be argued that, after all, one political column can't do everything, and that this one merely attempts to outline an important and current book. But this won't wash, because the column did not merely report; it sided with Mr. Reich and Consciousness III. And it never justified that choice. (The space limitations of a syndicated political column are cruel. But a writer who agrees to that limitation cannot then use that as an excuse for distortion or error.)

It should be obvious after consideration of the McGrory column and the *Times* editorial that analysis of political argument requires much more than cogent reasoning. The most brilliant logician in the world cannot deal adequately with typical political discussion if his mind is empty of thought on political matters. Political argument generally deals with broad topics which are the center of much controversy and which cannot all be argued about every time they are appealed to. To handle these broad topics we must bring to bear all sorts of previously accepted beliefs developed by prior thought on these matters. That's why careless thought is so deadly—it contaminates later attempts to think more carefully.

3. Political speeches

Political speeches generally are listened to rather than read. This makes critical analysis much more difficult, and margin notes impossible except on written versions. Let's analyze twelve short passages from a rather long speech (too long to be studied here in its entirety) which President Nixon delivered at Kansas State University on September 16, 1970. Here is the first excerpt:[7]

> *1. There are those who protest that if the verdict of democracy goes against them, democracy itself is at fault, the system is at fault; who say that if they don't get their own way, the answer is to burn or bomb a building.*

This occurs near the beginning of the speech, and sets the tone for the rest. It attacks the tiniest sliver of his opponents who (right or wrong) were extremely vulnerable, while ignoring those with more plausible objections and less extreme behavior. This is a typical device used by politicians of all sorts and parties. Nevertheless, it constitutes shoddy argument, and indeed amounts to a version of the fallacy of the *straw man*. It is true that a few people hold the position described and attacked by President Nixon. But it is almost always possible to find a few opponents who conveniently hold vulnerable positions. If you always (or usually) attack your weaker opponents, while ignoring those who have stronger objections, you are guilty of the fallacy of the *straw man,* because ultimately you convey the impression that you are attacking your strongest opponents.

The hope of politicians who employ this kind of *straw man* is that many people with meagre information will conclude falsely that there are only two serious alternatives, the one espoused by those the politician attacks and

---

[7] The interested reader may want to consult the more extensive *New York Times* excerpts, which appear on p. 28 of their September 17, 1970 edition.

the one held by the politician himself. In other words, they employ *straw man* in order to invite commission of the fallacy of *false dilemma.*

"Blockbuster" terms such as "radical liberal" (or Agnew's "radiclib") also serve to persuade the uninformed that there are only two alternatives. For the politician need only attack a few of the group, for instance, the few radical liberals (whatever that means) who believe in violence, in order to tar all the others with belief in violence. And what is worse, in so doing, the politician can expect, or at least hope, that many will unwittingly widen membership in the radiclib camp to include not-so-radical liberals as well.

Here is a second excerpt from Nixon's speech:

> 2. *When Palestinian guerrillas hijacked four airliners in flight,* [and] . . . *held their hundreds of passengers hostage under threat of murder, they sent shock waves of alarm around the world at the spreading disease of violence and terror and its use as a political tactic.*
>
> *That same cancerous disease has been spreading over the world and here in the United States.*
>
> *We saw it three weeks ago in the vicious bombing at the University of Wisconsin.* . . . *We have seen it in other bombings and burnings on our campuses and our cities, in the wanton shootings of policemen, in the attacks on school buses, in the destruction of offices, the seizure and harassment of college officials, the use of force and coercion to bar students and teachers from classrooms and even to close down whole campuses.*
>
> *Consider just a few items in the news. A courtroom spectator pulls out a gun. He halts the trial, gives arms to the defendants, takes the judge and four other hostages, moves to a waiting getaway van, and in the gunfight that follows four die, including the judge.*
>
> *A man walks into the guardhouse of a city park, pumps five bullets into a police sergeant sitting quietly at his desk.* . . . .

The chief fallacy here is that of *suppressed evidence,* or *biased selection of facts,* always an easy one to be guilty of in political arguments, because there must be *some* evidence in favor of your position. (Even the worst politicians rarely espouse that for which no evidence whatever exists.) So you can always cite the evidence favorable to your position, while ignoring that which runs contrary to it.

In this case, Mr. Nixon provided instances of *nongovernmental* violence, much of which could plausibly be attributed to the violent radiclibs. But he overlooked governmental violence, in particular violence by police, which his opponents with some justification believed to be both unlawful and unnecessary in defending true law and order.

The mark of such a one-sided presentation of evidence is the ease with which opponents can construct arguments similarly biased in their choice of facts. For instance, "radical liberals" easily could have constructed the following paraphrase of the above section of Nixon's speech:

> *When U.S. soldiers murdered women and children at My Lai in Vietnam, they sent shock waves of alarm around the world at the spreading disease of violence and terror and its use as a political tactic. That same cancerous disease has been spreading over the world and here in the United States.*
>
> *We saw it in the vicious police attack on Chicago Black Panthers asleep in their own homes. We have seen it in other police attacks in Chicago, in the wanton shooting of other Panthers in Oakland and elsewhere, in the overturning of school buses by racists condoned by onlooking police, in the destruction in private homes by police in New Jersey, mentioned in the Kerner Commission report, in the harassment of college officials at the State University of New York at Buffalo, in the use of force and coercion to bar students and teachers from the Ohio State University campus, as well as others.*
>
> *Consider just a few items in the news. Policemen at Jackson State University pull out guns. They fire at students without provocation, killing two.*
>
> *A student walks across the campus at Kent State University. National guardsmen, firing wildly at demonstrators, kill that student and three others, none of whom participated in any of the disorders at Kent State at the time.*

The game is too easy. To the list could be added police violence at Orangeburg, South Carolina, Lawrence, Kansas, Augusta, Georgia, and hundreds of other places. With good research, it would be easy to construct a dossier with thousands of cases in which reasonable men might conclude that police had used violence beyond that necessary to preserve law and order.

But it, too, would be a biased list. The proverbial man from Mars, coming down to earth and hearing only this recitation of police violence would not have a true picture of the situation in the United States, nor any understanding of the causes or cures of its problems. But neither would he if he had heard President Nixon's Kansas State address. Yet, Nixon's remarks were typical of the level of political rhetoric in the United States.

> 3. *The time has come for us to recognize that violence and terror have no place in a free society, whatever the purported cause or the perpetrators may be. And this is the fundamental lesson for us to remember: In a system like ours, which provides the means for peaceful change, no cause justifies violence in the name of change.*

This time the chief fallacy is a variation of the general category called the *all-some* fallacy. This fallacy takes what is sometimes or even usually true and elevates it to a universal.[8]

In this case, one wonders if Nixon, or anyone else reared in the spirit of the American Revolution and the Declaration of Independence, really believes that *no conceivable* cause could justify violence.

But once it is admitted that some causes might justify violence, evasion of the true issue is more difficult. For the true issue that the speech distorts was that those few who espoused violence, both on the right and the left, did so in the belief that the situation in 1970 was in fact one of those unusual cases in which violence was justified. The President of the United States would have done better to explain why 1970 was not one of those times, rather than mouthing universals that few other than complete pacifists really believe.

This passage also contains a subtle dual ambiguity, specifically in Mr. Nixon's phrase, "In a system like ours, which provides the means for peaceful change. . . ." the first ambiguity concerns the existence of means for peaceful change. Does he mean *formal* means? If so he obviously is correct. Or does he, rather, mean *effective* means for peaceful change? In that case, the question is debatable, as many of his opponents would contend.

The second ambiguity concerns the fact that peaceful change can be for better or for worse. Did the President mean *mere* peaceful change, or peaceful change for the better? The point is important. Since the Civil War, there

---

[8] Some versions of this fallacy rest on the ambiguity resulting from the *omission* of quantifying phrases such as "all" and "some." In English, we can often omit these terms as understood; for example, we can say, "Police do engage in unjustified violence," omitting the word "some." If we get someone to agree to a statement like this because he construes it to mean *some* policemen are unnecessarily violent, but later use this sentence to assert that *all* policemen engage in unjustified violence, then we are guilty of the *all-some* fallacy, as are those taken in by our ploy. Commission of this fallacy is made easier by the fact that the word "all" often is used when "almost all" is meant, as in the sentence "Negroes all voted against Max Rafferty in the 1970 California election."

have been means for peaceful change in the status of the Negro, but only occasionally (and recently) has change for the better been possible. In the 1870s and 1880s, for instance, peaceful change was all for the worse, leading to the legalization of segregation, Plessy vs. Ferguson, and all the rest.

> *4. What corrodes a society even more deeply than violence itself is the acceptance of violence, the condoning of terror, excusing of inhuman acts in a misguided effort to accommodate the community's standards to those of the violent few.*

Again, we have a rhetorical device just as easily used by the other side:

> *What corrodes a society even more deeply than police violence itself is the acceptance of police violence, the condoning of police terror, excusing of inhuman police actions in a misguided effort to keep those with legitimate grievances from airing their views.*

> *5. Yet we all know that at some of the great universities small bands of destructionists have been allowed to impose their own rule of arbitrary force.*
> *Because of this, we today face the greatest crisis in the history of American education. In times past we've had crises in education. . . . We faced shortages of classrooms, shortages of teachers; shortages that could always be made up, however, by appropriating more money.*
> *These material shortages are nothing compared to the crisis of the spirit which rocks hundreds of campuses across the country today.*

It's hard to know where to start when confronted with a passage like this one. In the first place, there is the suppression of "facts" similar to those presented which, however, would tend to move the hearer in the other direction. Mr. Nixon mentioned classroom and teacher shortages as examples of past crises, all of which could be made up by spending more money. But he neglected the worst evil ever in our schools, namely racial segregation, which could *not* be made up by spending more money.

He then refers to the "crisis of the spirit" on campuses today as a much greater problem than those we faced in the past. This has some plausibility to it, *if* we consider only the problems Mr. Nixon considered. But once we mention segregated schools, which effectively denied decent education to over 10 percent of our population for several generations, then the college crisis which started in the late 1960s has to take a back seat.

In addition, President Nixon begged the question as to the *cause* of this crisis of spirit (greatly exaggerated anyway). He assumed, but did not attempt to prove, that the cause of the crisis was campus violence and "a small band of destructionists" who were "allowed to impose their own rule of arbitrary force" on these campuses. He may have been right. But many at the time contended that it was Vietnam and internal failure to live up to our ideals which caused students to have their faith in America shaken, and caused them to turn away from the traditional theoretical disciplines to more "relevant" topics. Others felt it was the failure of students to accomplish quick changes in America during the 1960s which caused many young people to turn to drugs and a few to turn to violence. It isn't that Nixon was right or wrong, but rather that he didn't *argue* for his conclusions.

Finally, Mr. Nixon took advantage (as we all do) of the ambiguity of the English word "some," as well as the quirk in English which permits omission of *quantifiers*. The word "some" can mean anything from "just a few" to "all but one." It was true that (some) students took over some universities, because they took over a very few, not because they took over many.

And by omitting a *time quantifier*, the President gave the impression that destructionists at some universities were frequently or constantly allowed to impose their own rule of force, whereas this was never more than a fairly isolated happening at even the most troubled school.

> 6. *And it is time for the responsible university and college administrators, faculty and student leaders to stand up and be counted, because we must remember only they can save higher education in America. It cannot be by government.*

This time it's platitudes plus a begged question. Most generations see themselves as in a time of crisis or important events. It is almost always "time to stand up and be counted." The question is what specifically is to be done to solve the problem. In addition, Mr. Nixon told college administrators it was their job and not to count on government. But he neglected to argue for that view. If the problems of higher education stemmed from something internal to the system of higher education, he may have been right. But if the problem stemmed from external pressures (Vietnam, racial strife, etc.), then he was probably wrong. However, in either case, the President begged the question.

> 7. *The destructive activists at our universities and colleges are a small minority, but their voices have been allowed to drown out—my*

text at this point reads, "The voices of the small minority have been allowed to drown out the responsible majority." That may be true in some places, but not at Kansas State!

This is just playing to the crowd, whipping up emotions, appealing to prejudice, appealing to loyalty, the fallacy of *provincialism*. It's on a par with Nixon's wearing a purple and white tie at a school where the football coach wanted the football turf dyed purple.

> 8. *Automatic conformity with the older generation . . . is wrong. At the same time, it is just as wrong to fall into a* **slavish conformity** *with those who* **falsely** *claim to be leaders of a new generation, out of fear to be unpopular or considered square not to follow their lead. It would be a great tragedy for the . . . new generation to become simply parrots for the slogans of protests, uniformly chanting the same few phrases and often the same four-letter words.*

In the first place, the use of the phrase "slavish conformity" is unjustified, as is the word "falsely." These are value expressions which require argument. For instance, if he believes others are the true leaders of the younger generation, he should say who they are and explain why he thinks so.

But in addition, this is one of those pat passages which are so easy to turn in the other direction. Could we not just as easily accuse Mr. Nixon's "silent majority" of slavish conformity, for instance in their pasting flags on car windows and radio antennas. Couldn't we just as easily accuse them of the fear of being unpopular? (Who isn't afraid of being unpopular?)

> 9. *We see a natural environment. True, it's been damaged by careless nuisances and misuses of technology. But we also see that that same technology gives us the ability to clean up that environment, to restore the clean air, the clean water, the open spaces that are our rightful heritage. And I pledge we shall do that and can do it in America.*

Mr. Nixon pledges, like his predecessor, to reduce pollution. What politician would say otherwise? The question is whether his *actions* mirrored or contradicted his words, and the answer is clear from the tiny amount of money requested by the President for pollution control and in the fact that pollution increased during his administration just as it had under previous presidents.

> *10. Look at our nation. We are rich, and sometimes that is condemned because wealth can sometimes be used improperly. But because of our wealth, it means that today we in America cannot just talk about, but can plan for a program in which everyone in this nation, willing and able to work, can earn a decent living and so that we can care for those who are not able to do so on some basis.*

There is only one word for what it took to utter this remark—*chutzpah!* Or to put it more academically, this remark was *inconsistent* with the *actions* taken by the President to reduce inflation which also were expected to, and did, cause an increase in unemployment—in fact, the highest level of unemployment in many years. The point is that a president who deliberately increases unemployment (even to reduce inflation) cannot consistently pose as a champion of the unemployed.

> *11. It requires that the members of the academic community rise firmly in defense of the free pursuit of truth, that they defend it as zealously today against threats from within as they have in the past defended it against threats from without. . . . the final test of idealism lies in the respect each shows for the rights of others.*

Again, empty platitudes. Everyone is for the free pursuit of truth *in the abstract*. What counts is how they line up on the nitty gritty details. This paragraph could be inserted intact into a speech by any one of the presidents of a number of state universities harassed by state legislators, or in the case of Kent State, SUNY at Buffalo, Jackson State University, and many others, harassed by local governmental officials.

But any paragraph that can be used so widely *in toto* obviously hasn't gotten down to the details that make all the difference.

> *12. I speak here today on the campus of a great university, and I recall one of the great sons of Kansas, Dwight David Eisenhower. I recall the eloquent address he made at London's famous Guildhall immediately after victory in Europe.*

And on that day the huge assemblage of all the leading dignitaries of Britain were there to honor him.

And in his few remarks, one of the most eloquent speeches in the history of English eloquence, he said very simply, "I come from the heart of America."

Now, 25 years later, as I speak in the heart of America, I can truly say to you here today: You are the heart of America—and the heart of America is strong. The heart of America is good. The heart of America is sound.

This passage came very close to the end of Mr. Nixon's speech, and its intent is obvious. He appealed to the loyalty of the students as Kansans, who would be proud of a U.S. president who came from Kansas, who in particular was a military hero. The appeal was a *provincial* one. And he flattered them further by playing on the ambiguity of the word "heart," since Kansas *is* the heart of America in the sense that it is the geographic center of the United States (minus Hawaii and Alaska).

Notice how foolish it all sounds when the word "heart" is replaced by "geographic center": "I speak in the geographic center of America. I can truly say to you here today: You are the geographic center of America." And so on.

A typical political speech: selection of facts favorable to your side; distortion of the position of one's opponents; suppression of facts favorable to their position; and a bit of provincial appeal to whip up the crowd. But no carefully reasoned argument about the details that make all the difference.

Summary of Chapter Five

Chapter Five dealt with the analysis of lengthier arguments—an editorial, a political column, and a political speech. The margin note-summary method was introduced for use in analyzing extended passages. This method consists in making notes (in the margins or elsewhere) as an aid in the construction of an itemized summary of the main points in the passage to be analyzed. The passage then is analyzed through an analysis of the summary. In constructing a summary, care should be taken not to misrepresent the passage.

Exercise for Chapter Five

*1.   Here is a fairly typical editorial of the *New York Daily News*,[9]
      by far the largest-selling newspaper in the United States. Using
      the margin note-summary method (or a similar method of your
      own), analyze and evaluate this editorial:

The "White Flag Amendment"

*—which masquerades as the "amendment to end the war" comes be-
fore the Senate tomorrow for a showdown vote.*

   *This bugout scheme is co-sponsored by Sens. George McGovern
(D-S.D.) and Mark Hatfield (R-Ore.). And despite some last-minute
chopping and changing to sucker fence-sitting senators, the proposal
remains what it has always been, a blueprint for a U.S. surrender in
Vietnam.*

   *It would force a pell-mell pullout of American forces there by cut-
ting off all funds for the Vietnam war as of Dec. 31, 1971. It represents
the kind of simple—and simple-minded—solution to Vietnam for
which arch-doves and pacifists (as well as the defeatists and Reds who
lurk behind them) have long clamored.*

   *This amendment wears the phony tag of a "peace" plan. More
accurately, it constitutes a first step toward whittling Uncle Sam down
to pygmy size in the world power scales; it would fill our enemies with
glee and our friends with dismay.*

   *McGovern-Hatfield might appear a cheap out from Vietnam. But
we would pay for it dearly later in other challenges and confrontations
as the Communists probe, as they inevitably do at any sign of weakness, to determine the exact jelly content of America's spine.*

   *The McGoverns, Hatfields, Fulbrights, Goodells and their ilk would
have the nation believe that its only choice lies between their skedaddle
scheme and an endless war. That is a lie.*

   *President Richard M. Nixon has a program for ending America's
commitment in Vietnam, and it is now under way. It involves an
orderly cutback in U.S. forces.*

   *The White House method assures the South Vietnamese at least a
fighting chance to stand on their own feet and determine their own
future after we leave.*

   Equally important, it tells the world the U.S. is not about to pull the

---

[9] © 1970, by the *New York Daily News*. Reprinted by permission.

covers over its head and duck out on its responsibilities as leader of the free world.

We urge the Senate to slap down the McGovern-Hatfield amendment, and scuttle with it any notion that America is willing to buy off noisy dissidents at the price of its honor.

2. Here is an editorial from the *Hartford Courant* (October 26, 1970).[10] Using the margin note-summary method (or a similar method of your own) analyze and evaluate this editorial:

The Pornography Report

There is no surprise in the fact that President Nixon has rejected the report of the Commission on Obscenity and Pornography. The report was not officially released until the last of September. But as early as mid-August the White House had told reporters that Mr. Nixon had opinions at variance with those of the commission, and "believes pornography relates to adverse social conduct."

What a majority of commission members agreed upon was that "there is no causal relation between erotic materials and sex crime, and they recommended repeal of pornography laws for adults."

"Research indicates," they said, "that erotic materials do not contribute to the development of character deficits, nor operate as a significant factor in antisocial behavior, or in crime and delinquency causation. . . . There is no evidence that exposure to pornography operates as a cause of misconduct in either youths or adults."

Mr. Nixon's rejection of the report on the weekend was far stronger than his previous "variance of opinion." His rejection this time is total and categorically opposed to its "morally bankrupt conclusions and major recommendations." Against the theory that dissemination of pornography among adults has no lasting harmful effect, Mr. Nixon said if that were true, "it must also be true that great books, great paintings and great plays have no ennobling effect on a man's conduct. Centuries of civilization and ten minutes of common sense tell us otherwise."

Many persons are going to agree with the President's strong condemnation of the warped and brutal portrayal of sex in books, plays, magazines and movies. Indeed members of the commission itself were the first to reject the majority report. They went to court and got an injunction preventing release of the report until they could prepare

[10] Reprinted by permission of the *Hartford Courant*.

dissenting opinions. They charged that the commission had not carried on Congress' mandate to recommend means to regulate effectively the traffic in obscenity and pornography, but on the contrary had spent over two years and almost two million dollars to prove the preconceived notions of one man (chairman of the commission), and the small group of Americans he represents. They termed the commission report a magna carta for pornographers. They commented on the "negative effects" that should have been considered in studying pornography—"spectacular increase in VD in the last five years; divorce rate highest in 25 years; aggressive rape (great percentage increase); premarital pregnancies (spectacular ten-year increase)."

As the old saw has it, there are two sides to a question, and they are both set down in the majority and minority reports of the commission. But much of the American public will agree with the President and the minority dissenters. For whatever reason, Western civilization is in a morass of sex. Even if it is not a promoter of crime, it is an obsession to the point where it is a way of life, especially for the young. Pornography and obscenity are not going to abate it. Whatever they may do to "normal" adults, they are going to make worse those who already have sick ideas, and there are plenty of them.

With Mr. Nixon, we are all well aware of the importance of protecting freedom of expression. But most will agree with him that "pornography is to freedom of expression what anarchy is to liberty." Even the liberal-tending Supreme Court has held that obscenity is not within the area of protected speech or press. Everyone hollers for clean air, clean water. Let there be some yelling, too, for clean minds.

*3.   The following is part of a political column by the nationally syndicated columnist Jenkin Lloyd Jones on "law and order." [11] Using the margin note-summary method (or your own method) analyze and evaluate this political column:

In his recent speech to the American Bar Assn., an authentic card-carrying "liberal," Hubert Humphrey, said it is high time his fellow liberals got over on the side of law and order.

Four days later, as if to illustrate his point, the federal office building in his home town, Minneapolis, was rocked by a blast that shattered windows blocks away. This building which contained a military

---

[11] By Jenkin Lloyd Jones, © 1970, General Features Corp., Los Angeles Times Syndicate. Reprinted by permission.

induction center has been a favorite target of antiwar demonstrators.

The former Vice President warned that attempts to describe as "well-meaning" all authors of violence and disruption are creating a credibility gap from which political liberals are suffering.

"Police brutality"—which has come, in the fevered imaginations of some, to mean any attempt by police to resist snipers and rioters—degenerates into unreal polemics as the arsenals of the Black Panthers and the Weathermen are revealed and the bodies of policemen pile up.

There has been no public recantation from those free-swinging libertarians who had been crying out to heaven that the painful and only barely successful effort to pry the communist professor, Angela Davis, loose from the state university payroll in California was a violation of academic freedom. But since her guns were allegedly used in the murder of four persons at the Marin County Courthouse we haven't heard a peep from the apologists.

The incredible presidential Commission on Pornography, appointed by Lyndon Johnson, has spent $2 million and come in with a preliminary report, written by the staff, which concludes that wide-open, anything-goes pornography has no relation to sex crimes.

This ignores the latest FBI report that states that in 1969 over 1968 rapes rose 17 percent, the biggest increase in any major crime category except larceny. Dr. Victor B. Cline, professor of clinical psychology at the University of Utah, has damned the report as "an almost Alice in Wonderland distortion of the evidence." . . .

Hubert Humphrey is right. Anarchy leads inevitably to repression. There is neither freedom nor social progress outside of law and order.

4. Analyze and evaluate the following political column by William F. Buckley, Jr.:[12]

The Victory of Cesar Chavez

The Cesar Chavez people appear to have won their fight to unionize the grape-pickers in Southern California, and it is worth a moment to meditate on the means through which they succeeded in winning, and the consequences of their victory.

1. It is easy enough to say simply that it cannot be other than glad tidings that the grape-pickers in Southern California will be earning 20 percent more than they earned before. But of course there are those

---

[12] *On the Right*, © 1970, Washington Star Syndicate, Inc. Reprinted by permission.

who will remind themselves that economics doesn't work that way, else—for instance—we would send Cesar Chavez to India, to call for a general strike because, over there, the hourly pay of a Ph.D. is less than the hourly pay of a grape-picker in Southern California.

The emotional difficulty with any discussion in this area is obvious. If it is established that the hourly pay of the grape-picker in Southern California is, say $1.67, the temptation is to say that so insufficient a wage ought not to be condoned.

But the free market does not dispose of moral judgments. The question has been whether (a) you permit migrant workers, many of whom come in from Mexico, to continue to work at a price which is acceptable to employer and employees; or (b) you simply forbid said workers to come in to work at wages we consider to be too low.

The trouble with siding automatically with the apparently benevolent side of this argument is simply this: if the price of labor is raised, by political pressures, say by 50 percent, then of course the extra cost is passed along to the grape buyers. Since the desire for grapes is not inflexible, it follows that there will be those who reject the new price; and their rejection will mean, according to the terms of the economic argument, very simply: fewer grapes sold, fewer migratory workers hired.

2. But even if in the long run the grape-pickers lose, you have to hand it to Cesar Chavez, who succeeded in intimidating everybody you ever heard of not to buy California grapes. Indeed, non-California grape-eating was indisputably the single most important thing that a lot of people, primarily eastern seaboard blue bloods, were able to manage during 1969–1970.

Mr. Chavez's campaign was effective, reaching even to the airlines, although their boycott was less than candid.

TWA—for instance—reported through a vice president to one inquirer last May that although it theoretically isn't proper for an airline to take sides on a political controversy, "We were well aware that this is a case where, in effect, one can take sides by inaction as well as action." The solution? ". . . We had decided to remove fruit baskets from our domestic flights on June 15. We will substitute a so-called Fruit Bowl au Kirsch; grapes will not be utilized in this concoction."

A few weeks later another vice president of TWA wrote to a different inquirer, "I . . . appreciate this opportunity to discuss the reports which appeared in the press to the effect that TWA was 'boycotting' grapes. The change which apparently gave rise to this erroneous and unfortunate report involved, among other things, the substitution of a so-called Fruit Bowl au Kirsch for a fresh fruit tray which we had been offering under the previous menu. The recipe for this fruit bowl was developed in an effort to make the dish taste good; that was the only criterion used in its development. The fruit tray for which it substituted included, in addition to grapes, things like oranges, apples, pears and bananas."

So that, depending on what you want to hear, official A says: *We're cutting down on grapes, because if we use grapes we are in effect siding with the pro-grape people;* and official B of the same company says: *You're crazy if you think our nongrape position has anything to do with Cesar Chavez.*

3. *Will Mr. Chavez now rest? Or will he move on to unionize farm workers in general? If he calls for a more general boycott, the poor people in Southampton—and in TWA—may find that they are reduced to a diet of Fruit Bowl au Kirsch made up exclusively of grapes.*

Chapter Six

The Selling of the Candidate

> You can say this Administration will have the first far-reaching attack on the problem of hunger in history. Use all the rhetoric, so long as it doesn't cost any money.
>
> **Richard M. Nixon,** *at a 1969 White House meeting a few weeks before calling for "an end to hunger in America for all time" (quoted in* Look *magazine, Dec. 2, 1969).*

By now, just about everyone knows that political candidates are marketed pretty much like breakfast foods or laundry detergents. And that might be all right if the appeals in breakfast food and detergent advertising were rational. But they aren't, and thus the need for this chapter.

1. Some remarks about advertising

A profession seemingly without a product constantly needs to defend itself. The classical justification for advertising is that it informs the public of the availability and quality of products. In other words, the product of advertising is said to be simply *product information.* But it hasn't worked that way. Ads do occasionally inform, but that is not their primary purpose.

    a.   Ads never tell what is wrong with a product. No product is perfect. Hence the completely informative ad would mention at least some *drawbacks* of the product. But no one has yet seen an ad which deliberately said anything negative about a product.[1] As David Ogilvy, one of the biggest

---

[1] Except when employing "reverse twist" trying to make a virtue out of an apparent defect. The Avis Rent A Car campaign—"We try harder (because we're only number two)"—is an example.

ad executives, stated in his best seller on advertising,[2] "Surely it is asking too much to expect the advertiser to describe the shortcomings of his product." And that is exactly the point, for this means that practically every ad is guilty of the fallacy of *suppressed evidence* by concealing some negative information about the product.

This is a good deal more important than it sounds when you consider that the information suppressed may be about serious side effects of a drug (for example, birth control pills), or the relatively poor food value of commercial breads and breakfast foods (for example, Wonder Bread and Kellogg's Corn Flakes).

   b.   *Some ads say things about the product that are simply false.* Whatever "tired blood" was, Geritol was not good for it. Toothpastes on the market before the age of fluorides advertised reductions in tooth decay, but they didn't deliver. Ads for hair restorers "guarantee" to restore lost hair, but nothing yet discovered can do that. Diet pills advertise weight loss without cutting down on favorite foods (impossible—if you consume too many calories, you get fat—pills or no pills). Thousands of commercials have shown celebrities "using" products they wouldn't ordinarily touch with a ten-foot pole. A TV commercial for a shaving cream shows sandpaper being shaved, only it's really sand thrown on a piece of plexiglass.

   c.   *Advertisements frequently employ meaningless jargon.* We're all familiar with this from cosmetic ads. But the practice is much more widespread than is realized, because most ads of this kind *appear* to make sense. However, what does it *mean,* really, to say that a brand of detergent gets clothes "whiter than white," or "beyond white"? Or to say that a product is *better* (better than what?), or *genuine* (genuine what?).

   d.   *Many, perhaps most, ads are literally true, but imply falsehoods.* The Shell Platformate ad mentioned in Chapter One is an example. It implied, but never said, that *only* Shell has Platformate. But the Shell ad is not at all unusual. The cigarette ad trumpeting the fact that Brand X is lowest in tar and nicotine *implies* the falsehood that the difference between Brand X and the next brand is a significant one. (Old Gold touched bottom in this game when it used a *Reader's Digest* report indicating it was lowest in nicotine without mentioning that the difference was a completely negligible $1/177,187$ of an ounce per cigarette!)

The Armour Star frank ad which correctly stated that one pound of Armour franks and one pound of steak are equal in nourishment *implied* that a hot dog *meal* is just as nourishing as a steak meal. But did you ever try eating *ten* Armour franks at one sitting? In one Bayer aspirin TV

---

[2] *Confessions of an Advertising Man,* Atheneum, New York, 1963, p. 158. The succeeding Ogilvy references are from this book also.

commercial, an announcer holding a bottle of Bayer aspirin stated that doctors recommend aspirin for pain relief. He didn't say that doctors recommend Bayer's, but the *implication* was there.

One of the great geniuses of advertising, Claude Hopkins, was the first advertising man to understand and use a beautiful variation on the false implication gambit. Hopkins believed it was a waste of money to claim your product is the best, or pure, or anything so general. He tried to understand his product sufficiently to be able to provide more specific "reasons why" a person should buy that product. This may sound as though his ads really did inform the public about the product, and Hopkins himself may have believed this. But it didn't work that way.

One of Hopkins' early and famous ad campaigns illustrates this well. When he was put to work on Schlitz Beer ads, he discovered that each Schlitz bottle was sterilized with live steam. So he built his campaign around headlines such as "Washed with Live Steam!," omitting the fact that all breweries used live steam. He knew that competitors couldn't then advertise that they too used live steam—that claim had been preempted for Schlitz. And he knew that most readers would *assume* that only Schlitz washed their bottles with live steam. (He was right; Schlitz sales went from fifth to first in short order.)

Most ads that claim a certain quality for their product without explicitly asserting its uniqueness to that product are designed to make you *assume* that only their product has that quality. If you make that assumption, you reason fallaciously.

    e. The appeal of most ads is emotional, not rational. Information appeals to *reason,* but advertisements play to *emotions.* One of the classics of advertising history is built around a headline which for a time became a part of the language:

> *They Laughed when I Sat Down at the Piano*
> *But when I Started to Play! . . .*

The appeal of this ad was to the desire to shine at parties. In the fine print, having put the prospective customer in the proper emotional frame, the ad promises to teach piano playing quickly and with "no laborious scales— no heartless exercises—no tiresome practicing." *Reason* would caution the reader. How, after all, is it possible to learn to play the piano without lots of practicing? But no matter; emotions sufficiently worked-on override rationality—in a sufficient number of cases. This famous ad was a tremendous money-maker.[3]

Ads for deodorants and mouthwashes play on our *fear* of offending when we get close to others. Yet they rarely provide rational grounds for choosing the brand advertised. The same is true of cigarette and beer ads. Very few beer drinkers can tell "their" brand from other brands (easily proved by conducting blindfold taste tests). So beer ads have to appeal to emotions, since there aren't any rational grounds for drinking one standard brand of beer rather than another of the same type.

Early ads for automobiles stressed mechanical qualities of the cars advertised. But by the 1920s, auto ads had by and large switched to the emotional appeal that still is used. One of the first great auto ads was for a small company, the Jordan Motor Car Co., which put out a car called the Playboy. The ad pictured a young woman in a Playboy, mountains in the distance, and a cowboy on horseback being overtaken and passed. The caption read: "Somewhere West of Laramie," and then the copy started: "Somewhere west of Laramie, there's a broncho-busting, steer-roping girl who knows what I'm talking about. She can tell what a sassy pony. . . ." And on and on. Jordan made millions.

Critics of advertising often claim that *competitive* advertising, designed to switch people from one brand to another, is wasteful and undesirable, although *informative* advertising is legitimate.[4] Defenders of advertising (David Ogilvy is typical) generally reply by claiming that *good* advertising is truly informative. Ogilvy, for instance, claimed that uninformative competitive advertising is of *poor* quality and won't sell the product anyway.

This sounds fine until you begin to look at Mr. Ogilvy's own ads. What information is imparted by the black eye patch in the famous Hathaway Shirt ads? Did Mr. Ogilvy really believe Hathaway shirts were superior to those made by Arrow and Van Heusen? Weren't his great ads for Shell

---

[3] The headline on the ad became so well known, and remained so, that Frank Rowsome, Jr., used its opening phrase as the title of his delightful book on advertising, *They Laughed When I Sat Down*, Bonanza Books, New York, 1959. Some of the other examples used in this chapter also appear in Mr. Rowsome's book.

But an ad can be both competitive and informative, a point many advertising critics overlook. There is nothing wrong with *informative* competitive ads. If Schlitz really does have a particular edge on its competition, an ad saying so would be unobjectionable. The trouble with Hopkins' Schlitz ad, discussed above, was that all major brands washed their empties with live steam, so Hopkins' "reasons why" was not a good reason to switch to Schlitz. The ad was not usefully informative.

gasoline and Schweppes uninformative competitive ads designed to switch readers from one brand to another? How, for instance, could an ad for Shell gasoline show why Shell is better than its competitor if it isn't better?

The fact is that in spite of the advertising industry's claims to the contrary, most successful ads have not been truly informative. Bayer aspirin is not better than other aspirin; it only costs more. There isn't any reason to have Schaeffer beer instead of Schlitz, Ballantine, or dozens of others, "when you're having more than one." There is no detergent which gets clothes noticeably whiter than all of its competitors. You're not more likely to get the job if you use Listerine, because Listerine doesn't cure bad breath, much of which originates in the lungs and stomach anyway. Whatever Winstons taste like (or as?), they don't taste better than all of their competitors; even experts would have difficulty telling Winstons from competing brands. And if Avis tries harder than Hertz, it doesn't seem to make a noticeable difference when you rent an auto.

When you cut through all the malarky about advertising principles, you find that most successful ads follow two (or perhaps three) basic principles.[5] The first is that successful ads are directed towards selfish human desires and motives. The second is that even in appealing to human selfishness the appeal should be emotional, not rational.

Claude Hopkins explained the reason for the first rule as follows:

> *The people you address are selfish, as we all are. They care nothing about your interest or your profit. They seek service for themselves. Ignoring this fact is a common mistake and a costly mistake in advertising. Ads say in effect, "Buy my brand. Give me the trade you give to others. Let me have the money." That is not a popular appeal. Whatever people do they do to please themselves.*

Although Hopkins' psychology is not quite correct (people *sometimes* act from altruistic motives), almost every successful ad does appeal somehow or other to human selfishness.[6]

---

[5] Omitting technical principles of composition, type face, page placement, etc.

[6] One of the greatest ads ever, in the opinion of this writer, was the one that began, "If you have to kill children, it's nicer to let them starve than to put them into a gas oven. This is about the war on page 12 of your newspapers . . . ," and then told about the war in Biafra. This ad drew as well as others on the Biafra war, but did not produce the hoped-for flood of letters to the president. It's simply much more difficult to sell people by appeal to altruistic motives.

But it is the second principle of successful advertising that is of special interest here. One would suppose that the best ad would be one which makes a rational appeal to some selfish interest. If autos were symbols of freedom and abandon to the young generation of the 1920s, then an ad which demonstrated that a particular auto was best for those qualities ought to sell best.

But when we examine the most successful ads appealing to youth in the 1920s, we find that they contain few *facts* demonstrating any kind of superiority. The Jordan Playboy ads appealed directly to the desire to roam the world, to sexual adventure, and to freedom for women (the automatic starter had just made it practical for women to operate autos by themselves). But nowhere in these ads were there any facts about the car's construction which would justify buying a Playboy rather than a competing model.

Or consider the recent highly successful Schlitz ads which shouted at the listener to grab all the gusto in life he could, because "you only get one go around in life." The appeal was hedonistic, following rule one. But it also was an emotional appeal, devoid of reasons for drinking *Schlitz* rather than a competitor, following rule two. Examine a hundred successful ads and you'll find that the vast majority follow these two principles.

This brings us to a very disputed third rule of successful advertising, which is simply to repeat the message ad nauseum. The late George Washington Hill of the American Tobacco Company was the champion of this idea, with the result that for years on radio and in newspapers and magazines the nation was bombarded with the message that "L.S.M.F.T.— Lucky Strike means fine tobacco." (Track coaches throughout the nation changed that one to read "Less smoking means finer trackmen," which at least had the virtue of being *true*.)

But whether or not *endless* repetition is effective, there does seem to be some value in limited repetition. This is true not merely in promoting belief in the message, but, more importantly, in promoting belief which results in *action*.

2. The candidate as product

The subject of repetition brings us to the selling of politicians. In some areas of the country, local candidates campaign by lawn signs, billboards, and bumper stickers as much as in any other way. In general, lawn signs carry only the name of the candidate and (sometimes) party affiliation. Billboards and bumper stickers rarely have room for more, but when they do, the extra material is a slogan (slogans are discussed next).

And yet, a man's name never constitutes a good reason for voting for
him. And only occasionally is his party affiliation a good reason (it almost
never is a *sufficient* reason).

At work in these cases is the psychological mechanism that lies behind
the commission of the fallacy of *popularity,* namely familiarity and the
desire to be one of the crowd. Psychologically, voting for a familiar name
is little different from buying a product because advertising has made it
familiar and because so many other people are buying it.

Billboard ads come in for particularly heavy use during political campaigns, and generally consist of the candidate's name, party affiliation,
picture (sometimes), and a slogan. Here are a few slogans used on billboards in the 1970 elections in just one state (Connecticut):

> *Keep a Strong Voice in Congress (Kilbourne, running for U.S. Con-
> gress)*
>
> *Because you care . . . (Uccelo, running for U.S. Congress)*
>
> *Ella Grasso Cares (Grasso, running for U.S. Congress)*
>
> *One man can make a difference (Duffey, running for the Democratic
> nomination for the U.S. Senate)*
>
> *Put your confidence in a man with guts (Weicker, running for U.S.
> Senate)*
>
> *All the people must be heard (Daddario, running for Governor)*

None of these provided the slightest reason for voting for the touted candidate. One man sometimes *can* make a difference. But was Duffey that
man? A slogan can't tell us that. All the people *ought* to be heard. But
would they get heard if Daddario were elected? Again a slogan can't tell
us that.

In Tennessee in 1970, Senator Albert Gore ran against William Brock,
III, the Brock candy heir. One of Gore's more effective lines was that "I
came up here with Tennessee dirt on my hands, not chocolate." True, and
Gore may have been the better man. But dirt rather than chocolate didn't
prove it.

In the 1960 presidential campaign, John Kennedy projected the image
of youthful vigor, and repeated over and over the slogan that he wanted to

"get the country moving again." In all fairness, he did explain to some small degree *how* he would get it moving again, but by and large he won by projecting the *image* of a young, virile man who would get us moving again. His slogan mirrored that image and thus contributed to his election.[7]

But it is television on which most advertising money and effort has been lavished in major political campaigns in recent years.

In the 1970 New York State Senatorial campaign, Congressman Richard Ottinger, not well-known in the state outside of his own territory, won the Democratic nomination by making himself well-known via television. He then came very close to victory in the November elections even though he was one of two liberals running against one conservative. In both the primary and general elections, he spent millions on TV advertising.

In the 1970 New York race for Governor (which he won quite handily), Nelson Rockefeller used the most massive television campaign in New York history.

And yet, there is extremely little that is informative in TV ads for political candidates.

The chief political ad device on TV is the spot commercial, which generally runs from thirty to sixty seconds. It is almost impossible to say anything that is truly informative on any controversial topic in sixty seconds or less. Senator Philip Hart, of Michigan, who used TV ads in his successful 1970 campaign, put it perfectly, "How the hell can you describe in 30 seconds why you think a volunteer army is necessary?" [8]

In the 1968 campaign, the democratic presidential candidate Hubert Humphrey made the spot commercial his chief TV venture. Humphrey was advised to stop talking about his Marshall Plan for cities and start talking about law and order. So one of his spots showed a mother holding a baby, and musing to herself, "I wonder what he'll be like when he's older. I hope he won't be afraid the way we are." Then an announcer's voice said, "Hubert Humphrey has said that every American has a right to a safe neighborhood. . . ."

Of course, Humphrey was not ahead of Richard Nixon on this issue. One of Nixon's commercials showed scenes of violence and fear, followed by Nixon, who stated:

[7] Of course, he ran in a year when a Democrat had a good chance to win. In 1964, when Senator Goldwater ran as a conservative Republican, the liberal tide was strong. His silly slogan, "In your heart you know he's right" was countered by the even sillier back room liberal response, "In your guts you know he's nuts."

[8] Quoted in *Time* magazine, September 21, 1970.

It is time for some honest talk about the problem of order in the United States. Dissent is a necessary ingredient for change. But in a system that provides for peaceful change—there is no cause that justifies resort to violence. There is no cause that justifies rule by mob instead of reason.

The commercial ended with an announcer saying "This time vote like your whole world depended on it," while the name "Nixon" appeared on screen. (Does this sound like Nixon's 1970 Kansas State University speech discussed in Chapter Five?)

If both candidates say just about the same thing, and that amounts to little more than platitudes playing on the public's fears, then how can an intelligent voter make a decision between them?

Still, these spot commercials were better than the ones created for the 1952 Eisenhower campaign, the first presidential campaign in which TV ads played an important role. In that campaign, General Eisenhower would read from letters received from "citizens" asking questions which Eisenhower then "answered." Here is an example: [9]

Citizen: *Mr. Eisenhower, what about the high cost of living?*
General Eisenhower: *My wife Mamie worries about the same thing. I tell her it's our job to change that on November 14th.*

The appeal here is to Eisenhower the father figure who will set things right just as daddy used to. (Appeal to a father figure may well be the most effective version of *appeal to authority*.) You don't have to know *how* papa fixes things, and you didn't have to know how Eisenhower was going to reduce prices. (He didn't, of course; but that's hindsight.) All you had to know was that if you voted for him, he would be on the job after the election doing something about the high cost of living.

Perhaps the most effective Nixon spot was his first, which ran often while the Humphrey campaign was bogged down. The video portion of the spot consisted of shots from Vietnam cleverly dovetailed with Mr. Nixon's voice:

---

[9] Quoted by David Ogilvy in *Confessions of an Advertising Man*, p. 159. Ogilvy quotes Eisenhower as moaning between TV takes, "To think an old soldier should come to this."

Never has so much military, economic, and diplomatic power been used as ineffectively as in Vietnam. And if, after all of this time and all of this support, there is still no end in sight, then I say the time has come for the American people to turn to new leadership, not tied to the policies and mistakes of the past. I pledge to you: we will have an honorable end to the war in Vietnam.

(An ironic commercial, given what transpired in Vietnam after Nixon took office.) Notice, however, that the punch line, the promise to get us out of Vietnam, is extremely *vague*. In particular, he doesn't tell us *when* or *how* he will get us out, except that it will be honorable. Yet the tone of the commercial gives the viewer the impression that Nixon will get us out *quickly*.

· Many of Humphrey's 1968 spot commercials were directed against his opponents, Nixon and Wallace. One series of commercials had pictures of bubbles as their main video prop. As the announcer burst a political bubble, a visual bubble also would burst. For instance, Wallace stressed law and order, so one bubble commercial presented the following fact:

Fact:
Alabama:
Highest
Murder Rate

Thus exploding another bubble (that Alabama Governor Wallace would reduce crime in the U.S. if elected president). Another hit Nixon on the health issue:

Nixon:
Opposes Medicare

Another burst bubble (that Nixon would improve health care in the U.S. if elected).

These ads were very simple and very effective. But they tell the TV viewer almost nothing about what a vote for Humphrey would amount to. And they were misleading. To be sure, Nixon opposed Medicare; but he did have a program to improve medical care in America. The question was whether his plan or Humphrey's was better, and whether either program was likely to be carried out. Humphrey's TV spots never went into such details.

The same is true of his commercial which played on the fact that Nixon had chosen as his running mate a man who was almost unknown outside of his home state of Maryland, a man who happened to have the unusual name "Agnew." Democrats at the time often bucked up their sagging spirits by asking each other, "Spiro *who?*" So Humphrey's TV advertising geniuses concocted a TV spot consisting of almost a minute of laughter, with a voice saying, "Agnew for Vice President?" and at the end the video reading, "This would be funny if it weren't so serious. . . ." All of which amounts to nothing other than an *ad hominem* argument directed against Spiro Agnew.

Perhaps the most effective TV political spot of the sixties was the one made by the Democrats in 1964 to emphasize their claim that their man was a peace candidate, while the Republican candidate Barry Goldwater was a violent hawk. (Lyndon Johnson as peace candidate seems foolish now, but, again, that's hindsight.) The commercial shows a cute little girl plucking the petals from a flower one by one while on the sound track we hear, "Ten, nine, eight, seven, six, five, four, three, two, one," at which point an atomic fireball flashes on the screen. A very informative commercial.

In the 1968 campaign, the Republicans also made hay on TV with several hour-long question-answer panel shows. The format was pretty uniform: A "balanced" panel of voters, variously composed of a housewife, *one* Negro (generally light skinned), a "senior citizen," a Jewish professional man, a working man, etc., would ask questions of Mr. Nixon.

For him, it amounted to a press conference with two important and comforting differences: the audiences were hand-picked and guaranteed to applaud his every word; and the panelists were "safe," or in any event inexperienced (except for occasional newsmen), and tended to be overawed by Mr. Nixon, as most of us would be. In addition, the format was designed to gain sympathy for Mr. Nixon. He stood alone on a platform, without props, facing the six or seven panelists who surrounded him. The program was live; he had no way of knowing which questions would be asked. The result was that the viewer did tend to sympathize with Nixon, and hope he wouldn't be trapped or flub an answer.

Of course, there was no need for anxiety. Predictable questions were asked (with one exception out of the hundreds of questions on the many shows). The first question on the first panel show was typical. It was asked by a Jewish attorney on this balanced panel:[10]

---

[10] For a much more complete and revealing account of the Nixon TV campaign and in particular the panel shows and spot commercials, see the book, *The Selling of the President 1968,* by Joe McGinniss, Trident Press, New York, 1969 (also in Pocket Book paperback, 1970).

Question: *Would you comment on the accusation which was made from time to time that your views have shifted and that they are based on expediencies?*

Nixon: *I suppose what you are referring to is: Is there a new Nixon or is there an old Nixon? I suppose I could counter by saying, "Which Humphrey shall we listen to today?"* [applause] *I do want to say this: There certainly is a new Nixon. I realize too that as a man gets older he learns something. If I haven't learned something, I am not worth anything in public life.*

We live in a new world. Half the nations in the world were born since World War II. Half the people living in the world today were born since World War II. The problems are different, and I think I have had the good sense—I trust the intelligence—to travel the world since I left the office of Vice President and to bring my views up to date to deal with the new world. I think my principles are consistent. I believe very deeply in the American system. I think I have some ideas as to how we can promote peace, ideas that are different from what they were eight years ago; not because I have changed, but because the problems have changed. . . .

The question was about the frequently heard charge of expediency—that Nixon's views "blow with the winds of popularity." Much of his answer was irrelevant to that question, and what was relevant said what he could be expected to say, namely that his underlying principles remained the same, changes in his opinions resulting from changes in the situation.

Thus, nowhere did we get the crucial details. The format ruled against that for at least three reasons. The first was lack of time; every panelist had to ask two or three questions, and answers had to be short. The second was that the panelists were not professionals, and lacked knowledge of the details that make all the difference.

Instead of this first question we needed one giving *details* of Nixon's switches which could reasonably be construed as motivated by expediency. But it wouldn't have mattered in any case. For the third impediment to a truly informative session was that Nixon's answers tended to be vague and general, floating above any specific probe, and the questioners were psychologically indisposed to press for a better answer. (It takes a very strong character indeed to push forward in such an intimidating situation. Only one panelist—Jack McKinney—had what it takes to try it, and that was someone with a great deal of experience on the airwaves.)

Let's include one more example of political campaigning on TV, to illustrate again the evils of the "no-comeback" feature of political campaigning by advertising. It concerns a TV spot for Nelson Rockefeller in his successful 1966 race for Governor of New York. Rockefeller, as usual, outspent his opponent by a wide margin. During the last ten days of that campaign, Rockefeller "saturated the air waves" [11] with the following spot:

> *Frank O'Connor, the man who led the fight against the New York State Thruway, is running for Governor* [against Rockefeller, of course]. *Get in your car and drive down to the polls and vote.*

O'Connor did *not* lead the fight against the New York State Thruway; he didn't even oppose its construction. But he did oppose *Rockefeller* on the Thruway; O'Connor wanted it to be free, while Rockefeller insisted on a toll. So the concealment and distortion is that O'Connor opposed *Rockefeller's* thruway proposal. (The distorted position constituted, of course, a *straw man.*)

The main evil of such political advertisement is that the other side rarely can strike back and effectively explain the facts. In this case, the TV spots ran near the end of the campaign, so that the other side had little time to prepare a professional reply based on effective advertising techniques. And in any event such denials would have been drowned out by the sheer volume of the Rockefeller barrage. Rockefeller had tremendous *repetition* going for him, just as did Lucky Strike cigarettes at an earlier time. "M.C.M.R.C.: More commercials mean richer candidates."

Summary of Chapter Six

Chapter Six dealt with advertising, and in particular political advertising, as a form of argument. Advertising is designed to sell a product, but not necessarily by providing useful information about it.

1. Ads never tell about the bad features of a product.
   Example: Ads for Wheaties don't tell you what vitamins and minerals are removed in processing the wheat from which Wheaties are made.
2. Some ads say false things about the product.
   Example: Ads for diet pills falsely claim you can lose weight without reducing food intake.

---

[11] To borrow a phrase used by Jack Newfield in his *Village Voice* article "Nelson Rockefeller: The Chutzpah King," October 8, 1970.

3. Ads often contain meaningless jargon.

   Example: Some detergent ads claim the product gets clothes "whiter than white."

4. Many ads, although literally true, strongly imply falsehoods.

   , *Example:* Shell ads implied that only Shell has Platformate.

5. The appeal of most ads is emotional, not rational.

   Example: Mouthwash ads play on the fear of offending with bad breath.

Most successful ads follow two or three basic principles:

1. They are directed towards selfish human motives.
2. The appeal to these motives is emotional, not rational.
3. They are repeated over and over again.

Political candidates now are sold in much the same way as any other product. Billboards repeat the same emotional appeals over and over.

Example: "Put your confidence in a man with guts." Sixty-second commercials appeal to fears and prejudices, not to reason.

Example: Hubert Humphrey's 1968 TV spot showing a mother holding a baby and saying to herself "I wonder what he'll be like when he's older. I hope he won't be afraid the way we are," followed by an announcer saying "Hubert Humphrey has said that every American has a right to a safe neighborhood." And longer programs are used to improve the candidate's image rather than to inform the electorate on the issues.

Example: The 1968 panel shows used by Richard Nixon.

Exercise for Chapter Six

Find five ads, each of which either:

1. contains meaningless jargon; or
2. although literally true, strongly implies something false; or
3. appeals to the emotions, not reason.

At least one of the five ads should illustrate (1), (2), and (3) respectively. Be sure to explain your choices.

Chapter Seven

Managing the News

When a dog bites a man, that is not news, because it happens so often. But if a man bites a dog, that is news.

John B. Bogart

Except for logic and mathematics, which consist solely of deductive reasoning, rational thought requires factual knowledge. That is why the success of a democratic form of government depends on a *well-informed* electorate.

The thesis of this chapter is that the American mass media (newspapers, mass magazines, radio, and TV) do not adequately or accurately inform their readers and listeners about the great difference between the way our system is supposed to work (the ideal—the "official story") and the way it actually works.[1] It's to be hoped that a person who has some understanding of the mass media will be better able to deal with them, and will realize that to be well-informed (and thus to reason well about political matters), one must turn to other sources of information. It is almost impossible for the person who is not well-informed—at least of the basic facts about his society—to avoid being taken in by fallacious political rhetoric.

Most of our examples are drawn from newspapers, but what they illustrate is true of all the mass media. Most people read their daily newspapers to find out about the day's news, at least after they've finished the funnies or sports page. Do they find out what of importance has been happening in the U.S. and around the world? To some extent, they obviously do. They read about election results, presidential speeches, bills passed by Congress (occasionally), and battles won or lost (usually).

But newspaper readers do not find out what, in a sense, *really* is happen-

---

[1] Chapters Eight and Nine concern the same theme and another branch of the "mass media" establishment, public school textbooks.

146

ing. Moreover, what readers do find out frequently is not presented in a very usable fashion, making intelligent reasoning about political matters that much more difficult. The same is true for all of the mass media. Here are some of the main reasons why.

1. Incorrect theory of news reporting

The mass media tend to employ an incorrect theory of news reporting. In the first place, *the unusual is considered to be news; the usual is not.* Consequently, everyday evils tend not to get reported, *ever.* Since they're not special news today—or tomorrow or yesterday—there is no day on which they are appropriately reported.

A perfect example is our appalling system of justice, which sentenced one man (Negro, of course) to half a lifetime in prison for possession of one marijuana cigarette (which he claimed was planted on him by police), while giving the son of Robert Kennedy a suspended sentence for a similar offense. Under the present judicial system, people who appear before criminal courts in many big cities find that they must bargain away their right to a fair trial in return for pleading guilty to a lesser crime carrying a lesser penalty.[2]

Yet little of this ever gets into the news, because it happens every day. (The Kennedy case, of course, made headlines, because it isn't every day a *Kennedy* is charged with a crime.) And yet, the most important "news" about our nation is how it operates day in and day out.

Newsmen, again theorizing incorrectly, also seem to believe that *in reporting the news, objectivity requires them to give the facts, not draw conclusions or make value judgments:* Facts are objective, conclusions or value judgments subjective. (Even J. Edgar Hoover subscribes to this view. Witness his motto that the F.B.I. does not draw conclusions, it only reports the facts.)

But this view is mistaken. *All* reports of facts depend on the *judgment* that they are facts. The reporter must *conclude* that they are facts. Take the following excerpts from an Associated Press story carried in the *Lawrence Daily Journal World* (October 30, 1970) on the alleged riot in San Jose, California, prior to the November 1970, elections:

---

[2] See Chapter Eight for a brief account of this, or the article "Crime in the Courts: Assembly Line Justice," by Leonard Downie, Jr., *Washington Monthly,* May 1970, or the *New York Times* article on plea bargaining, December 13, 1970, p. 26. (The *Times* article was an unusual one, even for the *Times;* for most other newspapers, an article of this kind would be extremely rare.)

> *President Nixon, the target of rocks, bricks, bottles, eggs, red flags
> and other missiles hurled by antiwar demonstrators. . . .*
>
> *The San Jose violence was the most serious aimed at any president in this country since the assassination of President John Kennedy. . . .*
>
> [Nixon's] *limousine and other vehicles in the cavalcade were hit repeatedly by large rocks and other objects.*

It is obvious that the reporter did not *see* that the alleged attack on President Nixon was the worst attack on a President since the assassination of President Kennedy. He had to *conclude* to that fact—if it *is* a fact—by using judgment as well as eyesight.

But it is often overlooked that judgment and conclusion-drawing are required even in reporting more immediate facts. Did the AP reporter—or any AP reporter—actually *see* rocks hit the President's limousine? If not, who did? Are those who think they did sure no visual distortion was at work? Did they hear a crunch as the rocks hit the car? These questions are not academic; it is well known that honest reports by onlookers frequently differ seriously about what took place. In this case, many eyewitnesses, including TV and newspaper reporters, say that *nothing* was thrown at the presidential limousine, although objects were thrown at the press corps bus.[3]

A great deal of reporting is of this kind. If the reporter is not an eyewitness, he must draw a *conclusion* about what happened from what he is told by others. If he is an eyewitness, what he thinks he has seen needs to be checked with what others have seen and with later evidence (e.g., if he thinks he saw rocks thrown, there should be rock fragments on the pavement at the correct location[4]).

So the idea that reporters must stick to facts and not draw conclusions is a myth. One must *reason to the facts* just as one reasons to anything else.

---

[3] See, for instance, the *Village Voice* article by Tom Devries, November 5, 1970, in which Mike Mills, a TV reporter, when asked why his films of the event show no flying objects, stated, "That is because nothing was thrown." The article quoted several other reporters who support or repeat this statement. And the San Jose police chief confirmed reporters' claims.

[4] Mr. Devries, the *Village Voice* reporter, wrote that he later checked the area for loose rocks and broken glass and found none. This does not mean that we can conclude he is right that rocks were not thrown at the President's auto, for he had to *conclude* no rocks were thrown, and he too could be wrong. But his failure to find such debris is evidence that no rocks were thrown at the President's vehicle.

Similarly, the idea that newspapers must not and do not make value judgments is a myth. When we read of the death of a famous movie star on page one of our morning newspaper, but read nothing of the death of the eminent philosopher, Rudolf Carnap (reported in the obituary section of the *New York Times* but ignored in most papers), it becomes obvious that newspapers have to make *value judgments* to determine what is important and what is not. The same is true when a hurricane on the Gulf Coast that kills two dozen people receives much greater space than reports of the My Lai 4 massacre in Vietnam, to say nothing of the slaughter in Biafra.

In other words, *editing,* one of the chief tasks of any newspaper, requires value judgments to be made about the relative importance of events. And, incidentally, *moral* value judgments often are required as well as others. The starvation of little children in the U.S. should be news precisely because it is so horribly *wrong* and *ought* to be corrected.

Newsmen believe *objectivity requires that "in-depth" reporting be separate from current news.* Nothing is more important in making decisions than facts. But the mere unordered acquisition of facts leaves one a long way from intelligent opinion. Facts need working on, and in particular comparison with related facts. In general, because reporting of current news lacks *depth,* it is rendered much less useful than it could be in forming opinions. For example, an Associated Press photo captioned "Lawmen and Indians Fight," showing policemen apparently beating Indians, appeared on page one of the *Hartford Courant,* October 29, 1970. Below the caption was a brief story about the fight between lawmen and Pit River Indian tribesmen, started, lawmen said, when the Indians tried to publicize their claim to the land by building on it "illegally." The story identified the police units and where the fight occurred. It also stated that the Indians claimed the land was taken from them back in the Gold Rush days.

But we weren't told enough for us to deal intelligently with this news. Did the Indians resist arrest? Was police force necessary? Is there anything to the Indian land claim? Have they tried to gain redress via the courts? The picture seems to show a policeman beating someone with a long nightstick. Is he? If so, was this force necessary to subdue the person? The caption says lawmen and *Indians* fight. Did the Indians do any fighting? We aren't given the answers to any of these questions.

And yet it is impossible to form an intelligent opinion on the events described if we don't know at least some of these facts. Not that this deterred most readers. Some no doubt shrugged and muttered about drunken Indians acting up again, while others commented about more pig brutality. The story as presented justifies neither of these conclusions. In fact, it doesn't justify any conclusion at all. But it does give readers an opportunity to vent their prejudices and thus become further polarized.

Inadequately reported news stories occur in newspapers every day, increasing misunderstanding and polarization. Reports that Georgia Governor Lester Maddox's son was sentenced for burglary of a service station to six months of weekends in jail plus a $500 fine omitted the crucial information about the same judge's normal penalty for similar crimes. And the sentence of another man convicted for the same crime with Mr. Maddox's son was not even reported.

Yet one thing that splits this nation into factions is the question of equal treatment before the law. Millions of Americans believe that, by and large, justice in America is fair, while other millions believe it is not. At least one side must be wrong; but the matter will never be settled by appeal to the content of daily newspapers, or TV, for that matter.

One last example of the lack of in-depth reporting. The *Boston Herald Traveler* (November 14, 1970) contained a story on charges by the Massachusetts Bar Association that Massachusetts' no-fault auto insurance law would result in "legal chaos" if allowed to go into effect. The story cited a paper in the Massachusetts Law Quarterly which stated that the law is "both inconsistent and incomprehensible." But the newspaper article failed to quote a single relevant reason *why* legal chaos would result, or in what way the law is inconsistent and incomprehensible. Instead, it quoted the claim of the president of the Massachusetts Bar Association that legal chaos would result if the law went into effect: It cited an authority's opinion on a controversial matter, but failed to provide any of his reasons. It thus invited the reader to commit the fallacy of *appeal to authority*.

To make matters worse, the newspaper article failed to point out that lawyers have a special interest in fighting this law, namely to maintain one of their most lucrative sources of income: auto accident litigation. Instead, it quoted the charge of M.B.A. President Donahue that the law would "result in both increasing claims and increasing rates," again without furnishing any evidence pro or con. Nowhere in the article is there any mention of the frequently cited statistic that lawyers get as large a slice of auto insurance premiums as do those suffering losses in accidents, a slice of the pie that no-fault insurance laws greatly reduce. Yet, how can anyone get any benefit from a story on the Massachusetts "no fault" insurance law without at least some of these facts?

Even when newspapers attempt to give greater depth to the news, we still generally are not told all in one place what we need to know. One story

on law and order, entitled "The Cops—Victims of Ghetto Ambush," [5]
contained a long tally of police deaths attributed to "black and white revolutionaries," and provided evidence that underground newspapers en-
courage such violent acts.

But the story was hopelessly inadequate to help us understand anything.
In the first place, it was a completely one-sided story. It gave interesting
and important statistics on police deaths (16 in the first 8 months of 1970
against 4.3 per year in the sixties), but not the equally important statistics
on "black and white revolutionaries" killed by police. It described one
cause—left-wing encouragement—for police killings, but not what moti-
vates the radical left to be against police (e.g., alleged police brutality and
prejudice).

In other words, the story divorced police killings from their settings,
leaving the reader with no idea *why* anyone would want to risk his life to
kill policemen. Could the average newspaper reader tell us, for instance,
why so many more policemen are killed in the U.S. than in England?

An interesting postscript is that the newspaper which published this one-
sided account had previously published several news stories on police
brutality—for instance, at the Chicago Democratic Convention in 1968,
as well as the later Chicago Black Panther shootings. But all this relevant
information on the subject was never put together in one place.

Occasionally, newspapers do intersperse a current news story with pertinent background information. An example is the *New Britain Herald*
(October 27, 1970) AP story about a Boeing 747 jumbo jet, one of whose
engines burst into flames in flight. This story also contained information
about the running battle between the Federal Aviation Administration and
the National Transportation Board over the latter's claim that 747 engines
dangerously overheat, thus giving the reader some inkling of the import
of the event reported on. There is no *good* reason why newspapers could
not always provide such background information.

*Good citizenship and social convention are believed to require political
self-censorship.* A *Washington Post* reporter[6] learned that two Army intelligence officers claimed the C.I.A. and Army Intelligence were training
men in torture and assassination techniques to be used against National
Liberation Front members in Vietnam. But his story never appeared in
the *Washington Post,* an apparent victim of self-censorship by that newspaper.

---

[5] *The Hartford Times,* September 6, 1970, by Richard Lemon, Newsweek Service.
[6] George Wilson. See the *Village Voice* article "The Fourth Estate as the Fourth
Branch," January 1, 1970.

Though unusual, self-censorship is not rare. The nation's major newspapers, which have large investigative staffs, tend to engage in self-censorship more often than other newspapers, no doubt because they have access to more sensitive information. Perhaps the most famous example of this kind is the *New York Times'* decision to go easy on the Bay of Pigs story during the Kennedy administration.[7]

Another revealing example is the 1970 U.S. incursion into Cambodia. Associated Press reporters[8] with U.S. troops on this invasion wrote that U.S. troops engaged in much looting during the venture. But newspapers on the AP wire never received this portion of the report from Cambodia, which apparently was edited out partly because the AP wanted their men during that troubled period to report news that is "down the middle and subdues emotion," and because "in present context this [the report of looting] can be inflammatory."

Self-censorship due to respect for social conventions usually is relatively unimportant in each particular case, but in the aggregate may be quite important. Unfortunately, it is hard to know when such censorship is being practiced, and when not. All that can be pointed to in most cases is the lack of certain kinds of news.

One unfortunate aspect of this kind of self-censorship is that there seem to be no strict ground rules for what should be printed and what should not be. The result is, for example, that newspapers all over the country printed and even headlined a story about the alleged homosexuality of an aide to President Johnson, but rarely report on the alcoholism of local and state officials, or of senators and congressmen. Yet, homosexuality does not render one less able to perform public duties, while alcoholism does.[9]

Up to this point in our survey, we've been concerned with failures of news reporting resulting primarily from poor theory *about* news reporting. Let's now turn to an allied topic.

---

[7] President Kennedy is alleged later to have had the "chutzpah" to take the *Times* to task for this censorship on grounds that publication of the story by the *Times* might have resulted in calling off that ill-fated venture! The June 1971 publication by the *New York Times* of excerpts from a classified Pentagon report, which describes behind-the-scenes planning for the Vietnam War, was an exception to the usual self-censorship of newspapers; but we can hope that it represents a permanent policy change.

[8] According to a story in the September 1970 issue of the *AP Review*.

[9] Readers inclined to believe that the lack of reporting on this topic is due to a lack of things to report should recall that most Americans were unaware of the late Senator Joseph R. McCarthy's problems with the bottle until in defeat he became fair game for everyone. Even then, many newspapers never mentioned McCarthy's drinking problem.

2. Poor customs and practices

Customs and practices do not develop in a vacuum. They are the result of all kinds of pressures and forces, even though those forces do not dictate practice in any absolute fashion. The chief force at work in the development of news gathering practices is the ease with which certain kinds of news can be obtained. The result is what may well be the greatest bar of all to adequate news reporting.

Most news is given to reporters, not discovered by them. Check the front page of almost any newspaper and you will find as often as not that the vast majority of items on that page were acquired by that newspaper (or by the wire services—AP and UPI) from someone-or-other's press release, press conference, or speech. Thus, most news stories report what someone, usually someone powerful, has said about the news, rather than what reporters have discovered for themselves.

Two recent *N.Y. Times* front pages chosen at random (September 3, 1970, and November 1, 1970) contained altogether nineteen front-page stories. Of these, four were reports of speeches or announcements by local government officials (e.g., Mayor Lindsay unveiling plans to employ unused Hudson River piers as recreation centers), three were reports of speeches or announcements by federal government officials (e.g., a Vice President Agnew speech before the American Legion at Portland, Oregon), one concerned a speech by a foreign government official (President Thieu of South Vietnam), three were reports of federal-government agency announcements, with a mixture of statements by particular agency officials or "informed sources" (e.g., a N.A.S.A. announcement of space cutbacks due to lack of funds), and one was a report on an announcement of a panel of experts (on college entrance exams).

That accounts for thirteen of the nineteen stories. Only the other six represent any real effort at legwork by newspaper reporters. Of these, three were on the November 3 elections (e.g., a story that Arthur Goldberg's family would be joining him in his campaign for a senate seat), and three represented an attempt to get the "news behind the news" (e.g., a story on Nixon's moves to reorganize the vast federal science complex).

Remember that this is the box score for two front pages from one of the best newspapers in the country. The average newspaper front page would be likely to have a few more straight news stories (of murders, catastrophes, battles, etc.) taken from police and other government handouts, and rather less on the news behind the news.

There is a natural human tendency to allow theory to be influenced by practice, and (as stated before) to allow practice to be influenced by the path of least resistance. The unfortunate result is that theory tends to legitimatize whatever is easier, thus reinforcing the already-strong tendency most of us have to choose the easier way.

All of this is beautifully illustrated by the newspaper business. Newspaper practice, resulting from the ease with which it can be done, dictates reporting on the press handout of whoever speaks from power or authority. Take the story, described above, about Massachusetts' no-fault auto insurance law: The "authority" was an interested party, the president of the Massachusetts Bar Association, who gave his opinions on the law but not (presumably) his reasons for holding them—that is, not his defense of those opinions. So that's what the *Boston Herald Traveler* printed as news.

One would have supposed that the real news was not these undefended opinions printed as news, but the truth of the matter, that is, what the no-fault auto insurance law said, as well as a description of its likely operation (or at least a comparison of reasonable arguments pro and con). But no, at this point the theory of objective reporting enters the picture. While objectivity would permit the printing of the law itself, or portions thereof, it would not permit any statements about how the law would work in practice. For, even if such statements later turned out to be correct, still, at the time they were only *opinion,* and hence not objective. Similarly, it would be improper to bring together in one place all the pertinent arguments for and against the law, perhaps because any such effort requires that value judgments be made in assembling the relevant information.[10] But it is an objective fact that the president of the Massachusetts Bar Association did make a speech; hence reports of *his* opinions stay within the bounds of objectivity.

The result is that newspapers act as mere loudspeakers for the opinions and pronouncements of the powerful or "authoritative" in our society, and much of what we read has little to do with the truth. The news is *used* for all sorts of private gain. A president of the United States who wonders what will be the response to a particular proposed action of his need only try it out in the press and assess the results. Whether he will choose to use the "informed White House source" routine, have an underling make the proposal, or risk coming out with it himself depends on particular circumstances. But in any case, he is assured that newspapers all over the country will play up his trial balloon as news, even though nothing much of anything has happened.

Similarly, a labor leader, big business executive, or the president of the Massachusetts Bar Association can sound off with his own opinions, how-

---

[10] On this last point there seems to be some difference of opinion, leading to the hope that some day it may be common practice for newspapers to *assemble* a news story rather than act merely as funnels through which it passes.

ever self-serving, confident that they will be reported as news, however much they may be designed to fog an issue. These men also can be confident that no matter how far from the truth their statements may be, they need not worry that this will be pointed out to readers. For that would constitute opinion, not objective news, no matter how correct, whereas the *opinions* of the powerful are news, no matter how foolish or false they may be.

As a consequence, *newspapers tend to report primarily the "establishment" viewpoint.* Radicals of both the right and left have long complained about the lack of newspaper coverage of their views, and in particular of the slanting of news towards establishment middle ground. But it would be wrong to assign this bias solely to malice or prejudice on the part of news editors. Editors no doubt do exhibit a certain amount of prejudice against far-out opinions; people holding extreme views, no matter how right they may ultimately turn out to be, seldom become editors. But that doesn't begin to account for the facts. We also need to consider the *method* newspapers employ in gathering the news. For it is those with power or authority in the nation who comprise the establishment (if that concept is to have any meaning at all), and it is exactly these people whose opinions automatically are news according to the theory and practice of news reporting. If (per impossible) the President of the United States (or of G.M.) were to propound the views of Norman Thomas, then the socialist position would be heard. And if the vice president of G.M. or the president of Stanford University were to start sounding like members of the John Birch Society or the new libertarian conservative group (the "new right"), then these right-wing positions would become news.

Several other factors lead to the exclusion of opinions which stray too far from the center, including the desire not to annoy readers.[11] A person tends to tone down his opinions to match those of the group he finds himself in, because of the natural human tendency to court the approval of others. Similarly, newspapers court readers by trying to offend them as little as possible. As a result they tend to print the safe pabulum of establishment opinions and viewpoints.[12]

"In-depth" reporting on the drug scene in America furnishes a good example of the desire of the mass media to avoid offending their readers

---

[11] Another factor is the desire not to annoy large advertisers. Recall that the exposé of Bell Telephone discussed in Chapter Four ran in *Ramparts,* a non-mass-media magazine, not in *Time, Look,* or *Life.*

[12] Textbook writers tend to react just like newspaper writers on this score, with similar results, as will be seen in Chapter Eight.

by voicing nonestablishment opinions. By the late sixties, a whole subculture of drugs had arisen in the United States. While there was disagree-
ment on the relative merits or dangers of LSD, speed, etc., there was overwhelming conviction in this subculture in favor of marijuana. Yet almost
no mass media stories on drugs played it that way.

Typical was the AP story titled "Ex-Pot User Anti-Drug Crusade,"
(carried in the *Topeka Capital-Journal,* July 5, 1970), in which newspaper
objectivity was preserved by putting anti-marijuana opinions into the mouth
of a reformed seventeen-year-old pot smoker. But who recalls an article
built upon the opinions of even one of the hundreds of thousands of satisfied grass fans?

This push to the middle in order not to offend readers is evident in every
aspect of the typical newspaper. Advice columns, such as those of Ann
Landers and Abigail Van Buren, inevitably reflect the safe middle position.
A typical column of this kind will deal with a young man of 17 in love with
a divorced woman of 35 (or perhaps a married woman of 25) who is advised to try someone his own age (or someone who is single).

Or a young reader will write in that according to his experience, marijuana, unlike heroin, LSD, etc., is neither harmful nor habit-forming, and
on the whole is great fun. The inevitable "Dear Abby" reply will be that it
is inadvisable for anyone to try marijuana. Over the years there have been
thousands of questions answered on these topics, always as much as possible within the established limits of opinion current at the time. Imagine,
if you can, Ann Landers advising a 17 year-old teenager that love con-
quers all, and wishing him good luck with the 35 year-old divorcee next
door; or agreeing with her young reader hipped on grass that marijuana
isn't habit-forming or dangerous, is great fun, doesn't result in hangovers
(unlike alcohol), and consequently is something everyone ought to try at
least once in a lifetime.[13]

Even advertisements are forced to fit the mold. Few if any newspapers
would run an ad for a female willing to share bed and board with a male
in the latter's summer cottage (although circumlocution sometimes is permitted to accomplish the same result).

---

[13] The only advice column of any kind this writer has ever seen that tweaks the
establishment's nose is that of Dr. William Brady, M.D. In what other advice column
could we read, for instance, that "Some people are woefully ignorant and some
doctors take advantage of this ignorance" (*Hartford Courant,* January 9, 1971), or
"Three kinds or classes of physicians worry patients about cholesterol in the diet;
. . . those who are shrewdly aware how much such dietary advice impresses cus-
tomers . . . [those] who go along with the fad because they can't stand seeing their
patients running from one specialist to another . . . [and those] who think there
may be something in the theory . . ." (*Hartford Courant,* January 11, 1971)?

Earlier, we pointed out that newspapers tend to separate in-depth articles from news reports, most of which are nothing but handouts. An unfortunate consequence of this practice is that newspapers typically do not check up on the handouts they print: Not only do newspapers separate in-depth reporting from news reporting, but they also generally neglect to do in-depth investigation on these news stories even to verify alleged facts.

In 1970, the House Internal Security Committee compiled a list of 65 college-campus speakers and their alleged organizational memberships, citing the speakers as among "the radical rhetoricians of the new left promoting violence and encouraging the destruction of our system of government." On October 13, 1970, the committee was put under a temporary court order restraining distribution of the list. On October 15, the *Washington Post* published a story about the list, citing three persons on it, without revealing their alleged affiliations. But that same day, the *New York Times* published the entire list including the alleged political affiliations. In particular, its account contained the statement: "Among those not generally considered extremists were . . . ," followed by five names.

Among the names on the entire list but absent from the *Times* list of five nonextremists was that of Nat Hentoff. Hentoff then wrote two articles for the non-mass-media *Village Voice* (October 22 and 29, 1970) which presented the facts as he saw them, and drew unflattering conclusions about the *Times*. These articles represented exactly the sort of in-depth reporting the mass media generally avoid as being not "objective."

According to Hentoff, no one on the *Times* queried him or anyone else listed to determine whether the House committee allegations about them were true. Nor did *Times'* reporters do their own investigating of other sources on the matter. Mr. Hentoff claimed he was not a member of any of the three organizations the House Committee listed him as belonging to. The *Times* could have checked up on that simply by asking him. But it didn't, with great harm to him as well as to others on the list.

So far, we've dealt with two major reasons why newspapers are a poor source of real news: incorrect theories of news reporting and poor practices of news coverage. Let's now turn to a third reason.

3. Devices which distort the news

The mass media use devices which (deliberately or accidentally) distort the news. Among the most important is *the use of misleading or unfair headlines*. It is well known that many more people read the headline on a story than the story itself. So even if the story is accurate, a misleading headline results in a distorted picture of the news for many readers.

Here are some typical examples:

Hartford Courant (September 17, 1970, p. 29):

SECRET REPORT SAYS SUPERSONIC TRANSPORT MAY BE HARMFUL

Washington (AP)—The Dept. of Transportation concedes in a confidential report to the White House that the much disputed supersonic transport may have some harmful effects on the environment. **But it says they would be minor.**

Hartford Times (September 18, 1970), headline, p. 1:

$500 MILLION U.S. AID TO ISRAEL

But below, in the AP story, we learned that:

President Nixon **reportedly** *was preparing today to promise Israel Premier Golda Meir . . . officials say* **no final decision on exactly what the package will contain has been made.**

Hartford Times (September 13, 1970), headline on story, p. 1B:

ADDITIVES ALMOST ALL GONE NOW

Headline on continuation of same story, p. 2B:

CYCLAMATE FOOD STILL ON SHELVES

New Britain [Conn.] *Herald* (January 7, 1971):

FEW TROOPS TO STAY IN VIET AFTER MAY 1

Only a few thousand American combat troops will remain in Vietnam past May 1, 1971. . . . [Further down in the story, we learn that Air force pilots, artillery men, etc., were not considered combat men with respect to this announcement.]

Kansas City Star (June 28, 1970):

DRUG SMUGGLER "EDUCATED" BY REDS

The story below told of a 22-year-old student caught smuggling dope into Russia who was "educated" by his two years in Russian jails. But the quick reader may well have gotten the false impression that the Soviets had educated the young man in drug smuggling.

Lawrence [Kansas] *Daily Journal World*:

MAGAZINE STORY ON KING REFUTED

The story below indicated that *Time* magazine's account was *challenged* by Martin Luther King's widow and other King associates, not refuted.

Lawrence [Kansas] *Outlook* (October 10, 1968):

KU BUSYBODIES JOIN IN BLACK-LHS HASSLE

In the story below, the University of Kansas "busybodies" who joined in on the black students vs. Lawrence High School hassle turned out to be primarily Floyd Horowitz, English Professor and President of the local American Civil Liberties Union (ACLU).

Hartford Times (September 6, 1970):

MOST REAL ESTATE SALES BASED
ON NEWSPAPER ADS

The story below started out:

> *When it comes to buying a house, the average homeowner seems to get most of his help from newspapers* **and real estate agents**.

In addition to deceptive headlines, readers have to put up with the fact that *often the story below the headline also is slanted one way or another*. Misleading headlines frequently are matched with misleading or unnecessarily biased stories, in spite of the official theory of objective reporting:

New Britain [Conn.] *Herald* (November 5, 1970):

BRUCE REBUKES THUY FOR **INSULTING** CHARGE NIXON LIED TO PEOPLE

The story below was in the same vein, ignoring the factual issue (whether Nixon did in fact lie to the people on the issue in question).

New Britain Herald (September 19, 1970):

Demands Missile Removal:

MRS. MEIR JOLTS HOPES BY BARRING PEACE TALKS

Hartford Courant (same day):

(Under a picture of a smiling Mrs. Meir conferring with President Nixon):

MRS. MEIR, ROGERS SEE TALKS DELAYED

The stories both were built on AP releases on the same events and overlapped a great deal. But they selected and emphasized material so as to support their respective headlines.

New Britain Herald (October 27, 1970):

NIXON SIGNS DRUG BILL TO SAVE YOUNG LIVES

The story was built on statements made by President Nixon as he signed the bill into law. Ignored were the many who objected that the bill wouldn't save any lives or substantially reduce the use of drugs, but *would* violate civil rights. This example also illustrates the intertwining of the various factors already mentioned that lead to poor reporting—in particular, how the primary method of obtaining news (the official handout) leads to distortion in favor of the establishment viewpoint.

In playing a story one way or another, the headline obviously is most important (next to its location), since it is read by many who never read further. But in addition, the first few paragraphs are more important than what follows, for the same reason: Readership drops off after that point. A TV debate between three candidates for the U.S. Senate from Connecticut was played quite differently by means of headline and lead-paragraph distortion. Here is the story in the *Hartford Courant* (October 28, 1970):

DODD SAYS FEAR GRIPS U.S., CENSURE "A GRAVE INJUSTICE"

New Haven—U.S. Senator Thomas J. Dodd Tuesday admitted he is running on a platform of fear.

"Yes, I am, I'm afraid. And the vast majority of our people are afraid. . . . There never has been such violence in this country," he declared during his only debate with his two opponents during the current senatorial campaign.

Not a word in the headline or first two paragraphs (nor in the third) about the other two candidates, one of whom was an easy victor in the election itself.

Now see how the same debate was handled by the *New York Times* (Oct. 28, 1970):

WEICKER ASSAILS TWO RIVALS IN CONNECTICUT SENATE-RACE DEBATE

New Haven, Oct. 27, 1970—In the only scheduled debate for all three candidates, . . . the Republican lashed out today at both his opponents.

The Republican, Representative Lowell P. Weicker, Jr., who describes himself as a moderate, charged that Senator Thomas J. Dodd's censure by his colleagues three years ago for misuse of campaign funds had damaged his effectiveness, and he accused the Rev. Joseph D. Duffey of contributing to the division in American society.

It was not until the sixth paragraph that the *Times* reported a single word about the performance of Senator Dodd in the debate; Mr. Duffey had to wait until the ninth paragraph. (Curiously, a *Times* editorial then endorsed Duffey, while declaring that Weicker was also a good man.)

But the *New Britain Herald* story distorted the TV debate even more. In the debate itself, Senator Dodd attempted several times to project himself as the main issue of the campaign, because the other two candidates had battled primarily against each other, saying little of Dodd's censure by the U.S. Senate. The TV debate definitely did not center around the Dodd censure issue.

Yet the *New Britain Herald* headlined their story:

DODD'S CENSURE A MAJOR ISSUE IN DEBATE OF SENATE CANDIDATES

And they centered their story on the censure issue. Not until the tenth paragraph was any other issue mentioned. Weicker was not quoted on any other topic until the sixteenth paragraph. (Curiously, a *New Britain Herald* editorial endorsed Weicker on the same day the TV debate story appeared.)

Many newspapers subscribe to both major wire services, AP and UPI. So they sometimes have a choice of different basic story structure and slant. But usually AP and UPI stories are quite similar. In addition, a given wire service may issue more than one story on the same event. Usually, these multiple stories will be quite similar. But on certain kinds of controversial issues, one and the same wire service will provide its subscribers with material suitable for slanting in several directions.

The 1970 right-wing July 4 celebration in Washington, D.C., was such an event. The *Topeka Daily Capital* (July 3, 1970), began its story on the upcoming event:

EVANGELIST URGES HONORING AMERICA

Washington (AP)—The Rev. Billy Graham said Thursday the purpose of Honor America Day July 4th is to say "there are some good things about America."

Its story continued in the same vein.

On the other hand, the *Lawrence* [Kansas] *Daily Journal World* tried to be objective by running two separate stories based on AP releases. The first was headlined:

BIG JULY 4 EVENTS SLATED

The story described the event in glowing patriotic terms. But the second account, placed right below the first, was headlined:

EVENT LIKENED TO NAZISM

And the AP account described the event as "the kind of thing that took place in Hitler's Germany." Same event, same wire service, radically different account. In other words, *within establishment limits,* a newspaper can portray an event just about any way it wants to. So much for the myth of objectivity.

So far, we've illustrated how the news is slanted for political purposes or out of ignorance. (In a given case, it's hard to know which, because it's hard to know what is on a reporter's or editor's mind.) But news is slanted for other reasons. One such reason is *circulation.*

The *Los Angeles Times*[14] relegated a particularly shocking murder to the bottom of page one in its home-delivered morning edition, with a rather small-type headline. But its morning street edition gave the story its main headline, in extremely large type:

ZODIAC KILLS NO. 5

While not wishing to offend any of its regular readers, the L.A. *Times* evidently wanted the added sales of a sensational street edition.

Newspapers have other devices with which to distort the news. For instance, they not only can play an account in favor of one side or another, but they also can play it *up* or *down.* Where objectivity is supposed to reign, who is to say how important an issue really is? The play of the Zodiac killer story by the L.A. *Times* is an example. But it isn't only with respect to murders, catastrophes and the like that this occurs. For years, reporters sent daily accounts of small military engagements in Vietnam. One was not much different in importance from many others. Yet some of these accounts made page-one headlines in certain newspapers, while others were relegated to the back pages.

News is played up for many reasons. Perhaps the most common reason is that nothing out of the ordinary happened on a particular day. Manchester Boddy, of the old *Los Angeles Daily News,* once remarked that one of his ambitions was to print a headline stating something like "No Important News Today." But he didn't, and neither has anyone else. Instead, when nothing flashy is available, newspapers raise the ordinary to headline status and make it appear more important than it really is.

[14] October 16, 1969. This example and others are mentioned in an excellent article by John Corry on the *Los Angeles Times* in the December 1969 issue of *Harper's Magazine.*

Newspapers also employ value-tinged words quite frequently in reporting the news—not just in editorials.[15] Recall, for instance, the *New Britain Herald* headline: "Mrs. Meir **jolts hopes** by barring peace talks." Or their headline: "Bruce rebukes Thuy for **insulting** charge Nixon lied to people." But these are all gross cases. The really subtle ones are much more damaging, precisely because they pass by almost unnoticed. How many of us noticed, for instance, when reports from Vietnam referred to our victories as "battles" while referring to those of the communists as "massacres"? [16]

John P. Roche pointed out an interesting example of this kind in one of his political columns (August 1970). He noticed that volunteers for *our* army are referred to quite correctly as "volunteers," while volunteers for other armies often are referred to as "mercenaries." He voiced his objection to statements such as "The Khmer Krom, a group of American trained **mercenaries**, are providing cadres for the Royal Cambodian Army." And he asked us to "just suppose for a minute that a newspaperman back in World War II had sent a dispatch beginning 'American mercenaries today seized the airfield at Guadalcanal.'" Yet, the U.S. marines in question were volunteers, just as were the Khmer Krom. If the latter are mercenaries, why not the former?

The point, of course, is that the term "mercenary" has negative connotations, while "volunteer" sounds rather inspiring. So a newspaper can use the term "mercenary" in a news story, thus injecting its own opinion, while still appearing to be objective. (Notice that there then is no need to *justify* an opinion so masked, since officially no opinion has been stated.)

Even when they try hard to be objective and unbiased, newspapers may still distort the news (however slightly) by means of value-tinged words. The reason for this is that practically every word in a natural language such as English is value-tinged.

The *National Review* (August 11, 1970)[17] pointed out that:

> The New York Times (*e.g., July 24*) *in reporting the trial in New Haven for the murder of Alex Rackley, refers throughout to Warren*

---

[15] Recall the *New York Daily News* editorial, used as an exercise in Chapter Five, which contained such emotive expressions as "skedaddle scheme," "sucker," and "pell-mell pullout."

[16] The one big exception to this was My Lai, which finally had to be called a massacre when the true nature of that event became clear.

[17] © 1970, *National Review*. Reprinted by permission.

*Kimbro, the government witness, as "Kimbro," to George Sams, as "Sams"—and to Bobby Seale, head of the Black Panther Party and a co-defendant, as "**Mr**. Seale."*

Newspapers also manage the news through their power to print or fail to print letters to the editor.

Here is a letter to the editor of the *New York Times* protesting their publication of a House Internal Security Committee's list (referred to on p. 157), which the *Times* chose not to print (but which the *Village Voice* did print—on November 19, 1970):[18]

On October 14 the House Internal Security Committee branded 65 individuals as "radical" speakers at college campuses. On October 15, the Times *compounded this blatant infringement of constitutional rights by publishing the list in full—the names and alleged affiliations of the 65.*

As Nat Hentoff, one of the victims, reported in the Village Voice *(October 22), the* Times *did not first check the veracity of the accusations with the accused. (Mr. Hentoff notes he was falsely charged as being affiliated with three organizations.)*

Even more significant than these lapses in fair reporting is the fact that the Times *published the "blacklist." As the* Times *emphasized in its editorial of October 24, the Committee's promulgation of the list violated the First Amendment freedoms of speech and press. The purpose and effect of the list are to intimidate universities into closing their doors to those on the list; to deny the accused the right to speak at educational institutions; and to deny students and faculties the right to hear them.*

The blacklist is also a warning to others not to utter viewpoints inimical to the Committee's political philosophy at pain of being listed in the future. Its effect, as always, is to suppress freedom of expression and also, not insignificantly, to punish those listed, without trial or hearing. The Times *owes the First Amendment more than the lip service paid in editorials. It also owes the affirmative loyalty not to serve as an instrument to suppress the rights of free speech and press. By broadcasting the Committee's blacklist, the* Times *has struck a heavy blow against those rights, and the 65 individuals who were pilloried by the Committee. The* Times *was not faced with the choice of burying the story or printing the names. It could have reported the*

---

[18] Reprinted by permission of Jerome Weidman, and by permission of the *Village Voice*. Copyrighted by the Village Voice, Inc., 1970.

Committee's action in violation of the District Court's temporary in-
junction against the publication without printing the blacklist itself.
                                              Jerome Weidman
                                              President
                                              Authors League of America

Here is a letter (whose authorship you ought to be able to guess) critical
of Walter Cronkite, "objective" reporting, and (indirectly) of *Look* magazine, which *Look* chose not to print:

Oriana Fallaci ended her conversation with Walter Cronkite (What
Does Walter Cronkite Really Think," LOOK, November 17) with the
remark that Cronkite "really is a person you can respect." If there is
anyone on TV this very occasional TV viewer could respect, it is
Walter Cronkite.

But I wonder if the discussion did not reveal a hidden difficulty in
his views on the role of a TV reporter. Perhaps his idea that the prod-
uct—news—he reports on is objective *is a myth:*

1.   The number of "facts" to report on each day is indefinitely
large. Yet he can report only a very few. Could it be that the job of
editing requires Mr. Cronkite to employ *value judgments? Doesn't he*
have to decide that one fact is more important *than another? And*
shouldn't it often be more important because of moral *considerations?*
(Surely, the starvation of thousands of children in the U.S. each year
is an important fact to report precisely because it is so immoral to
permit such a thing.)

2.   A careful TV viewer will notice that much of the news consists
in what someone says about *the world: presidential speeches on law*
and order, blasts by the Soviet government, Senator Phogbound, etc.
TV reports an expert's attack on the food industry. But wasn't it an
objective fact that breakfast cereals were nutritionally poor before the
expert's pronouncement? Weren't children in the U.S. starving to
death before an expert (and senators) made it known?

3.   TV news reporters seem to feel that unusual evils—such as
prison riots—are news, but not the day to day horror we call our
prison system. At least we rarely hear of this horror except when
prisoners riot. But isn't the everyday brutal treatment of prisoners
just as objective and factual as a prison riot?

I suggest Mr. Cronkite consider the possibility that objectivity can
be used all too easily as a mask behind which lurks the fact *that in*
editing the news value judgments must be made, and the possibility

that editing the way he and his fellow TV newsmen do plays into the hands of those who would hide the great gap in America between noble ideals and much less than noble actual practice.

Newspaper editors also keep things under their own control by judicious employment of replies to critical letters. Of course, the practice of having running battles between staff writers and those writing letters to the editor is a good one, on the whole. But the cards are stacked against the man in the street who writes in to a newspaper or magazine, because the publication or its writers always have the right of last reply.

Similarly, it is common for newspapers and magazines to edit letters to the editor, even though this may result in distortion. The letter by C. W. Griffin to the editor of the *New York Times Magazine* mentioned in the discussion of *questionable analogies* in Chapter Three is a typical (although fairly innocuous) example. The *Times* printed the first part of Mr. Griffin's letter, which drew an analogy between belief in *laissez faire* economics and literal belief in the Garden of Eden. But it omitted the second portion, which explained *why* the analogy was a good one. It thus robbed the letter of its true import. Here is the letter with the omitted portions included:[19]

> *Milton Friedman's defense of pure Adam Smith is like Billy Graham's defense of the literal truth of Genesis. To believe that a* laissez-faire *economic theory offers any hope of promoting a viable society is as naive as the belief that Adam and Eve were the first man and woman.*

The *Times* printed the above portion of the letter, omitting the meat:

> *Consider the issue of air and water pollution, which is overwhelmingly an industry-created problem. Despite the lying propaganda of their public relations campaigns, American industry has perennially fought and delayed pollution control by all levels of government— federal, state, and local. Industry's tactics have included economic pressures—threats to move where local authorities were more "understanding"—and massive political lobbying. This lobbying is actually subsidized by U.S. taxpayers; years ago the lobbyists pressed Congress into treating lobbying expenses as tax-deductible business ex-*

[19] Printed here with the permission of the author and (the first part) the *New York Times.*

*penses. When Mr. Friedman implies that use of "political mechanisms
. . . to determine the allocation of resources" is a peculiarly socialistic
practice, one wonders who is kidding whom. But perhaps he has never
heard of the highway lobby or the military-industrial complex.*

There are any number of possible reasons why the *Times* deleted the
second, and more interesting, half of Mr. Griffin's letter. Space may have
run short; or perhaps the *Times* didn't want Mr. Friedman's article to be
subjected to criticisms with such broad import to the whole of our capitalis-
tic system. The reason is problematic; that distortion resulted is not. (Incidentally, the *Times* neglected to provide those essential three little dots
indicating that they had not printed the entire letter.)

Among devices which distort the news there is, finally, the use of "informed sources" in news articles, editorials, and political columns. The
Hartford Courant (November 9, 1970), and many other newspapers picked
up a story from *Time* magazine in which President Nixon was quoted as
informing his cabinet and top advisors that Republican chances in the 1972
elections would be good; the Vietnam war would be over, crime would be
on the downturn, and the economy would be strong. But *Time* stated that
no source could be given for these statements.

This is a typical use of the informed source. There is no way to know the
motives of the person who "leaked" this information to *Time* magazine.
But such leaks frequently are employed by political officials for all sorts of
devious purposes other than informing the press of the truth. Imagine that
you were president of the United States and wanted to assure loyal Republicans around the country that all would be well in 1972 without at the same
time going out on a limb. You could easily have arranged to have a report
to this effect leaked to the press through an anonymous informed source
(i.e., someone who allegedly was there). If your predictions turned out to
be true, you could then take credit for them. If they turned out to be false,
you could always deny them, something it would be impossible to do if you
had stated them in public.

The informed source can be used for many other purposes. President
Johnson is said (by informed sources) to have used informed source leaks
quite frequently as trial balloons. They also (according to insiders) are used
to inform foreign powers about our government's position on an issue when,
for one reason or another, the president can't come right out with it. *None*
of these uses has anything to do with the truth, except accidentally. Yet,

newspapers eagerly print informed-source leaks, perhaps because they sound important and make newspapers appear to have a great deal more inside information than in fact is the case.

We have already mentioned the use of second-hand information in page-one news stories (when discussing two *New York Times* front pages). The lead story on one of these front pages used the phrases "according to officials here," "high sources in the Administration," and "data made available here by authoritative sources," which is typical of most news reports on foreign affairs. So the reader had no way of knowing whether the story itself was important, or just a plant intended to satisfy someone's private purpose.

Political columnists also use informed sources as their stock in trade. Here is an example from a column by Marquis Childs (August 1970):

> *One factor* **Western Diplomats** *count solidly on the side of success. That is the conviction that Egypt's President Gamal Nasser wants peace. A strong motivation,* **according to informed sources**, *is Nasser's desire to get rid of the 10,000 or more Soviet technicians and pilots. . . .*
>
> *The same* **knowledgeable sources** *believe. . . .*

But Evans and Novak seem to be the current informed-source champs; their column specializes in inside information. Here are several examples culled from a few November 1970 issues of the *Lawrence Daily Journal World:*

> *(November 5, 1970) Most important,* **as seen by objective Republican politicians**, *the President's inner circle has become almost pathological in its protection of Mr. Nixon. . . .*

> *(November 7, 1970) With a surprising unanimity that crosses ideological and geographic lines,* **Republican leaders** *agree that: Mr. Nixon's ill advised campaign has damaged his credibility. . . .*

> *(November 12, 1970) Shortly after emerging from a rosy-hued White House post-mortem on the election, a* **top Republican strategist** *said out loud. . . .*

> *(November 13, 1970) Although* [Senator] *Byrd is a longshot* [for Sen. Kennedy's Majority Whip post], **Kennedy's most knowledgeable supporters** *in the Senate believe. . . .*

So frequent is their use of inside information from unnamed sources that Evans and Novak often omit even the mention of "top Republican strategists" or "Kennedy's most knowledgeable supporters." Here is a typical example (*Lawrence* [Kansas] *Daily Journal World,* November 2, 1970) in which the source (assuming it was not a case of mental telepathy) is never mentioned:

> . . . *President Nixon is now plotting a precisely opposite diplomatic course designed to force Israeli withdrawal from most of the Israeli occupied land.*

4. False aura of authority

Way back in the 1920s and 1930s *Time* magazine developed a "you are *there*" style of news reporting which became an essential part of the "*Time*-style" which all newsmagazines have copied at one time or another. *Time*-style is currently less in evidence than formerly, even in *Time* itself. But it hasn't entirely disappeared, nor is it likely to, because, for one thing, it lends an *aura of authority* to news reports.

A *Newsweek* report (November 2, 1970) on the 1970 elections is typical. The story was simply that Republican Mayor Lindsay of New York had announced he would support the Democratic gubernatorial candidate Arthur Goldberg. But Newsweek's article starts it with inside information, a call from Lindsay to Goldberg:

> *Hello, Arthur?*
> *With a single late-night phone call last week, New York's liberal Mayor John V. Lindsay paid off an old political debt. . . .*
> *The call, at 1 a.m., roused Democratic gubernatorial candidate Arthur Goldberg . . .*

Time, incidentally, reported Lindsay's endorsement straight, omitting the 1 a.m. phone call.

Not that *Time* has given up completely on *Time*style, although sleek black Rolls Royces and Cadillacs don't drive up to No. 10 Downing Street or the White House steps as frequently as they used to. In their November

2, 1970 issue, *Time* began its article on the My Lai trials with a typical insider's irrelevant detail:

> *A sudden susurrus of shock ran through the Fort Hood, Texas, military courtroom. Defense Attorney Ossie Brown reacted as if someone had pinched his neck. . . .*

In the same issue, *Time* ran a story whose main point was to emphasize how much of our air effort in Vietnam had been turned over to the South Vietnamese. *Time* reported that:

> *"The target today is a suspected enemy location near the gully behind that clump of trees," says the American Forward Air Controller (FAC) from a tiny spotter plane just above the treetops some 30 miles northwest of Saigon. . . .*

Obviously, if *Time* reporters are so knowledgeable that they can quote word for word the remark of a FAC man in action, they surely must have been correct about the main point of their article (which happened to be quite controversial: Many claimed at the time that Vietnamization of our air effort was nothing but a token gesture).

But *Newsweek* is up to *Time* in *Time*style. The same issue of *Newsweek* mentioned above contained a long article on Gov. Ronald Reagan which began:

> *The head at a boyish tilt, the blue eyes batting modestly, the huckleberry grin crinkling the age-resistant fan-mag face. Gosh—Ronald Reagan. He slides out of the back of a gray Lincoln hard-top and glides into the crowd. . . .*

In addition to using their insider's "you are there" style, newsmagazine writers and others in the mass media often write or speak with an aura of expertness they frequently lack. The November 2, 1970 issue of *Time* contained an article on Charles Reich's book, *The Greening of America,* which started out:

> *Sociology has spawned more games than Parker Brothers. But all the* divertissements *rest upon a single process—the breakup of phenomena into categories. It has been so ever since Auguste Comte in-*

> *vented the "science" and divided human progress into three stages,*
> *theological, metaphysical and positive. . . .*

Forgetting the question whether any one man invented sociology, does the *Time* writer really understand the complex philosophy of Comte to which he so blithely refers?

Whatever the answer may be in that particular case, it seems true that experts in various fields frequently find errors when *Time* and *Newsweek* report on their own areas of knowledge. This fact casts serious doubt on the general competence of newsmagazine writers to talk so flippantly of technical matters. Here is a particularly revealing flub which occurred in *Time*'s April 14, 1967, review of the autobiography of the great philosopher Bertrand Russell. Wrote the *Time* reviewer:[20]

> [Russell's] *historic collaboration with Alfred North Whitehead . . .*
> *that resulted, after ten years' labor, in the publication of* Principia
> Mathematica, *named after Newton's great work,* **which in many re-**
> **pects it superseded.** *. . .*

Needless to say, the writer didn't mention in *which* respects Russell's work superseded Newton's *Principia,* since there aren't any. Newton's *Principia* formed the foundation of *mechanics,* a topic on which Russell's *Principia* has nothing to say.

5. The peculiar time problem of the air waves

What we have said so far about newspapers and, to a lesser extent, magazines also applies to TV and radio, which show the same lack of in-depth reporting and the same questionable ideas about objectivity. (They also slant the news, although headline slanting obviously is not an important device in their arsenal.)

A July 1970 *Life* magazine interview with Chet Huntley, shortly before Huntley retired, quoted him as saying of President Nixon, "I've seen him

---

[20] Pointed out to me by a *knowledgeable* layman, C. W. Griffin, Denville, New Jersey.

under many conditions. The shallowness of the man overwhelms me; the fact that he is President frightens me." He also is quoted as saying "Spiro Agnew is appealing to the most base elements." But if Nixon was shallow, wasn't that news? While he was a newscaster, shouldn't Huntley have given his listeners at least the evidence on which he based his opinion, if not a hint of the opinion? And if Agnew appealed to "the most base elements," shouldn't listeners have been informed of this? The answer, of course, is "no." Huntley was forbidden to do so by the theories and practices we have just discussed. (Of course, if Senator Blowhard had called a press conference and said the very same things, *then* Huntley could have quoted Blowhard on the Huntley-Brinkley Show.)

But TV and radio have a particular problem that newspapers and magazines don't have. For a given station can show only one thing at a time (and once it has been shown it is gone). A newspaper that prints a long article need not fear that the person who quits reading it after two paragraphs will turn to a competing paper; he's more likely to turn to another article. But when a TV program loses the interest of a viewer, his response often as not will be to flick to a competing channel.

Consequently, serious TV programs tend to be much too short for the purpose at hand, making true in-depth accounts of anything very difficult and unlikely.[21]

The TV debate between Emelio Q. Daddario and Thomas J. Meskill, candidates for the governorship of Connecticut in 1970, illustrates the problem. Each candidate had ninety seconds (!) to answer questions on such complex topics as a proposed state income tax, use of the national guard on college campuses, and widespread pornography. The result was that both men had to restrict their answers to quick capsule *conclusions,* with no chance whatever to present *reasons* for their conclusions. For instance, Daddario used his ninety seconds on the question of proposed annual sessions of the state legislature to say that the present state government was a "mishmash." When asked to answer the question, he said "I am in favor of annual sessions." So was Meskill. So what?

So here we have the two candidates for governor with the largest audience of the campaign; yet they had no chance to *explain* their positions, no chance to present any of the complexities of issues without which voters cannot vote intelligently. After all, one dull stretch of two or three minutes might well result in thousands of sets being turned to other channels.

[21] The great expense involved in a mass-audience TV show also makes for poor coverage intellectually, because mass audiences are less likely to prefer programs which delve into the true complexities of issues.

6. An example of poor coverage

We've now considered all sorts of reasons why news media operate as they do, and also discussed devices used to distort the news. Let's present one more example to sum up a great deal of what we have said by showing the reader material which generally does not get printed in American newspapers.

When Biafra fell in January 1970, that war was page-one news in newspapers and magazines all over the country for a week or two. There were big stories of the massive aid the U.S. and international relief agencies were going to send to the people starving in Biafra. There were also stories to the effect that Nigerian government officials would see to it that things got back to normal quickly and that food and seeds were sent to the hungry. But fairly rapidly Biafra receded from page one through to the back pages and then disappeared entirely. Occasional stories of isolated atrocities were printed, as well as rosy accounts of great improvements in food supplies and the health picture.

Typical was the *New York Times* editorial of June 5, 1970, which mentioned that the Nigerian government would make a flat payment of $56 to each of 200,000 Biafrans who had turned in Biafran currency when the war ended. The editorial also mentioned other economic measures to be taken. The *Times* editorial was optimistic and gave no indication that things were going other than well in Eastern Nigeria.

But all was very likely not going well in Biafra. At least there was good evidence at the time that it was not, which American newspaper and magazine readers (to say nothing of TV viewers) never were exposed to. Here are a very few excerpts from one such piece of evidence, a report by a Holy Ghost father who was part of the Catholic relief mission in Biafra during the Nigerian civil war, and who could be expected to know the situation there after the war as well as any Westerner.[22] Note that this report concerns the situation in *September* 1970, long after most Americans had for-

[22] The report was written by Father Michael Doheney, C.S.Sp., after a visit to Nigeria from September 1 to September 26, 1970, nineteen days of which were spent in the part of Nigeria that had been Biafra during the war. Father Doheney wished it understood that his report had nothing to do with politics. He believed then that the problem should be taken out of the political realm, and felt that the whole report, from which the above is taken, in particular his recommendations about what had to be done at the time, were consistent with Nigerian policy. He further stated in the report that relief efforts should be under the aegis of the Nigerian government and the relief agencies they sanction. This statement appears here to satisfy Father Doheney's desire that his report not be quoted without such comments.

gotten all about Biafra, because they had been led to believe starvation no longer existed there:

While in some areas the situation is relatively good . . . in other areas the situation is still desperate. For instance, while I was in one sick bay, on the day I was there six people died. How many might have died in the same situation before? Maybe one. In another parish 50 people, mostly children or old people, are dying per week. This is far far more than the average death rate in the area. There still is malnutrition. There still is Kwashiorkor.[23] **In places it is not less than it was at the worst time in the last three years.** *I met it without going to look for it. I saw cases come in from a place called Obosi. They were worse than anything I have ever seen. I met one woman on her way into a hospital with her child in her arms. I stopped and talked to her and I said "What is wrong with the child, Mrs.?" She said "The child is hungry." I said "How long has the child been hungry"? She said "The child has been hungry for 2½ years." This is to convey some idea of what the situation is like. Malnutrition, Kwashiorkor, Hepatitis is rampant. One medical worker told me that in her area the figure she would estimate was that 75% of the people had TB. It may not be as bad as that in all areas, but it gives you an idea of the magnitude of the danger. I heard of leprosy in at least four places with up to 200 miles between them. . . .*

A great need, the greatest need of all, I think, which is the key to all the needs, is money. If one has money, one can get medicines and drugs and equipment, one can get food in most places, but not everywhere —for instance in Okpala there are no yams [the staple food of the area], *because all the seeds were destroyed during the war. . . . Needless to say, few Biafrans in the East Central Region had any money. . . . The great era of reconstruction has not begun. We had great promises during the war of all that would be given for reconstruction. But what is being done? Practically nothing.*

So that was the situation in Biafra in September 1970, according to a reputable observer. Yet, as early as February of that year, newspaper accounts carrying official stories about what was happening conveyed the impression that rapid progress was being made, and that starvation had been

---

[23] A protein-deficiency type of starvation which first attacks the nervous system and eventually results in death.

virtually eliminated. Even William Borders, of the *New York Times,* one of
the better reporters on Biafra, wrote on February 14 that there was little
starvation and that the relief efforts which got off to a slow start were beginning to work. (There was almost no coverage in the mass media on the
fact that during the first few months after the war, little of the "massive U.S.
aid" ever reached the worst starvation areas, or any parts of Biafra at all,
for that matter.) By June 1970, reports from Biafra frequently did not mention starvation, or even the terrible malnutrition which left Biafrans in many
areas wide open to disease, with the results Father Doheney found in September of that year.

The gap between reality and what is reported in the mass media often is
grotesquely large. No wonder then that the public tolerates such a dismally
low level of political rhetoric. It simply is not possible for the public to reason cogently about political matters without knowing (in some detail, at
least) the true state of affairs in their own country and around the world.

Summary of Chapter Seven

The American mass media fail to inform their audience about the gap
between our political principles and our actual practices.
1. The media employ an erroneous theory of news reporting, according to
    which: (a) The unusual is news, not the usual; (b) objectivity forbids
    newsmen to draw conclusions or to state their own opinions; (c) objec-
    tivity requires separation of current news from in-depth reporting; and
    (d) good citizenship sometimes requires political self-censorship.
2. The mass media have evolved poor customs and practices: (a) They
    are given most news, rather than seeking it out; and (b) they tend
    therefore to report the establishment viewpoint, because establishment
    views are more readily available.
3. The mass media use devices which distort the news: (a) misleading
    headlines; (b) misleading lead paragraphs on stories; (c) manipula-
    tion of a story's apparent importance; (d) use of subtly value-tinged
    words; (e) selection and editing of letters to the editor and of feature
    columns; and (f) use of the "informed source" leak in news stories and
    in political columns.
4. The mass media exude a false aura of authority, e.g., via the use of
    "*Time*style."
In addition, radio and TV have a special time problem, in that the listener
cannot choose the time he wants to listen to a particular program. If he is
bored for a minute, he turns to another station; consequently the news is

truncated, at the expense of thoroughness and complexity, so as not to lose the viewer's interest.

Exercises for Chapter Seven

1. Obtain a copy of your local newspaper, and evaluate its coverage of one particular event or issue with respect to (1) objectivity; (2) original vs. second-hand reporting of the news; (3) use of headlines; (4) "establishment" viewpoint; and (5) any of the other matters discussed in this chapter. (Be sure to pick an issue of national importance.)
2. Do the same for a recent issue of *Time* or *Newsweek* magazine, including an account of their use (if any) of "*Time*style."

Chapter Eight

Textbooks and Indoctrination

It is often easier to fight for principles than to live up to them.

Adlai Stevenson

1. History textbooks

The need for students to know the history of their own nation is, of course, one reason for the great emphasis on American history in our public schools. But in view of the actual content of the history texts used, it can hardly be the only reason.

Given the portrayal of American history in typical public school textbooks, it seems reasonable to conclude that history is taught to public school children as much to *indoctrinate* them as to teach them the truth about the history of their own land:

1. History as a subject matter is inherently value-tinged, first in the very selection of "facts" to be presented, and second in discussing the quality of political and social systems. History also is inherently *controversial,* unless all controversial topics are ignored, in which case we have pabulum. Yet these texts have an "objective" and "evenhanded" tone, which is used to create the impression that it is an *objective fact* we as a nation hold and *live up to* the highest ideals, and in general are the greatest nation on earth.

2. This impression is enhanced by omission of as much as possible that is sordid in our past (the fallacy of *suppressed evidence*), and by playing up all that is good (the fallacy of *distortion*). In general, the skeletons in our national closet that cannot be ignored are discussed only at the point in history when they have somehow been corrected or atoned for, or else, on a note of optimism, as being in process of solution.

3. Minority groups, in particular those we have treated the worst, are

made as close to "invisible" as possible. The exceptions to this are "token" figures, such as Indian guides, Susan B. Anthony, Booker T. Washington, and George Washington Carver.

These sorry facts would be out of place in a book on reasoning, argument, and political rhetoric were it not for the subtle (often not so subtle) bias most of us bring to many political arguments in later life, a bias produced in part by the history and civics textbook brainwashing we all suffer through as youngsters. We are ill-prepared to face the problems of today because we were never taught the evils of the past which in large part produced them.

In addition, history texts ill prepare students to face today's challenges because they perpetuate falsehoods about the relative importance of events and (in particular) people. They portray the great men in our history as (roughly in descending order of importance) U.S. presidents, other politicians, explorers and adventurers, military men, inventors, businessmen, settlers (pioneers), religious leaders and, last, artists, scientists, and "intellectuals." In the elementary school text to be discussed, we are told about every president, twenty-two other politicians, twenty explorers, fifteen military men (excluding those who later became politicians), sixteen inventors, three businessmen, ten settlers, and thirteen religious leaders. We are told about two social workers (white), five men granted land in what is now the U.S., one adventurer, one "bad man," and two Wild West types. But we read the names of only one labor leader, two artists, four Indians (three friendly to white men), three scientists (none of them theoretical scientists, or of the first rank), two (token) Negroes, and no philosophers whatsoever.

Let's now take a look at a fairly typical elementary school textbook,[1] chosen *because* it is fairly typical and was published by a major textbook publisher prior to 1965. It thus represents the kind of textbook most young adults in the U.S. today were exposed to in elementary school.

a. The Indian in elementary school history textbooks

When the "white man" came from Europe to what is now the United States, the land was inhabited by hundreds of American Indian tribes. They owned the land in every sense of that term, except perhaps that they did

---

[1] *The United States of America,* by Jack Allen and Adeline Howland, Prentice-Hall, Inc., Englewood Cliffs, N.J., 1964.

not have legal deeds filed in local courthouses. Today, the descendants of those Indians own an insignificantly small and relatively undesirable portion of the nation's real estate.[2] And yet, only a tiny amount of land was ever purchased from the Indians by the white man or given to him without severe arm twisting.

The problem for public school textbook writers (not to mention most others writing on U.S. history) is to get around the obvious fact that if we didn't buy the land from the Indians, and they didn't give it to us, then we must have obtained it by grand theft rivaling any other case in history. In general, this problem is solved in the text under discussion (let's refer to it by its authors' names—Allen and Howland) in four ways:

1.   Much is made of the famous but rare cases in which land actually was purchased from the Indians. Examples are the sale of Manhattan Island for $24 and Roger Williams' purchase of land around Providence Bay. Questions about whether the Indians clearly understood what was happening are never discussed. Similarly, it is never mentioned that after purchasing land the settlers just kept pushing outward from that land without regard for the Indians, who had just made an effort to live in peace with the white man.

2.   The entire book is written in a "factual," "objective" manner (with a few significant but rare exceptions) designed to impart a note of authority and fairness. One of the few lapses from "objectivity" occurs in the description of the $24 Manhattan Island deal. A transaction of this kind obviously needs justification, and here it is (p. 105):

> Governor Minuit bought the island of Manhattan from the Indians. He did not use money. He paid them with beads, bright colored cloth, pots and pans, knives and axes, blankets, and other articles. The articles were worth, in all, about twenty-four dollars in our United States money. We think this is quite a bargain. But to the Indians, and to Peter Minuit, it seemed like a fair price. **It probably was for that time**.

One of the few outright value judgments in the entire book,[3] and it's just flatly and patently *wrong*. But the student is told that it's "probably" right, and then the topic is shifted to the Dutch patroons settling up the Hudson River from Manhattan Island:

---

[2] Excluding the Far North of Alaska, where the Eskimos (not really Indians, anyway) are fighting a last-ditch battle for their share of the oil wealth in that area.

[3] The first 104 pages are full of stories of European explorers going all over the Western Hemisphere, defeating Indians, stealing their land, etc. Yet not once is a value judgment made as to the fairness of what they did.

Up the Hudson River another kind of settlement was taking place. Large pieces of land were offered **by the Dutch West India Company** *to rich men in the Netherlands if they would agree to send groups of settlers to America.*

It isn't explained how the Dutch West India Company obtained the land from the Indian owners.

3. This last quoted passage illustrates another way the vexing land problem is solved. Simply *ignore the problem,* especially when there is no explanation compatible with our sense of morality which can be made plausible even to elementary school children.

4. Finally, the problem of the transfer of land ownership is solved also by mentioning treaties between Indians and whites in which land was ceded to the whites. Sometimes, the Indian motives for making such treaties are simply ignored. Occasionally, it is at least acknowledged that the treaties were forced on the Indians after defeat in battle. An example is the description of the settling of the Ohio country (pp. 193–194):

Certainly the Ohio country brought good luck to thousands of settlers. At first the Indians who lived there fought the settlers. The Indians were defeated in 1794, and gave up most of their lands. As soon as a treaty was signed with the Indian tribes, people began to move in by the thousands.

Clearly, if the purchase of Manhattan Island for just $24 requires justification, the Ohio country treaty does also. The trouble is that in this case there is no plausible explanation handy which is compatible with our sense of morality. So the authors simply ignore the question, hiding behind their usual mask of "objectivity."

But the objectivity is just a mask. There is no question here or anywhere in the text but that the authors are on the side of the white man. Even in passages where embarrassing facts must be glossed over, passages in which the authors may well have been particularly careful, subtle signs reveal their bias.

In the example just cited, the settling of the Ohio country "brought good luck to thousands of settlers"—*white* settlers, of course. The horrible suffering and death inflicted on the Indians who owned the land is not mentioned.

What is worse, the white men are never portrayed as breaking treaties with the Indians. Occasionally, however, *individual* whites (never the government) are portrayed as mistreating Indians (p. 118):

The Spanish soldiers [in what was to become California] *who came with* [Father Serra—a Spanish missionary] *began to treat the Indians badly. The Indians revolted. The wise priest quieted the Indians and worked to improve the way they were treated.*

Notice that even here the evil is discussed on a note of optimism; Father Serra "worked to improve" the treatment of the Indians.

The impression left with the reader of Allen and Howland is this: When the white men came to America, they found the country sparsely settled by backward peoples, the Indians. The whites slowly settled the land, moving from East to West, paying for some of the land and obtaining the rest by treaty. Some treaties resulted from wars between the whites and Indians, but it is never made clear who was right and who wrong in these wars. What is clear is that the whites always won, and gained land from the Indians. As the white man moved through a territory, the Indians just seemed to fade out of the picture. By 1890, they had faded away completely, later to be joined by other American minority groups who are "invisible" in our histories (the Puerto Ricans of New York, Cubans of Miami, Mexican-Americans of the West and Southwest—after these areas were "obtained" from Mexico, Spain, etc.).[4]

In general, the authors of this text use the least space possible in discussing the American Indian. Obviously, the Indians could not be omitted from the story entirely. But as just illustrated, the central facts about them could be and were omitted. Nowhere in the text does it say that their lands were *unjustly* taken from them by force and violence, that they endured great suffering, that thousands were slaughtered and their descendants relegated to third-class citizenship (usually on land no one else much wanted), or that almost all of the treaties they made with the white man were broken by the white man, and continue to be broken by the white man to this very

---

[4] This text also contains other, perhaps more subtle, evidence of bias against the Indian. For instance, land west of the white frontier is generally referred to as "unsettled wilderness"; Indian occupation apparently didn't count. Only a handful of Indians are mentioned by name in the entire book, and all but one (Tecumseh) are portrayed in the act of aiding the white man (for example, aiding Lewis and Clark explore the Northwest U.S.). White explorers keep "discovering" things Indians had known about for centuries—not excluding the whole Western Hemisphere. The terrible suffering needlessly inflicted on the Indians in the process of stealing their land is glossed over, or in general completely ignored (for example, the terrible treatment of the Cherokees). Finally, one gets the impression that things would have been much better for all concerned if the Indians had simply disappeared, leaving behind a few friendly guides and someone to tell the white man about corn, turkeys, Thanksgiving, and all that.

day. This constitutes the twin fallacies of *suppressed evidence* and *distortion* on a grand scale.

b. The Negro in elementary school history textbooks

Since the white man didn't steal the land from the Negroes as he had from the Indians, Negroes can be even closer to "invisible" in history texts than can Indians. And so they are in the text in question (except, of course, for the one period in our history when they cannot be hidden, the Civil War).

Negroes are first mentioned in relation to the settling of Virginia (p. 81):

> *Aboard ship* [1619, in Jamestown] *were twenty Negroes. They were put to work in the tobacco fields. The Negroes were good workers. Soon others were brought to the colony. They were sold as slaves. The number of slaves did not increase rapidly at first. Thirty years later there were only about 300 Negroes in all of Virginia.*

Exit the Negro from American history for 125 pages and about 200 years. Then (p. 206), having moved to the period 1817–1819, and to the Gulf Coast region of the South, we learn that:

> *Hundreds of Negro slaves worked in the cotton fields. Life there was like the life on some of the tobacco plantations in colonial Virginia. Most of the cotton growers, however, were small farmers who owned fewer than ten slaves. These farmers usually worked in the fields with their slaves.*

But not one word is said which would suggest that slaves were mistreated, that families were split by sale of individual members, or even that slavery is *wrong*. In fact, by implication, the slave's lot is portrayed as not so very different from that of small slave owners, since these owners "usually worked in the fields with their slaves."

Finally (p. 206), there is a hint of the darker side of the matter in one cryptic statement that "Florida was a place to which slaves could escape, and where they could hide." But the sentence is an aside in what is basically an account of the American government's troubles with Spain over Florida, and Negroes drop from sight for twenty more pages. We are given no reason why Negro slaves would take the great risk and endure the hardships of escape to Florida.

But now the story has moved close to the Civil War period; Negroes and slavery no longer can be ignored. Six passages concerning Negroes in one way or another, several of them longer than a paragraph, suffice to get us through the Civil War period. After that, American Negroes are mentioned only five times in the book's remaining 100 pages. The five passages state that (a) Negroes no longer worked as slaves in cotton fields in the South, but were now free (p. 237); (b) some settlers in Kansas believed in slavery while others didn't, which led to bloodshed (p. 247); (c) George Washington Carver discovered many products that could be made from Southern crops (p. 288); (d) Booker T. Washington, a Negro educator, persuaded Carver to attend the all-black Tuskegee Institute (p. 288); and, finally, (e) Negroes were given the right to vote after the Civil War (p. 300).

Only the section on George Washington Carver and Booker T. Washington runs to more than a sentence or two. And except for these two men, no Negroes are mentioned by name; all are virtually invisible as *people* throughout our history, mentioned only as tobacco and cottonfield hands and, of course, as the cause of the Civil War. Discrimination in the North against Negroes is *never* mentioned; in fact, the book never lets it be known (except that one passage about slavery in Kansas) that Negroes ever lived in any area outside the South, and not a word is said about their existence in the United States after 1877 other than the one small section on Carver and Booker T. Washington.

The evils of slavery are discussed only once in the entire text, and even this reference is veiled and weak. It concerns Abraham Lincoln's trip to New Orleans in about 1830:

> *On this trip, he saw slaves working at the wharves and in the fields. He saw slaves being bought and sold like cattle or bales of cotton. He did not like what he saw.*

The description of Negroes in the Civil War period (pp. 227–230) starts with a three-paragraph, factual and fairly accurate account of the connection between cotton and slavery, pointing out that many Southerners believed slaves were necessary to their economic system. It also mentions that:

there were more and more people in the North who objected to slavery. These people wanted to give the slaves their freedom.

But nothing is said here as to *why* Northerners objected. It is not stated that Northerners believed slavery to be immoral, much less that slavery is in fact immoral.

The treatment of the North and South on the slavery question and the Civil War is "objectively evenhanded." Perhaps this is inevitable if a textbook is to have truly nationwide distribution. At any rate, this evenhandedness results in two juxtaposed passages, one about a typical Northern soldier, Billy Yank, the other a typical Southern soldier, Johnny Reb. (There is no mention of *Negro* soldiers, either in the Civil War or any other war.) These passages seem intended to justify both sides in the Civil War.

Billy Yank is described as believing that "all people had a right to be free," and that it was wrong for a state to leave the union (a point which is ignored when discussing other civil wars, such as the one which resulted in the freedom of Texas from Mexico). Johnny Reb is described as follows (p. 230):

> *Johnny Reb had always known Negro slaves. They were as much a part of his life as eating and sleeping. Johnny liked the Negroes. He believed that he treated them well. They had rocked him to sleep when he was little. He had played with them as a boy. He probably had worked with them in the fields. But he still wanted to keep the Negroes as slaves.*[5]

These quotes illustrate the "evenhanded objectivity" the text employs with respect to the Northern and Southern views of slavery and secession. But, of course, these are *white* views. Nothing is said about whether blacks liked Johnny Reb, or wanted to remain slaves. "Evenhanded objectivity" seems to include the opinions of whites, but not blacks.

---

[5] We then are given Johnny Reb's answer to Billy Yank on secession:

> *The states, the first thirteen, had governments of their own before the government of the United States was established under our Constitution. Since each of these states had agreed to become a part of the national government, any or all of them had a right to withdraw from the government if they wished.*

There is a ring of rationality to this argument defending the right of secession. One wonders what Billy Yank would have said about it, but we aren't told.

The text quotes Billy Yank, Abraham Lincoln, and many Northerners as believing slavery is wrong. So at least the student is exposed to the idea that slavery existed in the U.S. and many believed it morally wrong. But nothing is said of *racial segregation* or *racial prejudice*. The proverbial "man from Mars" on reading this book would be justified in assuming that since the post-Civil War period, blacks in America have been treated the same as anyone else.

No mention is made of racially segregated public schools (although free public schools are discussed at length). The Supreme Court's 1896 "separate but equal" decision is passed over, as is its 1954 reversal, as is Dred Scott.

As stated before, the Negroes' legal right to vote is mentioned; but poll taxes and other devices which in fact have kept Negroes from voting are not. No mention is made of the Ku Klux Klan, "last hired first fired," Northern and Western big-city ghettos, or segregated restrooms, drinking fountains, transportation, or restaurants. And it goes without saying that lynching and slave rebellions are not part of the story.

Finally, it must be pointed out that the air of objectivity is enhanced by the device of *tokenism*. America's two favorite "token niggers," Booker T. Washington and George Washington Carver, are put on public display, perhaps to show that blacks are human too and are even capable of intelligence. But whatever the reason for the choice, the selection amounts to tokenism plain and simple. This conclusion is inescapable because Allen and Howland say nothing whatever about Frederick Douglass or W.E.B. DuBois, or even contemporary Negroes as innocuous (compared to Malcolm X, Rap Brown, Bobby Seale, etc.) as Walter White, Roy Wilkins, and Nobel Prize winner Ralph Bunche.[6]

It may be argued in defense of the textbook just discussed that it was designed, after all, for elementary school children. And it is true that this fact requires that the history of the United States be *simplified*. Obviously, many facts must be left out and many complex issues not completely explained.

But the charge leveled here against elementary school history textbooks is not simplification but rather *distortion,* and *suppression* of relevant facts. Of course, simplification always results in some distortion, but it clearly need not result in the distortion we have just cited. There is nothing com-

---

[6] The omission of black artists, such as Richard Wright and James Baldwin, is probably due neither to their being nonwhite nor to doubts about their eventual place in the literary sphere, but rather to their being *artists,* a group represented in this book by only two men (Ralph Waldo Emerson and Francis Scott Key), both of whom happened to write something patriotic.

plicated about the idea that white Europeans stole the land from the Indians or that white Americans have mistreated Negroes in many ways.

It may also be argued that the "errors" of omission cited above are better explained by limitations of space than by any intent to distort history. An elementary school textbook cannot be very long, perhaps because we haven't taught the average student to read that well.

But this defense has even less merit than the previous one. There are too many examples of relatively unimportant matters receiving great attention while important ones receive little attention or none at all. Lindbergh's solo flight across the Atlantic gets more space than the Supreme Court, all of their decisions, and the Bill of Rights, combined. He receives almost as much attention as the entire labor movement, Samuel Gompers included. (Gompers is the only labor leader mentioned in the text.) There is room in this text for mention of Lillian Wald, Benjamin Waterhouse, John A. Sutter, Charles Carroll, Samuel Slater, David Ira Sankey, Dwight L. Moody, William Brewster, Edward Rutledge, John Fitch, Thomas Hooker, Edward Jenner, and "Wild Bill" Hickok. We are treated to a stanza from that immortal gem "On the Banks of the Wabash," and of course a bit of "Yankee Doodle." We receive two pages on Mississippi river steamboats (but, alas, not a word about Sam Clemens). We must conclude, then, that the "lack of space" defense will not wash.

If we judge from the finished product (and what other pertinent evidence is available to us?), we seem forced to conclude that minority groups, or Indians and Negroes at any rate, do not get a fair shake in the elementary school history text we have just discussed. This is what would be expected if the intent in teaching American history were *indoctrination,* and not merely the teaching of the history of our nation.

c. The Indian in high school history textbooks

Let's again use one text as our example.[7] We must remember, though, that this text (let's refer to it as "Canfield and Wilder") runs to over 800 pages of double-column, rather small type, whereas the elementary school text just discussed was less than 350 pages in length and printed in large type. We must remember also that this text is designed for high school

---

[7] *The Making of Modern America,* by Leon H. Canfield and Howard B. Wilder. Houghton Mifflin Company, Boston, 1962.

students, who are at an age at which their grandfathers were considered
young adults.

In this textbook, the transfer of ownership of land in the United States
from Indian to white hands is handled in roughly the same way as in Allen
and Howland. William Penn is described as "even paying them [the In-
dians] for their land." Nothing is said about how much land was purchased,
or the conditions of sale (e.g., the price per acre, whether there was coer-
cion, etc.). (No text this writer has ever seen goes into these crucial details, except, of course, for Manhattan Island and $24, a story happily
omitted from Canfield and Wilder.)

Treaties in which Indians cede land are mentioned frequently, and,
sometimes, there is even mention of the force which usually preceded such
treaties. However, the *breaking* of treaties by white governments, although
admitted to in general, is not documented for specific cases. It certainly
is not made clear that almost every treaty was broken by the whites, usually
within a few years after being made.

This high school text, too, is written in what appears to be an objective,
evenhanded manner, although lapses from objectivity are more frequent
than in the elementary school text considered, and the entire text is prefaced
with a gigantic lapse entitled "Nation of Free People" in which the United
States is eulogized (with much exaggeration).

Yet, despite this pretense of objectivity, it is always clear that the authors are "rooting for" the white man, as most of us are (from second
nature) when we don't think about it carefully. Sioux and other tribes are
described as "fierce and warlike" (p. 344). Custer is "ambushed and wiped
out" (p. 354). The settlers' move westward is blocked by the "hostility
of the Indians" (p. 155). Tecumseh is a "dreaded Indian leader" (p. 176).

On the other hand, Indians are never "wiped out" or "ambushed"; they
tend to be "defeated." Whites, even soldiers, are portrayed as normal human beings, never as "fierce and warlike." And their military leaders are
never "dreaded"; they are revered and become U.S. presidents.

It is true that the text contains a few scattered sentences which describe
the Indians as being cheated, from which an intelligent reader might conclude that the Indians had a case, but the subject of the *rightness* or *wrong-
ness* of what has been described is discussed only once (pp. 352–353).
And as expected, this crucial topic receives an "evenhanded," "impartial"
treatment (p. 353):

> *The retreat of the Indians may be looked at from two points of view:
> that of the pioneer and that of the Indian himself.*

> *1.* [Whites] *looked upon the destruction of the "***savages***" as natural, inevitable, and even desirable. They argued that the Indian . . . had done little to develop the country and its resources. Now, they believed, he threatened to be a dangerous obstacle to* **progress**. *The settler saw nothing good in the Indians; he saw only their* **cunning**, *their* **ferocity**, *and their* **shocking cruelty**. *Along the whole frontier white settlers cried angrily, "There are no good Indians except dead Indians!"*
>
> *2. The red men . . . saw only that they were losing their land and their lives through the dishonesty or the greed of white men. Homes and* **hunting grounds granted** *to them by solemn treaties were overrun by fortune seekers. Corrupt government agents and dishonest traders and settlers added to their troubles. From the Indians' point of view, there was no choice but to fight for their right to live in the homeland of their ancestors.*

Several things need to be said about this passage. First, the words in boldface type are all loaded against the Indian. Indians are *cunning* in defending their land, not intelligent. And they use "shocking cruelty" (a phrase never used to describe the shocking cruelty of whites to Indians, which is never really mentioned anyway). They are an obstacle to "progress" (white man's progress). The phrase "hunting grounds" is used, and this is a phrase often used by writers who want to suggest that the Indians were nomadic and uncivilized, and thus not entitled to their lands.[8]

Second, Indians and their governments are treated as one, but whites and their governments are not. Thus, the reader is given the opportunity to conclude (falsely, of course) that it was individual white charlatans who were causing trouble for the Indians, not the United States government, not white society as a whole.

Third, notice that the Indians' hunting grounds are "granted" to the Indians by treaties with the white man. Since Indians, not whites, already owned the land, it couldn't have been "granted" by whites to anyone.

Fourth, the white man's argument is presented in as strong a manner as possible. But not that of the Indian, even ignoring the loaded words mentioned above. In particular, the savage horror of the *way* in which Indians were swept aside like so many herds of wild animals is omitted. Nor is the reader provided with this information elsewhere in the text, so that he might supply it here himself. (An example is the text's treatment of the

---

[8] Indeed, Canfield and Wilder do use this ploy several times, for example (p. 87): "The Indians [in the Ohio country] grew restless under the threat of losing their hunting grounds." What is called their "hunting grounds" is, of course, their land. They were threatened with loss of their land, tradition, culture, and lives.

period 1800–1850, which in general receives large coverage. The forced march, the infamous "Trail of Tears," is masked under the term "removal" of Indians to West of the Mississippi. And Andrew Jackson's massacre of Indian women and children at Horseshoe Bend is not mentioned at all.)

Finally, and perhaps most importantly, by presenting "both sides of the picture," the authors don the cloak of objectivity. Yet the passage cries out for evaluation. Surely it must be made clear to present-day Americans that the arguments defending the white man can be rebutted successfully, but those of the Indian cannot.

This last point is made quite well in another book critical of how the Indian is treated in history books:[9]

> *An effort to be "fair" is prominent in* [Canfield and Wilder]. *This would be praiseworthy if such fairness were justified. After all, one could present both sides of the Hitler crimes too.* [Needless to say, no such presentation is made in any *American* textbooks.] *This ideology is evidenced on page 353: "The retreat of the Indians may be looked at from two points of view. That of the pioneer and that of the Indian himself." This position is analogous to presenting the equal but opposite points of view of a holdup man and his victim.*

The perfect analogy—provided we add that when the victim realizes his very existence is threatened and fights back, he is described as "cunning" and "a dangerous obstacle to progress," and reference is made to his "ferocity" and "shocking cruelty." After all, there are no good victims except dead victims!

2. Civics as indoctrination

At this point, the reader may suspect that the dice have been just a little bit loaded. A great deal has been said about just two topics, and only two textbooks. Perhaps these texts are not typical (or perhaps not typical with respect to the two major topics we examined).

Well, then, let's look at some other secondary school texts, making our selection this time from a different but related field (civics). And let's examine several other controversial topics in one of these texts, in addition

---

[9] *Textbooks and the American Indian,* by the American Indian Historical Society, Indian Historian Press, 1970, p. 25. This excellent book is highly recommended, especially to anyone not convinced by the relatively short treatment given in this chapter.

to the two topics we have concentrated on so far. The purpose, of course, is to present more evidence for our main thesis that primary and secondary school textbooks indoctrinate as much as they teach the truth about our nation.[10]

To support this conclusion, we're going to present evidence for several related claims.

a. Actual practice is distorted. Civics textbooks concentrate on the *theoretical machinery* of government; what they say about actual practice is generally false or distorted, as it would be if civics texts were designed to confirm the false thesis that our system works just about as it's supposed to.

Here is an example from a recent typical textbook.[11] To illustrate how our court systems work, a fictionalized version of a real case is presented in which a "Hilda Gray" is accused and convicted of kidnapping. The case is appealed all the way to the Supreme Court, and the proper rules and procedures are followed in every instance.

The text in question then states (p. 105):

> *From the case you have just studied, you can see how fully "equal justice under the law" is enjoyed by citizens of the United States. At each step of the way, Hilda Gray was given her full legal rights. All of us can be thankful we live in a country where* **anyone** *accused of a crime has a right to receive a fair, public trial in a court of law.*

The Hilda Gray case concerns federal courts. But it is clear that the quoted paragraph, which ends discussion of the case, is meant to apply to all courts. Later in the text, similar cases are described in which both the letter and spirit of the law are scrupulously observed.

---

[10] Of course, there is no intent to argue that there are no good general textbooks on American history or civics. There are a few which are good with respect to certain key controversial topics, in particular the Negro in American life. The best example, and it is very good, that this writer has come across is *Discovering American History,* by Alan O. Knownslar and Donald B. Frizzle, Holt, Rinehart and Winston, New York, 1967. This text is unusual in its use of material from many sources, material which was definitely *not* written for textbooks. In this text, for instance, instead of a single dry paragraph in which lunch-counter sit-ins are mentioned (as in Canfield and Wilder), we are treated to excerpts from *Diary of a Sit-In,* by Merrill Proudfoot, The Univ. of North Carolina Press, 1962; we experience a sit-in through the eyes of a perceptive viewer on the scene. Excerpts of this kind, taken from many diverse sources, make it possible for the reader to get a better idea of what it has meant, day in and day out, to be a black person in America. We also are more likely to perceive the controversial nature of most of the subject matter discussed in history textbooks, and even be prepared to do a little conclusion-drawing for ourselves.

[11] *American Civics,* by William H. Hartley and William S. Vincent, Harcourt Brace Jovanovich, New York, 1967.

The trouble, of course, is that courts in the United States usually don't work that way. Hilda Gray appealed her case all the way to the Supreme Court; most people can't even afford a good lawyer for their original trial.

In fact, a great many Americans convicted of crimes (indeed probably most) don't even have a trial. They are never *proven* guilty: they *plead* guilty. And their plea of guilt has little or nothing to do with actual guilt or innocence, or even with possible evidence against them.[12] They plead guilty as a way of bargaining with the court. In return for the guilty plea, the court charges and convicts them for a lesser crime than they were originally charged with, for which the penalty is much lower.

This is the procedure in criminal courts in many, perhaps most, large cities in the United States. The typical accused person has insufficient time to confer with his lawyer. (Frequently, his lawyer is court-appointed, and is seen for the first time on the trial date.) The defendant has little or no money for an investigation which might reveal evidence in his favor. On the day he is to be tried, he is confronted with an offer (usually bargained for between the prosecutor and his court-appointed lawyer); he will be charged with a lesser crime in return for pleading guilty. He must decide whether to risk a long sentence in jail in the hope of being declared innocent or accept a shorter sentence in return for pleading guilty. If he is innocent, this means he must decide whether to gamble on receiving justice or accept a lesser penalty. The vast majority decide not to gamble on justice.

Here is a description of the process which you *won't* find in any current civics textbooks:[13]

> *Plea bargaining is what the lawyers call it. No trial. No jury of peers. No exhaustive search for truth. No exacting legal rules. . . .*
>
> *A lawyer who knows next to nothing about his client or the facts of the crime with which he is charged barters away a man's right to a trial. . . .*
>
> *A prosecutor who knows little more about the case than what a policeman tells him hurriedly trades off . . . the responsibility for providing for those charged . . . a full hearing. . . . The judge, who has abdicated his authority to bartering lawyers, acquiesces in all this and sanctifies it for "the record."*

[12] Since most never have a trial, statistics on the percentage who really are guilty are not much better than mere guesses.

[13] Taken from "Crime in the Courts: Assembly Line Justice," by Leonard Downie, Jr., *The Washington Monthly*, May 1970, pp. 28–29. The whole article runs to 14 pages and is well worth the attention of anyone who wants to understand how criminal courts work in America.

This system has developed because of crowded courtrooms, a shortage of judges, and the inability of the poor either to hire good lawyers or to spend the amount of time away from their jobs that snail-paced courtroom procedures require. But they don't tell you about such things in civics textbooks.

One more example of distortion from the same text: Unit Four concerns the American economy and how it works. It accurately describes the formal machinery of American business (in simplified form, of course). It explains about preferred and common stocks, bonds, legal monopolies, antitrust laws, etc. And it gives a simple account of an Adam Smith-type theory of the free market, which it says our economy operates under (excluding certain public utilities).

Neglecting for the moment the controversial nature of the free market theory, we can question the *accuracy* of the account. It simply isn't true that our system involves a free market in which the government is a referee. Think of labor union members and collective bargaining, or the way in which the federal government attempts to manage the economy by means of its fiscal and monetary policies.

In addition, the impression is given that there is genuine *price* competition among producers of a given product, as is required in a true *laissez faire* economy. But only a cursory examination of the prices of gasoline, automobiles, steel, etc., reveals that sometimes there is price competition, often there is not. How often, for instance, do standard-brand cigarettes of the same type differ in price by even one penny? How is it that when R. J. Reynolds or American Tobacco raise prices, the others always do also?

Needless to say, no mention is made of a single instance of outright collusion on the part of businessmen, such as the famous electrical conspiracy of the early 1960s, nor of the feebleness in actual practice of antitrust laws (for instance, the continued submission of identical bids on contracts for heavy electrical equipment construction even after the electrical conspiracy trial).[14]

b. Controversial theories are stated as facts. Civics textbooks describe all of the controversial theories of government and economics which have gained assent as our "official myths," or "official ideals," as though all sane, loyal Americans accept them, and, worse, as though they are *true*.

Yet, save perhaps religion and sex, nothing is more controversial than

[14] See, for instance, Fred J. Cook, *The Corrupted Land,* The Macmillan Co., New York, 1966, or "The Incredible Electrical Conspiracy," *Fortune* magazine, April–May, 1961, or the *Wall Street Journal,* January 9, 10, 12, and 13, 1961.

the topics these texts deal with. A perfect example is the *laissez faire* free-economy theory, which almost every civics text presents as though no informed American would doubt its correctness. One need only read the tiniest fragments from the writings of, say, Milton Friedman and Leon Keyserling to realize that the topic is drenched in controversy.

None of this comes through in civics texts. Instead, we generally read that Americans disagree with the peoples of other nations, chiefly Communists, on these matters, and no room is left for doubt about where the truth lies. But little or nothing is said about disagreements among Americans on these topics.

c. Objectivity is used to hide distortion. Civics texts, like history texts, indoctrinate by using the appearance of objectivity and evenhandedness to conceal the differences between our principles and our practices. And yet they need ways to avoid or at least negate those painful facts which cannot be totally ignored.

An example is racially segregated schools: A textbook may want to mention the 1954 Supreme Court decision, but this decision carries with it the implication that prior to 1954 there were segregated schools which were separate but *not* equal. The text in question solves the problem this poses by the device of the unrebutted "second party" opinion (p. 390):

> *This Supreme Court decision immediately led to a bitter controversy. Many school systems, particularly those in the Southern states, claimed that their separate schools for Negroes were equal to the schools attended by white students.*

The text thus does not actually *say* that the segregated Negro schools of the South were equal. Hence, it can't be accused of falsehood, since Southerners did claim they were equal. But it gets the thought across that perhaps many Negro schools in the South were equal to white schools, thus tending to uphold the "official truth" of freedom and *equality* for all Americans. The beauty of the ploy, of course, is that it preserves the "objectivity" of the textbook.

d. Minority groups are poorly dealt with. As might be expected, minority groups tend to be invisible in civics texts, and when they are mentioned, their treatment is distorted. Since we've concentrated so much on Indians and Negroes, this time let's first consider a few other minority groups which most people would now agree don't get a fair shake in the United States.

Many, perhaps most, civics texts (history texts, too, for that matter) don't even mention the migrant laborer, although they do say a great deal about farmers and farming. However, the text we have been examining does deal with migrant laborers—in exactly two sentences (pp. 324–325):

> *Others* [other sharecroppers] *move their families from farm to farm, making only a bare living. These day-to-day farm workers are called* migrant farm laborers.

The implication that only sharecroppers become migrant laborers is, of course, false. But the important error in this passage (which comes in the middle of a long section on farming) is the quick way in which migrants are passed over in two short, dry sentences. The reader is not told of the virtual peonage of the migrant. Nor is he told how they are denied their legal rights.[15]

By now it is generally recognized that women have been discriminated against in ways other than just the denial of the vote.[16] In particular, it is generally agreed that even today women sometimes receive less pay than men do for the same job; often are not seriously considered for "higher" positions in industry or government (witness the paucity of female cabinet members throughout our history, and the fact that in a recent year there was no tenured female faculty member at Harvard University); and are all-too-often counseled into the typing-shorthand track in high school (how many men do you see in shorthand classes?), so that they are trained for jobs which permit relatively little advancement.

A civics text which pointed out these facts, and perhaps urged bright women students to avoid the typing-steno route, would perform a useful service. But to do so it would have to admit that there is discrimination by sex, and very few texts seem willing to make that admission.

---

[15] See, for instance, "Peonage in Florida," by Robert Coles, *The New Republic,* January 11, 1969, and the *New York Times* article "Court Abuse of Migrants Charged in South Jersey," August 16, 1970, p. 1.

[16] Women constitute a curious "minority" group, since there are more women than men in the United States. In treating them as a minority group, we may appear to be committing the fallacy of *questionable classification,* since the category under discussion really is "oppressed group," not "minority group." The explanation is simply that the term "minority group" frequently gets interchanged with "oppressed group" in everyday life, because in the United States these days the most visible recipients of oppressive discrimination are minority groups.

The text we have been considering mentions women *qua* women many times. It mentions them as housewives, in the armed forces, on farms, etc. It mentions their attaining the right to vote. But only twice does it hint at current discrimination against women.

The first is a one-sentence snippet in a section on the Department of Labor (p. 81):

> *Working women get special help through the Department's Women's Bureau, which strives to promote good working conditions, wages, and hours for all women workers.*

Perhaps the average adult Russian, long trained in reading between the lines of Communist newspapers, would be able to conclude from this that working conditions, and wages and hours for women must not be as good as for men, otherwise there would be no need to strive to promote them. But the average American student is unlikely to be as perceptive.

The other reference to discrimination against women is rather more extended (pp. 348–349). But boiled down to its essentials it says that women once were discriminated against in employment, in particular in highly trained and professional jobs, but now all that is rapidly changing. The emphasis is on rapid change toward the official line, not on the past evil. Here are some excerpts (pp. 348–349):

> *Even in the 1920s and 1930s, . . . many Americans believed that a woman's place was in the home. Few careers, except teaching and nursing, were open to women.* **Now all this is changed**.

> . . . *what was said* [about career opportunities] **is equally true for both young men and young women**. *Even in the armed forces. . . .*

> *America's business firms are urging young women to train and study for many scientific and technical jobs that were* **once** *open only to men.*

Nothing is said about how junior high school and high school counselors (to say nothing of parents) urge young women to train for low-level office jobs, nor about the reality of the personnel man's almost automatic classification of women as typists, clerks, and secretaries.

Finally, here is a passage from the same section which may well reveal more about our ingrained deep-down discrimination against women than most males will care to admit to:

> *The profession of* nursing *is a field in which young* **women** *are urgently needed. The shortage of nurses is great at the present time.*

And what about easing that shortage with young *men?* (Men do serve successfully as nurses.) What of the even greater shortage of M.D.s? Why not urge young women to become M.D.s?

Nowhere in the text are statistics given comparing the percentage of female doctors with that of female nurses. The reason is obvious. The overwhelming number of doctors (and dentists) are men; the overwhelming number of nurses are women. The same sexual correlation is true for persons *training* to be physicians or nurses. But these facts tend to cast doubt on the official line that all of us, men and women, have equal opportunity in the United States.[17]

We've now provided a little information about the way in which migrants and women are dealt with in civics texts. Were we to do the same for Mexican-Americans, Puerto Ricans, Indians, and, in particular, homosexuals, the results would be similar; if anything, the discrimination against these groups receives even less attention.

e. Civics texts lag behind. If migrants, women, homosexuals, etc., tend to be invisible in civics texts, and their unfair treatment swept under the rug, so also do Negroes—but not to the extent that they used to be.

The difference is that starting soon after World War II American public opinion on Negroes began to change, and the Negroes' fight for their rights began to pay off, even if very slowly. Negroes became a political power, and their cause became much more popular.

The result has been a change in the way blacks are dealt with by all textbooks, including civics texts. Negroes get mentioned more often; greater effort is made to point out how particular kinds of discrimination (previously neglected in civics texts) have been or are being corrected; and Negroes even appear in photographs, on occasion.

Let's see how this has worked by examining two civics texts, treating two editions of each text.

The 1952 edition of the first of these texts, *Your Life as a Citizen,*[18] lists exactly three items in its index under the title "Negroes":

---

[17] An interesting sidelight on this topic is the fact that civics texts, in comparing our system to a communist one, do not mention that a far greater proportion of doctors in the Soviet Union are women than is true in the U.S.

[18] By Harriet Fullen Smith, Ginn and Co., 1952.

Negroes, and voting, 336; number of, in United States in 1810, 383;
spirituals *of, 397.*

Here are the text passages, in order of listing in the index:

> *The national government stepped in to settle two problems for the*
> *country as a whole: First, could Negroes vote? Second, could women*
> *vote? The Fifteenth Amendment to the Constitution says that the*
> *states cannot deny the right to vote "on account of race, color, or pre-*
> *vious condition of servitude."*

> [In a section on the ethnic makeup of the U.S. in 1810.]
> *There were more than a million Negroes in the country, but they*
> *worked in the households and on the plantations of their masters and*
> *had not yet faced the problem of making independent homes for them-*
> *selves.*

> [In a section on the origins of American dance and music.]
> *Of course, our Negro spirituals, acclaimed the world over as the most*
> *original of all American music, are sometimes said to·have their roots*
> *in Africa.*

In addition, a very few pictures contain people who are recognizably Negro
(never in closeup—although hundreds of whites are shown that way), and
the word "color" occurs in a quote by Abraham Lincoln on "reverence for
the laws" (p. 330) in which he says, "let the old and the young, the rich
and the poor, the grave and the gay of all sexes and tongues and [here it
comes] colors and conditions, sacrifice unceasingly upon its altars." [19] And
that's about *it* for the American Negro. Even slavery fails to make the
lineup.

Now let's jump ahead only nine years and examine the 1961 revised
edition of this text.[20] The three references indexed in the first edition are
indexed in the second, but they are described differently; the phrase "spirituals of" is deleted. And the sentence on spirituals in the text itself has
been updated (p. 95):

---

[19] Strangely, this is the only quote from Lincoln in the entire text. He is mentioned
in passing two or three other times, and otherwise ignored.
[20] Revised Edition by Harriet Fullen Smith and George G. Bruntz, 1961.

Of course our Negro spirituals, **work songs, and** *"***blues***" are folk songs of great popularity, too. They* **often are said** [21] *to be the most original of all American music.*

But the major changes are three additions. The first concerns slavery and the arrival of blacks in America as slaves (p. 93). The second concerns contributions of Negroes in recent years (p. 94). It is a token paragraph, the key sentences of which are:

They [Negroes] *have made lasting contributions in science, government, and education. They have contributed significantly in the fields of music and literature.*

This is *tokenism,* to be sure, but it is *there;* in 1952, even tokenism was not required.

The third important addition concerns the Fourteenth Amendment. (Neither of the two editions bothers to discuss the Thirteenth Amendment, which freed Negroes from slavery.) The first edition contains about two pages on the Fourteenth Amendment, but quotes only its first sentence, which states that everyone born or naturalized in the U.S. is a citizen. It manages to omit any mention of Negroes or of "equal protection of the law." The second edition (pp. 220–221) rectifies this error, stating that most important section of the Amendment and giving examples of its use by courts, including three involving Negro rights.

Thus, the changes in nine years are not great. The 1961 text clearly is not adequate in its treatment of the black man, but it is a definite improvement over its 1952 forerunner, and reflects changes in attitude which had already occurred among the vast majority of Americans.

Before drawing any more conclusions, let's examine two editions (1961 and 1966) of another textbook, *Building Citizenship,*[22] and see what we find. (There was also a 1965 edition, which is of interest only for the minor

---

[21] Is the phrase "often are said" a device that was added to attain greater objectivity? Or was it added to calm objections to the phrase, "acclaimed the world over as the most original of all American music," which occurred in the first edition?

[22] This text has been in use for a long time. The original author is Ray Osgood Hughes (Allyn & Bacon, Boston); its revisions, 1961 and 1966, are due to C. H. W. Pullen and James H. McCrocklin, the latter being responsible for both of the versions considered here.

differences between it and the 1966 edition. See footnote 26.) These editions were published only five years apart; yet there are interesting and
important differences in their treatment of the American Negro (although
in general there are very few other significant differences between the two).

The major change between the two editions is in photographs. There are
fifty-three such changes, out of hundreds of pictures (at least one photo-
graph, often more, appears on nearly every page). Of these, thirty-eight
show one or more persons recognizably Negro. Typical is the photo (p.
251) of a smiling Negro boy holding up a large fish he's just caught, which
replaces a picture of a smiling white boy doing exactly the same thing (the
caption remains the same).

Of the fifteen changes in which Negroes are not pictured, most are required by changing events (the new Supreme Court instead of the old; a
more current replacement for *Senator* Lyndon Johnson). Even so, over
two-thirds of the photo changes replace all-white scenes with ones that are
racially mixed (in one case, all black). In almost all of these changes, the
caption remains the same, because the picture's topic remains the same
(students in a classroom, a business conference, a nurse in action, policemen on duty, etc.). It should be mentioned that not one definitely recog-
nizable black face is pictured in the earlier (1961) edition. (There are two
or three borderline cases.)

Negroes are mentioned significantly about six or seven times in the 1961
edition, but over twenty times in the edition of 1966. It is true, however,
that most of these changes are one-liners. (We don't want to give the impression that the changes in the 1966 edition are more substantial than
they are.)

Still, they are interesting, even if only token gestures. Let's illustrate by
a bit of comparison shopping.

In the 1961 edition (p. 286), we read:

> *Some people found fault with Theodore Roosevelt because they said*
> *he acted as if he had discovered the Ten Commandments. Quite likely,*
> *however, many more people became interested in applying the Ten*
> *Commandments to present day life because they admired something*
> *in "T.R."*

This is changed in the 1966 edition (same page, same exact spot on the
page)[23] to read:

[23] Most pages in this text read word for word the same in both editions, and are in
the very same type. The photos represent the only change that would justify a new
edition. This should be noted in assessing the changes concerning Negroes.

Some people find fault with [brace yourself] *Martin Luther King because he acts as if he had discovered the Ten Commandments. Quite likely, however, many more people have become interested in applying the Ten Commandments to present day life because they admire Dr. King's fight against racial discrimination.*

If there is any other reason for downgrading poor old "T.R." than the authors' desire to say something about Negroes (without getting too specific), it's hard to imagine what it is.

Masons and miners get eliminated à la Teddy Roosevelt in a discussion of causes of unemployment (p. 477). In 1961, we read: "The work of masons and miners, for example, is 'seasonal.'" This is changed in the 1966 edition to: "Racial discrimination sometimes illegally prevents individuals from getting jobs."

Several of the 1961 references to Negroes have been changed in the later edition. After mentioning good old Booker T. Washington and Tuskegee Institute, the 1961 version states (p. 204): "Poets, musicians, lawyers, doctors, and skilled tradesmen **of whom we are all proud** have arisen among the Negro people." Those too young to have seen former heavyweight champion Joe Louis in action aren't likely to appreciate the import of the phrase "of whom we are all proud." Mr. Louis (who, of course, was not then referred to in public as "Mr." Louis) almost always was introduced as "a credit to his race," or some such locution. The 1966 edition changes this passage to read: "Since their emancipation, outstanding Negroes have achieved in each major field of human endeavor." An odd locution, but it had to fit the space vacated by the sentence it replaced.

Material on the poll tax contains perhaps the most significant textual changes, at least for the theory that edition changes in general were just tacked-on token gestures, and not an attempt to portray life as it really is in America. The major change on the poll tax (p. 149) is simply deletion of the key paragraph (the one in which the term appears in italics and is explained), replaced by a paragraph on the sales tax. This seems innocent enough, and hardly connected to Negroes, since they aren't mentioned in either the deleted paragraph or its replacement. But this change begins to look peculiar when the reader follows a reference to Section 78 and discovers (p. 155) another paragraph on the sales tax which also seems to be the *key* paragraph on that tax. (For instance, it italicizes the term "sales tax," and uses that term in a sentence which makes its meaning clear.) The new paragraph on the sales tax, on p. 149, begins to look suspiciously like filler material.

But why did the paragraph on the poll tax have to be deleted or at least changed? The answer may be its last sentence (it contains only three others, all short):

> *Since people's wealth differs so much, this kind of tax does not agree with the principle of ability to pay;* **but taxes of this kind are seldom high enough to be a very great burden on anybody.**

The emphasized clause had to be changed, and not just because it is false. (It was just as false in 1961.) For it also contradicts two changes made elsewhere in the 1966 edition. The first is inserted into p. 18:

> *Our government is removing the last barriers which have kept many eligible Negroes from voting,* **such as poll taxes** *and literacy tests.*

The second is mention of the Twenty-fourth Amendment to the Constitution which abolishes poll taxes (p. 135):[24]

> *A few states required the payment of a poll tax before a person could vote. The Twenty-fourth Amendment, which was submitted to the states in 1962 and ratified in 1964, outlawed the poll tax as a voting requirement in federal elections. In many states a person may have to show that he can read, write, or understand the state constitution. New federal voting rights laws are designed to eliminate these provisions* **when they are used to prevent Negroes from voting.**

What we have shown so far is that two textbooks give greater and fairer treatment to Negroes in later editions than in earlier ones. If we were to compare the 1952 edition of the first text considered (*Your Life as a Citizen*) with the 1966 edition of the second text (*Building Citizenship*), this difference would be even more striking.

But two questions remain. First, why use the term "tokenism" even in reference to the 1966 text with all its pictures of Negroes and twenty-odd textual references? And second, why assume that the improved treatment of this minority group is due to the pressure of changed public opinion?

The first question is best answered by reference to what is omitted, as

---

[24] Obviously, we can't score the 1961 text for failing to mention a Constitutional amendment that didn't yet exist. But we can score it for failing to indicate the true intent of the poll tax, and for writing falsely about its effect.

well as by the one-line nature of most of the text changes. The 1966 text does not mention the 1954 Supreme Court decision outlawing segregated schools (omitted perhaps because segregated schools are not discussed), the KKK or White Citizen Councils, lynchings, segregated public facilities, and big-city ghettos. Of the few references to discrimination, most are made, as usual, in the process of explaining how they have been or are being eradicated. Finally, this text has room to discuss dozens of relatively unimportant governmental agencies, such as the National Youth Administration and Mothers' Pension Fund. It has room for the Knights of Labor, 4-H Clubs, The National Safety Council, Future Farmers of America, A.F. of L., C.I.O., C.C.C., National Grange, Universal Postal Union, American Farm Bureau Federation, R.O.T.C., and the good old P.T.A. But it discusses no Negro organizations in the text, and only one institution (Tuskegee Institute). A picture caption does describe Roy Wilkins (pictured with President Johnson at the 1964 Civil Rights signing) as "executive secretary of the National Association for the Advancement of Colored People." [25] But neither the N.A.A.C.P. nor any other group whose aim is the advancement of Negro rights is discussed in the text. Their existence or function is never explained.

Now let's deal with the second question: Why is it a fair assumption that better textbook treatment of blacks follows and results from the pressure of public opinion (rather than the reverse, as it should be if the function of schools is to teach the truth, not indoctrinate with the official story)?

In the first place, the nature of the textual and photo changes seems better explained by outside pressure than by any heartfelt need on the part of the authors (as we have gone to some pains to illustrate—think of the replacement of Teddy Roosevelt by Martin Luther King in the very same story). Even the existence of a 1966 edition seems to have no other explanation.

But equally important is the fact that textbook treatment of the Negro steadily improved after 1954, while that of other minorities did not, thus mirroring (with a small time-lag) the state of affairs in the United States in the last twenty years.

There are a great many groups discriminated against in the United States. But until a few years after the 1966 text was published, only one was a large center of controversy, and only one was the recipient of a publicly acknowledged and widespread "official" change in attitude. Americans in large numbers owned up to at least part of the evil of our treatment of

[25] The photo caption continues, "Looking on are some of the people who helped to steer the bill through Congress." And they are all white. The reader is left to wonder what Roy Wilkins or the N.A.A.C.P. have to do with passage of a Civil Rights bill.

blacks, and admitted it was wrong. In addition, Negroes have more political power than they did: an important fact, because they constitute over 10 percent of the population.

However, the situation did not change in this way for the other minority groups. There was publicity from time to time about them, but it never made a sufficient dent. The migrant laborer is a good example. So is that strange "minority" group, *women.*

We showed how discrimination against migrants and women was glossed over in one text (*American Civics*). It could be demonstrated for the two others we've considered as well. More importantly, it could be shown that no significant improvement occurred in the textual treatment of these groups from earlier to later editions. The job would be quite easy with respect to migrants, because, except for the two sentences referred to in Section d, above, they aren't mentioned at all in earlier *or* later editions of either text. It would be easy with respect to Mexican-Americans, Puerto Ricans on the mainland (for example, in New York), and many other minority groups, for the same reason. Even the American Indian receives only insignificantly improved treatment in revised editions.[26]

All of this does not prove the thesis at issue. But it does provide significant evidence. When public opinion and political pressure began to turn in favor of the Negro after remaining the same for many years, blacks then received fairer coverage in civics texts (in history texts too, although we haven't provided evidence of that). But during the period in question, public opinion and political pressure did not change nearly as much with respect to other minority groups. And textbook coverage of these groups in turn did not change as much as did that of the Negro.

The main thesis of the chapter has been that civics is taught in secondary schools chiefly to indoctrinate, and not to teach the truth about how our nation operates. We centered on one aspect of this indoctrination: the glossing over of our unfairness to minority groups. (See the summary, below.)

The textbooks of, say, 1976 will provide a good test of these theses, in particular the one which states that textbooks lag behind public opinion

[26] Additional evidence is furnished by examination of the 1965 edition of the text, *Building Citizenship.* This edition has some of the textual changes (from the 1961 edition) concerning Negroes which occur also in the 1966 edition. But the major difference between it and the 1966 edition, and apparently the only reason a 1966 edition was required, is in illustrations. Of the fifteen picture changes between 1961 and 1966 which do not concern Negroes, all but two occur in the 1965 edition. But not one of the thirty-eight changes which picture Negroes in the 1966 edition occurs in the 1965 edition. The picture changes from 1965 to 1966 seem best explained as an attempt to bring up to the level of public opinion a text which was sadly lagging behind.

and only change in response to it. For, subsequent to 1966 (the latest copyright date of any of the texts discussed), a great deal of agitation has occurred and is occurring on behalf of other minority groups. This is true particularly for migrants (think only of Cesar Chavez and the grape boycott), women, and American Indians. Of the three, women have the greatest political clout, simply because of their large number. It is reasonable to expect, then, that by about 1976 civics texts will have caught up with this change in public opinion and political reality, and will deal more equitably with these groups (in particular, women).

Summary of Chapter Eight

Given the content of primary and secondary school textbooks, it seems reasonable to conclude that history and civics are taught to indoctrinate as much as to furnish students with the truth about our nation. In defense of this thesis we demonstrated that:

1. Their "objective" tone is used to present as an objective *fact* the idea that we as a nation have, and still do, lived up to our high ideals.
2. This impression is enhanced by omission of the sordid in our past and our failings in the present—in other words, by *distortion* and by *suppression of evidence*. In particular, minority groups are dealt with poorly.
   a. American Indians tend to be "invisible" in history and civics texts, and the theft of their land by the white man played down or ignored. The same is true of the white man's massacre and subjugation of the Indian.
   b. American Negroes also tend to be invisible, except during the Civil War period. The evils of slavery are glossed over, as are the evils of the segregation and discrimination which developed after slavery was abolished. Indeed, in many cases, the very existence of a particular type of segregation or discrimination goes unmentioned unless and until it is in process of being eliminated.
   c. The plight of the migrant farm laborer is ignored in most civics texts. Indeed, many texts ignore migrants entirely.
   d. Civics texts generally fail to report discrimination against women in the U.S. For instance, they fail to indicate that women frequently receive less money than men for the same jobs. In addition, they contain the same stereotypes of the male and female roles: Men become doctors and engineers; women become nurses and secretaries.

Exercise for Chapter Eight

In college, the subject matter dealt with in high school civics classes becomes the province of political science and (to some extent) other social science courses. Along with this change in title, there is a broadening of subject matter and a change in motive. Indoctrination with the "American way" surely is not attempted in the typical social science course or text. But some social science texts still display a few of the defects we have been discussing, including an "objectivism" which hides a controversial point of view, distortion of the difference between theory and practice (often by ignoring practice that doesn't conform to theory), and an unconscious bias against certain groups (e.g., women). College history texts also often display these defects.

Examine one of your history, political science, or other relevant social science texts (or get one from the library) for evidence of bias, distortion, suppressed evidence, or "textbook objectivity," and write a brief paper on your findings. Be sure to *argue* (present evidence) for your conclusions, trying, of course, to avoid fallacious argument.

Chapter Nine

Textbooks and Fallacies

> Those who corrupt the public mind are just as evil as those who steal from the public purse.
> **Adlai Stevenson**

Textbooks contain about as many fallacies as most other writings. And their fallacies run nearly the whole range, omitting those involving strong emotions and (usually) *ad hominems*. But most of the time, they are guilty of the same few fallacies over and over. In addition, textbooks tend to employ fallacies in a rather subdued way. They aren't permitted, after all, to call Drew Pearson a liar, even if he's been called one by several presidents and countless senators. And when they finally get around to the women's liberation movement, they won't be able to dismiss the ladies as a "small band of bra-less bubbleheads." Nevertheless, the fallacies they commit are just as real and just as damaging.

1. *Distortion and suppressed evidence.* The fallacies most frequently committed by textbooks are, of course, *distortion* and *suppressed evidence*. In the last chapter we documented those two fallacies at length. So let's skip their further discussion as basic categories, and discuss just one interesting variation on the fallacy of *distortion*.

2. *Graph distortion.* Although less common in textbooks than it once was, **graph distortion** still occurs.

Your Life as a Citizen (1952 edition, p. 241) contains a typical example. A graph illustrating the increase in numbers of working women caused mainly by World War II depicts the increase between 1940 and 1950 by drawings of two women. The smaller figure represents the 1940 female work force, the larger figure the 1950 female work force. The figures are correctly labeled with the numbers 12,000,000 and 17,700,000, respectively, and the *height* of the second figure is about one-third greater than that of the first, correctly reflecting the difference between 12 million and 17.7 million. But their difference in *gross size* completely falsifies that ratio; the second figure appears to be well over twice the size of the first figure. (The reason for this is the geometric fact that area increases geometrically, not arithmetically. The area of a two-inch square is four square inches; the area of a four-inch square is sixteen square inches, not eight square inches.)

This same sort of geometric distortion occurs in at least five graphs in another text.[1] In one of these graphs, a soldier six times the height of another was used to illustrate the sixfold increase in manpower in the U.S. Armed Forces during World War II. In another, a ship almost 10 times as long as another ship was used to illustrate the WW II tenfold increase in total number of U.S. ships.

The *cutoff graph* also is used, on occasion. A typical textbook use of the cutoff graph[2] distorted the U.S. national budget for each year from 1953 to 1963 by cutting the first 50 billion dollars off the bottom of the chart. This gave the reader a distorted visual impression of the size of the change from year to year, because that change was not visually measured against the total national budget, but only against any excess of 50 billion dollars. Another chart omitted the first 5 billion of our gold reserves in illustrating the dollar drain.

3.   *Provincialism.* Though this fallacy wasn't explicitly mentioned by name there, the previous chapter illustrated the extreme provincialism which characterizes our history and civics texts, and how this provincialism results in distortion of facts. Recall, for instance, the treatment, in Allen and Howland, of the settling of the Ohio country; it "brought good luck" to the settlers, with no mention of "bad luck" to the Indians. But because this fallacy is so widespread, let's consider two more examples.

Most textbooks are guilty of the fallacy of *provincialism* in their treatment of the Russian role in World War II. The grade school text by Allen and Howland again is a good example. Since this text has a little less than two pages on WW II (pp. 330–331), it can't give many details; but the reader is left with the impression that the U.S. did all of the winning in that war. Our British ally is not mentioned at all, even as a mere participant, nor is our Russian ally—except later, in passing, in another context (p. 333):

---

[1] *This Is Our Nation,* by Paul F. Boller, Jr. and E. Jean Tilford, Webster Publishing Co., 1961.

[2] In *The United States: Story of a Free People,* by Samuel Steinberg, Allyn and Bacon, Inc., Boston, 1964, pp. 632 and 640.

The United States and Russia had fought together against Germany in WW II. Soon after the war Russia helped to force a communist form of government. . . .

But this text does have room to discuss the rise of the Communist dictatorship under Stalin (p. 330), the Cold War as an ideological fight against Communism (pp. 332–333), and NATO as a response to the Communist threat in Europe. No doubt, it will be suggested that this poor coverage is due to the small amount of space a grade school text can allow for such a complex event as WW II. And it is true that high school texts have more space and do a better job on this topic. But the improvement is still not sufficient to remove the charge of provincialism.

An example is the high school text[3] which devotes over sixteen pages (pp. 722–739) primarily to our part in WW II, including about five pages on the European-theater battles, but only has ten *sentences* on the entire Russian effort in that war. (This text also uses more space on the Yalta meeting and agreement than on the entire Russian War effort [pp. 736–737].) It lists our casualties in WW II and all of our other wars (p. 737). But it fails to contrast our WW II deaths, 405,399, almost all of military men on active duty, with the *millions* of Russian deaths. (Estimates of Russians killed in WW II range as high as 20 million, but no one really knows more than roughly.) It fails to mention that as a result of WW II many more Russian women and children died than did all the soldiers in all the wars in our entire history. (Can anyone understand the post-World War II period who does not know these vital facts?)

This text also fails to convey the fact that it was the Russian military forces which ground down most of the German army. Instead, it creates the impression (the same provincial falsehood conveyed by almost every history textbook written in the United States) that the United States military (in some texts the U.S. with a little British help) inflicted far more damage on the German military machine than did everyone else.

Well, perhaps this provincial treatment of World War II is due to the fact that these texts are histories of the *United States*. Do world-history texts give a less provincial account? Unfortunately, the answer seems to be "no." Consider an average world-history text,[4] which devotes twenty-six pages to World War II. Its "Keynote" section on WW II (p. 636) men-

[3] *Our American Nation,* by T. Harry Williams and Hazel C. Wolf, Charles Merrill Books, Inc., Columbus, Ohio, 1966.
[4] *A World History,* by Daniel Roselle, Ginn and Co., Boston, 1966.

tions as "Key People" in that war Winston Churchill, Franklin Roosevelt, General Erwin Rommel, and three American generals, but no Russians. It mentions fourteen "Key Places," none of them in Russia, but does mention two places (Finland and Poland) which were victims of Russian aggression. It lists six "Key Events," none of which concerns the Russian war effort.

The treatment in the body of the text is better, but still one-sided. The treatment of Germany's invasion of Russia prior to discussion of our entrance into the war (pp. 643–644) is about average (two paragraphs). It does mention "merciless bombing," "periods of **near** starvation," "terrible losses," "heroic defenses at Stalingrad and other cities," and ends by stating that "Russian armies were preparing counter-offensives to force the Germans to surrender."

But then it is time to discuss the U.S. participation in WW II, and all else shrinks into the background. Almost a page is spent on Pearl Harbor. D-day receives well over half a page. The Russians get these two sentences (p. 648): "**Meanwhile**, the Russians pushed back the Germans in the east. . . ." "And the Russians, under Marshal Zhukov, pushed on toward Berlin."

A map (on p. 646) correctly shows arrows converging towards the center of Germany, illustrating the armies advancing from the east (Russian) and south and west (British and American). But the caption above the map gives away the textbook's *provincialism:* "To combat the Axis, the Allies launched an invasion in North Africa and then in Sicily and Southern Italy. Finally, Allied forces invaded France." No mention whatever of Russian attacks in the East, which were launched against the most powerful segment of the German Army.

World War II and its immediate aftermath constitutes one of the most important periods in U.S. history. Almost all high school textbooks provide several of the basic facts, such as the viciousness of the Nazis, their initial successes and final defeat, the Japanese defeat, and postwar Communist violations of the Yalta agreements and their subjugation of Eastern Europe.

But *provincialism,* perhaps because of a desire to picture American troops as superior to all others, results in the omission of two extremely important facts about WW II, without which the postwar world cannot be adequately understood. The first, again, is the terrible punishment dealt Russia in that war (they suffered about as many deaths as all the other combatants combined). The second is that from June 1941, when Germany invaded Russia, until at least the last weeks of the war, the largest part of the German military machine always was concentrated on the Russian front; it was Russian military forces which defeated and destroyed that strongest segment of the German military machine (with the aid of much American equipment). The Russian role in defeating Hitler was much larger than ours, their suffering incomparably greater, and we should not let textbook provincialism obscure these points.

One last little example of textbook provincialism, away from current controversies. The grade school text, Allen and Howland, previously mentioned, has a section in its discussion of the Spanish-American War titled "A Splendid Little War," which states in part:

> It seemed so to **Americans** back home who were reading in their newspapers thrilling stories from the battle front. To **American** soldiers suffering in tropical heat . . . and dying of yellow fever, the war was anything but splendid.

All well and good. But don't *enemy* soldiers suffer in tropical heat and die of yellow fever? And what of the *Spanish* people and their government? The text is silent on these points.

4. *Ambiguity.* Most civics texts and many history texts start out with a section on democracy and freedom. They contain broad, unqualified statements such as the following:[5]

> We have the right to speak and to write freely, to go to school, to choose our occupations, to live wherever we desire, to join any church we like, and to do many other things without interference of any government.

This is the *theory,* the "official story" of how our system works. But many of us learn sooner or later that actual *practice* often is much different from theory. Negroes find that they cannot live in many areas; migrants, that their children aren't given much more than token schooling; and Jews, Negroes, and many others, that certain occupations discriminate against them.

But did the quoted passage refer to the *theory,* the ideal, of our system, or to actual practice? It is very hard, if not impossible, to tell. On this point, the text in question is guilty of the fallacy of *ambiguity.* In most

---

[5] From *Our Democracy at Work,* by Harris G. Warren, Harry D. Leinenweber, and Ruth O. M. Anderson, Prentice-Hall, Inc., 1963, p. 2.

texts, passages of this kind can be construed either way. The reader is not told that this is the theory, but actual practice is something else. He generally is left with the *impression* that theory and practice coincide. The few examples, encountered later in the text, of practices contrary to the bold pronouncements at the beginning may convince the perceptive reader that it is theory, not practice, that the author had in mind. But this is just the reader's guess; many students very likely never notice the problem at all.

5. *Inconsistency.* An equally likely explanation for the difference just cited is that the textbooks in question are just plain *inconsistent.* Since we cannot know for sure what is in the minds of textbook writers, we cannot state in each case whether a text is inconsistent or simply trading on the ambiguity of key statements about freedom and democracy. Perhaps the correct answer is inconsistency in some cases and ambiguity in others.

But in some texts, the scales are tipped toward *inconsistency,* because inconsistencies crop up in related topics. One civics text,[6] which contains the usual statements on freedom and democracy, has an interesting section on "The American Way Versus the Communist Way" (pp. 269–273). It compares economic systems, labeling ours a "free economy" and theirs a "command economy." The comparison, of course, is very flattering to us, and unflattering to the Communists' command economy. The reader is given to understand that our free system is far superior, both in theory and practice.

But the section ends with three paragraphs, intended perhaps to make better "cold warriors" of American students, but nevertheless inconsistent with what has gone before. These paragraphs cite "rapid gains" in Soviet industry, and "advances" in science and education, citing Sputnik I as an instance. In the last paragraph, we read:

> *The Soviet leaders have proved that a command economy may be a threat to our American way of life. If the United States is to continue to be the greatest nation in the world, we cannot sit back and relax our efforts.*

The reader is left to wonder why so much effort will be needed to stay ahead of the Communists if our system is so superior to theirs.

6. *Misleading statistics.* A typical example of the fallacy of *misleading statistics* occurs in the first edition of the text *Building Citizenship,* dis-

---

[6] *American Civics,* by William H. Hartley and William S. Vincent, Harcourt Brace Jovanovich, New York, 1967.

cussed in the previous chapter. In a section on "Who owns America's corporations?" (p. 268), it answers:

The Stockholders. But who are the stockholders? . . . The typical American stockholder . . . is under 40, married, has two children, and owns his own home. He goes to church on Sunday . . . and makes less than $9500 a year. . . . There are now more than 20 million stockholders in America. Another 100 million Americans are indirect stockholders, . . . because they have put their savings in life insurance, pension funds, or mutual savings banks.

The statistics cited in this passage no doubt are correct. But the passage inevitably is going to mislead students about the true nature of our system. For it gives the erroneous impression that American corporations are *controlled* by millions of Americans (the quoted passage occurs a few inches away from one in which the voting rights of common stockholders are mentioned). And it glosses over the utterly immense wealth that stock ownership gives to a very few in the U.S. The reader is given correct information, but he is seriously misled nevertheless.

The main reason he is misled is, of course, suppression of pertinent evidence. The student needs to know that "the top 2 percent of all American families own between two-thirds and three-quarters of all corporate stock, and . . . the top 2 percent of all income receivers enjoy incomes roughly ten times larger than the average received within the nation as a whole." [7] He needs to know that some of the 100 million living on pension funds, or life insurance, are living on the edge of poverty. The *average* income of stockholders is a relatively useless statistic all by itself.

A description of a "typical" stockholder is a foolish idea anyway, since stockholders differ so much one from another. We might just as well describe a typical animal as having a hard outer shell and six legs, since insects are so numerous: It is just as misleading to describe the typical stockholder as a married, home-owning churchgoer who makes less than $9500 per year.

7. *Use of stereotypes.* Textbooks make frequent use of misleading stereotypes, starting with Negroes and their spirituals, and cowboys and Indians. (One dictionary uses the cowboys and Indians bit as its example of stereotype.) But the use of stereotypes goes far beyond the cowboys and Indians category. The 1961 edition of *Your Life as a Citizen* (p. 303), in

[7] Robert Heilbroner, *The Limits of American Capitalism,* Harper and Row, New York, 1965.

a section titled "Do boys' interests differ from girls'?", answers that question by saying:

> *Each person's interests differ from every other person's. In addition, boys' interests as a group tend to be somewhat different from girls'. Boys, for example, tend to lean toward technical interests, **interests in things rather than persons**. Girls, on the other hand, **lean toward artistic interests** and **interests having to do with people, particularly how they think and feel.***

These are stereotypes, and like most stereotypes, are false or at least not proven.

What evidence is there that boys are any less interested in people than girls? And since almost all of the great artists in history and the majority of performers have been men, what reason is there to assume that girls more than boys lean towards artistic interests? The answer is the stereotype of fragile girls in frilly dresses sitting at the piano or gathered together playing house with their dolls and tea sets, while the future he-men are outside hunting, fishing, or climbing trees. How many men are there (this writer is one) who were surprised to find as they grew up that ballet and Mozart are not "sissy" things that only girls are interested in, but rather vibrant, alive, *human* arts?

8. *Dick and Jane ambiguity.* Let's end our discussion of textbook fallacies with a minor one which applies mainly to primary school textbooks. The sentences in most primary school texts are mostly written in simple subject-predicate form. Though there are many exceptions, even these are short sentences. In particular, there is an absence of compound sentences containing connecting words such as "because," "therefore," "however," etc.

This causes problems, **because** (as this very sentence indicates) compound sentences formed by words like "because" frequently are used in "grown-up" English to indicate *causal connections.* The "Dick and Jane" sentence-simplicity of most primary school texts makes for many fewer uses of these connections. The trouble is that *sentence juxtaposition* then becomes the primary way of indicating these connections. And, of course, this leads to *ambiguity.* Does the fact that a given sentence follows another one indicate a causal connection or doesn't it? Here is an example from Allen and Howland, the primary school text we've been considering (p. 330):

> *During World War I there had been a revolution in Russia. Russia turned to a form of government called communism. Only one political*

party was allowed, the Communist party. The leader of this party ran the government. The government owned and controlled almost everything. The Russian people had to do just as the government said. During the 1920s a dictator named Joseph Stalin became head of the Russian government.

All of which is more or less true if read sentence by sentence. But there is a natural tendency to suppose that sentences following one another may be connected, a tendency vastly increased by Dick and Jane sentence structure, leading the student to conclude perhaps that communism's coming to power *causes* dictatorship by the leader of the Communist party. The text does not say this, but it is an easy inference to draw from what it does say, plus the order in which the sentences occur. A student of, say, the early 1960s who made such an inference when reading Allen & Howland may well have responded differently to the 1970 Chilean elections (in which a communist was elected in a relatively free election) than he otherwise would have. If so, chalk up another triumph for Dick and Jane!

One final example before leaving textbooks for good. We have stated several times that the textbooks we've been dealing with are somewhere around average in quality. We cited a few much-better-than-average texts, although we didn't discuss them. But we haven't said anything about *bad* textbooks, and so the reader may suspect that some of the texts we have considered aren't average at all but rather belong in the well-below-average camp. To dispel any such idea, we offer one example from a fourth grade textbook that no doubt does merit the label below average:[8]

As you ride up beside the Negroes in the field they stop working long enough to look up, tip their hats and say, "Good morning, Master John." You like the friendly way they speak and smile; they show bright rows of white teeth. "How's it coming, Sam?", your father asks one of the old Negroes. "Fine, Marse Tom, jes fine. We got more cotton than we can pick." Then Sam chuckles to himself and goes back to picking as fast as he can.

If that sort of writing doesn't make *Your Life as a Citizen* look good then nothing will.

---

[8] Mentioned in the TRB column, the *New Republic*, July 25, 1970, and best left anonymous here.

Summary of Chapter Nine

Textbooks contain fallacies about as often as other writings, although they generally do so in a subdued way (they can't call Drew Pearson a liar).

1. The fallacies textbooks are most often guilty of are *distortion* and its companion *suppressed evidence*. (These general fallacy categories were documented in Chapter Eight.)
2. In addition to the standard varieties of *distortion*, textbooks sometimes employ *graph distortion*, which consists in misleading the reader by the way a graph is constructed.
    Example: The graph depicting the increase in female employment during WW II used drawings of two women to illustrate the increase; the figures were accurate in relative height but far from accurate in relative *area*, the more striking visual feature.
3. Textbooks also are guilty of large-scale *provincialism*.
    Example: Their treatment of the Russian role in World War II as compared to the American role.
4. They also are guilty of *ambiguity*.
    Example: It often is unclear in civics texts whether statements about freedom and equality are meant to tell the reader about American ideals or about actual practice.
5. Textbooks occasionally are guilty of the fallacy of *inconsistency*, although often ambiguity makes it impossible to be certain about this.
    Example: The civics texts which extolled the virtues of the American "free economy" and decried the defects of the Soviet "command economy," but then concluded by stating that the Soviet command economy posed a threat to our system.
6. Textbooks sometimes cite misleading statistics.
    Example: The statistic that the typical American stockholder makes $9500 per year.
7. They also make use of stereotypes.
    Example: Boys are interested in things rather than persons. Girls are interested in the arts and in persons.
8. Grade school texts tend to be written in "Dick and Jane" English: short sentences which do not contain words such as "because," "therefore," etc. The result is that sentence juxtaposition often is taken by the student to indicate causal connection.
    Example: A sentence about the rise of communism in Russia, followed by a sentence stating that the leader of the Communist party ran the government in Russia, which gave the impression that the com-

ing of communism to power *causes,* or is inevitably followed by, a dictatorship of the communist leader.

Exercise for the entire text

We've spent the last two chapters attempting to show that primary and secondary school textbooks are not models of correct inquiry. College texts (in the opinion of this author) are far superior. But college textbook writers are human, too, the present writer unfortunately not excepted. This text, as all others, has presuppositions (only some of them made explicit), and no doubt contains fallacious reasoning in spite of the author's best efforts to reason cogently. So, as a final exercise, write a brief critique of this textbook with respect to (1) its major presuppositions, and (2) possible fallacious arguments. (Be sure to *argue* for your findings.) And then, as part three of your paper, evaluate the presuppositions you discovered, and if you find them faulty, explain what (if anything) you would put in their place.

Appendix A

Valid Argument

The body of this text has concentrated on the detection of fallacious argument and the avoidance of false belief. Let's concentrate in this appendix on *valid* argument, the fundamental element of nonfallacious (correct) reasoning.

1. Two basic kinds of valid argument

Valid arguments divide into two main categories, *deductive* and *inductive*.[1] The essential property of a **valid deductive argument** is this: *If its premises are true, then its conclusion must be true also.* To put it another way, if the premises of a valid deductive argument are true, then its conclusion *cannot be false.*[2]

On the other hand, a **valid inductive argument** provides good *but not conclusive* grounds for the acceptance of its conclusion. The truth of the premises of a valid inductive argument does *not* guarantee the truth of its conclusion, although it does make the conclusion *probable.* (That's why the term "probability argument" often is used instead of "inductive argument.")

---

[1] The expression "valid inductive argument" has many meanings. It is used here as a near synonym for "valid but not deductive."

[2] Notice that this definition of valid deductive argument is so broad that it covers *arithmetic* reasoning also.

Here is an example of a valid inductive argument:

Premise:	1.	*So far, very few presidents of U.S. colleges and universities have been brilliant intellectuals.*

Conclusion:	2.	*Very few future presidents of U.S. colleges and universities will be brilliant intellectuals.*

There may be a few readers who will want to deny the truth of the premise of this argument. But even they will have to admit that *if* they were to accept it as true (on good grounds), then it would be reasonable to accept the argument's conclusion also. And yet, it is conceivable that the conclusion is false, even though the premise is true. For it is *conceivable,* however unlikely, that boards of overseers, regents, and state legislators change in time in a way which results in the selection of more intellectual college presidents.

Contrast the above inductive argument with the following *deductive* argument:

Premises:	1.	*Every U.S. president has gone against his principles at least once.*
	2.	*John Kennedy is[3] a U.S. President.*

Conclusion:	3.	*John Kennedy has gone against his principles at least once.*

Assuming for the moment that the first premise is true (we all know the second premise is true), it is *inconceivable* that the conclusion be false. It would be *inconsistent* to believe both premises yet deny the conclusion.

We have here the fundamental difference between deductive and inductive reasoning: The conclusion of a valid deductive argument is just as certain as its premises; the conclusion of a valid inductive argument is less certain than its premises. The negation of the conclusion of a valid deductive argument *contradicts* its premises; this is not true for inductive arguments. An inductive argument attaches to its conclusion an extra element of doubt (however slight) that does not adhere to its premises. Deductive arguments do not do this.

---

[3] Tense doesn't matter in this case.

2. More on the difference between inductive and deductive argument

Before proceeding to an examination of inductive reasoning, perhaps it would be wise to discuss a widespread but erroneous idea about the difference between induction and deduction. This is the idea that in deductive reasoning we proceed from the general to the particular, while in inductive reasoning we go from the particular to the general. This is false, because both kinds of reasoning proceed sometimes from the particular to the particular, sometimes from the particular to the general, sometimes from the general to the particular, and sometimes from the general to the general.

For instance, the valid deductive argument that infers from "All Democrats are grafters" to "All nongrafters are non-Democrats" goes from the general to the equally general. And the deductive argument from "Nixon is dishonest and successful" to "Nixon is successful" goes from the particular to the equally particular. So it is incorrect to say that *all* deductive arguments move from the general to the particular, although many do.

Similarly, it is incorrect to say that all inductive arguments move from the particular to the general, although some do. The valid inductive inference from "Nixon made promises in 1960 and 1968 he didn't intend to keep" to "Nixon will make promises in 1972 he doesn't intend to keep" moves from the particular to the *particular,* not from the particular to the general. And the inference from "All Democratic candidates so far have conned the electorate" to "The next Democrat who runs for office will con the electorate" moves from the general to the particular, not the other way around.

So there isn't any truth to this old idea about the difference between deduction and induction. The difference instead rests, roughly, on the fact that the conclusion of a valid deductive argument is, as we said before, just as certain as its premises, while a new possibility of error attaches to the conclusion of a valid inductive argument, over and above any doubt concerning its premises.

3. Valid inductive argument

Deductive logic is a very well worked-out branch of knowledge, an area in which the fundamentals are generally agreed upon. Inductive logic is another matter. This fact is unfortunate for us, because most everyday reasoning about political matters (in fact most everyday reasoning about any topic) is largely nondeductive.[4] So we need to say a few words about inductive logic, in spite of the controversial nature of almost everything we will say.

a. Low-level induction by enumeration. This is the simplest kind of inductive inference, and according to some experts the foundation of all the rest. In simple **induction by enumeration**, we infer from the fact that all *A*s observed so far are *B*s to the conclusion that all *A*s whatsoever are *B*s. For instance, a study of 100 senators and congressmen which revealed that all 100 misused their franking privilege would constitute good evidence for the inductive conclusion that *all* senators and congressmen misuse their franking privilege.[5] Similarly, if we check 15 secondary school civics texts published by major textbook houses, and find that they all falsify the difference between American ideals and actual practice (this is an actual case), then we are justified in concluding that all such texts falsify the difference in America between ideals and practice.

Obviously, some inductions of this kind are better than others. Unfortunately, there is no agreement about how to determine the **probability** attaching to the conclusion of an induction by simple enumeration. However, there is agreement on a few general points:

1. The more instances in a sample, the greater the probability of the conclusion. If our sample of textbooks had included 20 civics texts instead of 15, and if we had checked the mailing habits of 200 congressmen instead of 100, the conclusions we arrived at would be more probable.

2. Some theorists claim that we must consider not merely the size of the sample, but its size *relative* to the population from which it is drawn. And this does seem right with respect to cases in which the population in question is rather small. For instance, if the total number of civics texts put out by major publishers (the "population") totals 25, our sample of 15 constitutes much better evidence than if major publishers put out 50 civics texts.

3. Also, the *type* of instance is important. It won't do to ignore the

---

[4] Deductive inferences that do arise in daily life often are so trivial that they are omitted as understood. For instance, the Republican candidate who spends half an hour blasting the Democrats as pinko liberals and then points out that his opponent is a Democratic party regular doesn't ordinarily bother to come right out and call his opponent a pinko liberal. He leaves that obvious deductive conclusion to be drawn by members of his audience, who are quite able to do so for themselves, surprising as that may seem to logic teachers who have watched countless beginners in logic flub the same kind of reasoning on logic exams.

[5] The day after this was written, the author received a franked letter from a senator thanking him for a campaign contribution. So make that a sample of 101 senators and congressmen!

civics texts of a particular major publisher if we have any reason to suspect
that that company's texts might be better than the rest on the difference
between ideals and practice. Similarly, we don't want our sample of congressmen to contain only Republicans, or only Democrats, because of the
possibility (slim) that one party is more dedicated to thievery than the
other.

4. One *definite* counter-example to an enumerative induction shoots
it down. For instance, if we run across even one congressman who resists
the temptation to use his franking privilege to woo the voters back home,
then our theory that *all* congressmen abuse the franking privilege obviously
is false.

The problem is how to know for sure that a counter-instance is genuine.
Is the angelic-appearing congressman really on the square? Or is he just
clever at the game? Unless we examine all of his mail, which in practice
is impossible, we just can't be sure. That he is a counter-example to our
theory is itself a probability, which is one reason why two or more counter-
instances are better than one, and also why apparently disconfirmed theories
(theories for which there are apparent counter-instances) sometimes turn
out to be correct.

b. Higher-level induction by enumeration. There are two kinds of
higher-level enumerative induction. The first kind amounts merely to a
check on a particular kind of lower-level induction by enumeration. For
instance, if we use induction by enumeration to check up on our success
rate with lower-level inductions concerning election predictions, we might
discover that a certain political pundit who predicts the results of political
contests by "intuition" and "hunch" is more successful than the Gallup
Poll. We then could use higher-level induction to predict that he will out-
perform the Gallup Poll in future.

This sort of higher-level checking on lower-level inductions such as those
employed by the Gallup Poll is risky and should be avoided if other evidence is available. But in the absence of such evidence, it is legitimate.

The second kind of higher-level enumerative induction concerns the use
of one inductively supported theory to correct or support another one. Suppose, for instance, we find that every one of ten men convicted of rape
turns out to be an avid reader of pornography. This constitutes good low-
level evidence that pornography is a cause of rape. We could then test this
conclusion by looking into the reading habits of more rapists. But we can
do a better job by trying to determine *why* there might be (or perhaps why
there is not) such a connection. If we find, say, that children in a psychological experiment play more violently after seeing violence on TV, and
discover that in their youth convicted criminals in general read a great deal
of violent comic books and witnessed much violence on radio and TV,
then we might reason from these results to the conclusion that human

beings tend to mirror what they see and read. And this in turn would constitute evidence that men who read about sexual activities unavailable to them through ordinary means may be more likely to use unusual means such as rape.

On the other hand, by this test we might find that children exposed to violence on TV are less violent than those who don't watch the tube. And we might find that convicted criminals have been exposed to less violence in books and on the airwaves than the rest of us. Such results could be construed as evidence for the theory that exposure to simulated violence acts to "release" energy which might otherwise be directed toward violent activities. This would support a more general "release" theory applying to "sexual energy" also, which in turn would contradict the low-level induction that rape is linked to exposure to pornography.

It may seem strange that evidence about the behavior of children exposed to TV violence could be more important in deciding whether there is a link between pornography and rape than checking up on the habits of more rapists. But the explanation is fairly simple. First, even if we find that, say, ten more rapists are pornography regulars, it still is always possible that the connection between the two is through a third factor which causes both. In other words, the desire to rape and the need to read pornography may both be caused by something else, perhaps sexual problems between the parents of those prone to rape. By going to a higher-level theory to *explain* (or correct) the low-level results, we reduce the possibility that an as yet undetected third factor causes the other two. And second, if we can confirm a theory about the connection (or lack of connection) between rape and pornography by showing it to be a special case of a more general theory, then we make *varieties* of evidence relevant that would not otherwise be relevant, thus greatly increasing the probability of our initial theory by increasing **instance variety**.

A classic case of this occurs in physics: Newton uses evidence about the tides, and about objects falling toward the earth, as evidence for his very general laws of motion. These laws in turn imply Kepler's laws which describe the orbits of the planets around the sun as ellipses of a certain kind.[6] So evidence about the motion of the tides and the velocity of objects falling toward the earth confirms Kepler's laws by confirming Newton's higher-level laws of which Kepler's are a special case. The relevance of the reading habits of the young to adult rape is thus no more mysterious than the relevance of the tides to Kepler's laws about planetary motion.

   c.   Analogical reasoning. We reason analogically when we infer from a past connection between *A*s and *B*s to a single future connection. Thus,

---

[6] Actually, Newton shows that Kepler's laws are only very close approximations.

having caught 100 congressmen and senators improperly using franked mail at election time, we can conclude by analogy that our incumbent opponent in a forthcoming election is going to campaign via franked mail and thus have an advantage over our side.

Reasoning by analogy is safer than straight induction by enumeration, since the only difference between the two is that analogies have much weaker conclusions. For example, we inferred above that *one particular* congressman would abuse his right to free official mail, which clearly is far safer than predicting that all congressmen will abuse that privilege.

All of what we said about how to determine the probability of an induction by enumeration applies equally to analogies. The conclusion of an analogy is more probable if we have more instances in its support or have greater instance variety, and one fairly definite counter-example shoots it down entirely.

d. Statistical induction. Suppose that instead of misuse of the franking privilege, we were to investigate the kind of improper use of funds that resulted in the Senate censure of Senator Dodd of Connecticut. We are almost certain to find that some senators and congressmen don't seem ever to engage in that kind of thievery. Checking on 100 incumbents, we might find that only 68 seem ever to have engaged in such practices so far as we can tell. Then we can't conclude anything about what *all* incumbents do.

But we can conclude that about *68 percent* of all senators and congressmen improperly use government funds, based on the evidence that 68 percent of our sample seemed to do so. Such an inference is called a **statistical induction**.

It should be obvious that statistical induction is very much like induction by enumeration. In fact, some claim that induction by enumeration is just a special case of statistical induction in which the percentage of *A*s that are also *B*s just happens to be 100 percent. In other words, they interpret the "all" in the conclusion of an enumerative induction to mean "100 percent." [7]

If the conclusion of an induction by enumeration becomes more probable as we increase sample size and instance variety—because they make it more likely that our sample is *representative* of the population as a whole—the same is true of statistical induction. But *how* we get instance variety, and thus **representative samples**, is interesting.

First, we can divide our total sample into smaller groups of samples and

[7] This claim may seem obviously correct. But it isn't at all obvious with respect to the theoretically interesting case in which the population is *infinitely* large.

check the variation of one sample compared to another. (This is the general idea behind the mathematical concept called "standard deviation.") If the smaller samples differ but little from each other, and from the sample as a whole, then the sample as a whole is more likely to be representative of the population than otherwise. For instance, if we sample Congress in 1948, '50, . . . '68, '70, and find that the percentage of congressmen misusing funds always hovers roughly around 66 percent, then our statistical conclusion that two-thirds of all congressmen misuse government funds is more probable than it would be if many more misused funds in some sessions of Congress than in others, even though *overall* two-thirds misused funds.

There is a great deal of controversy over the efficacy of this procedure of dividing samples into smaller samples. However, most theorists accept this method as an important cornerstone of the theory of statistics.

And second, we assume a sample is representative of the population unless we have reason to think otherwise. One reason would be contrary higher-level induction. Thus, an election-poll sample of 1,000 voters, 500 rich and 500 poor, should be rejected on the grounds that there are more poor than rich voters *and* it is known that rich and poor tend to vote differently. This is just like the case for enumerative induction.

Polls often fail to make the right prediction because the sample they use is not representative. Two famous examples are the *Literary Digest* poll of 1936, which predicted Landon would defeat Roosevelt, and the 1948 Gallup Poll, which predicted that Dewey would defeat Truman. Gallup's error was very small, and his sample only slightly unrepresentative. But the *Literary Digest*'s error was a classic. They polled a sample of voters selected from telephone directories and auto registration lists, and of course were way off in their prediction, since in those unprosperous times large numbers of middle- and lower-class voters didn't have phones or automobiles. Their sample thus did not reflect the population it was supposed to represent, and was therefore worthless.

Statistical induction also is a bit different from induction by enumeration with respect to *negative* evidence. A single counter-instance is fairly deadly for an enumerative induction, but obviously not for a statistical induction. In our example, what any single congressman does with government funds neither greatly confirms nor disconfirms the statistical hypothesis that 68 percent of all congressmen misuse government funds. But it is highly disconfirming for the hypothesis that *all* congressmen misuse funds.

In addition, we have a problem in deciding whether statistical evidence supports or falsifies a statistical induction. Suppose our theory is that roughly two-thirds of all congressmen misuse funds. If we find that 65, 66,

67, or 68 do so, this would tend to confirm our theory. But what about 64,
63, 62, . . . ? When do we reach the point at which confirmation turns
to disconfirmation? There is no general agreement on the answer to this
question.

   e. Singular probability statement. Another extremely controversial topic
is the so-called "singular probability statement." The dispute concerns the
question how to interpret a statement like "The probability that it will rain
tomorrow is .9." One view is that a statement of this kind is really an
elliptical way of saying something *statistical,* namely that nine-tenths of
the time when conditions are what they are today, it rains the next day.
The other view is that the statement says it is reasonable to believe it will
rain tomorrow with a *strength of belief* equal to nine-tenths (using a scale
on which one is certitude and zero complete denial).

   But however we interpret such a sentence, *its* probability seems to be
increased or decreased in the same way as a statistical induction. For instance, we would be surer that the probability of rain tomorrow is nine-
tenths on the basis of evidence covering 100 years of weather experience
rather than only 20 or 30 years.

   In addition, the value nine-tenths is itself determined statistically. For
instance, we might conclude that the probability of rain is nine-tenths because in the past it rained nine times out of ten under similar circumstances.

   f. Causal connections. When we reason in any of the ways described
above, we usually are looking for explanations or causes. For example, in
relation to pornography and rape, what we would like to determine is
whether exposure to pornography *causes* men to rape. But we often must
be satisfied with less than a causal connection. Sometimes we must be satisfied with a merely statistical connection for which no *causal* efficacy is
claimed.

   To take a famous example, pretend we're living back in the days just
before Newton. So far as was then known, the earth was going to circle the
sun forever, revolving on its axis every 24 hours. The result would be a
constant connection between the occurrence of *night* and *day;* every time
night occurred, it would be followed by day. We have here a one-to-one
statistical correlation. But would we have been willing to say that this connection constituted a *causal* correlation? Would we have said that night
causes day, or that day causes night? Surely not.

   The reason is that even before Newton it was known that *if* (per impossible) the earth were to stop rotating on its axis, or stop revolving around
the sun, then night would *not* follow day, nor day night. Hence one could
not cause the other. But the two still are statistically correlated one-to-one.

The problem, then, is to decide when a statistical correlation is *merely* statistical, and when it is "significant," that is, when it is good evidence of a *causal* connection. There are several criteria:

1. In the first place, a statistical correlation is likely to indicate a causal connection if the statistics deviate from the norm or the expected. For instance, we suspect a causal connection between cigarette smoking and lung cancer because a greater percentage of smokers than nonsmokers gets lung cancer.

Notice that the percentage of smokers who get lung cancer is not what counts. And surely we are not just looking for percentages over fifty—even among heavy smokers the percentage of those who get lung cancer is far less than fifty. What does count is that many more people who smoke cigarettes get lung cancer than those who do not smoke.

A statistical correlation that does not satisfy this first criterion is not a good candidate for the status of causal connection.

2. The larger the sample for which a statistical correlation is significant by the first criterion, the more likely it is that it indicates a causal connection. For instance, if we find that more smokers get cancer than nonsmokers in a sample of 100,000 people, this is better evidence that smoking is a cause of lung cancer than similar results in a sample of only 10,000.

3. In the same way, the greater the *instance variety,* the more likely that the connection is causal. We can get greater instance variety in many ways. One is by checking samples of the total sample population for internal variations. Thus, if we break down a sample of 100,000 smokers into ten smaller groups of 10,000 each and find that the number who get lung cancer is roughly the same in each of the smaller samples, then (according to some experts) it is more likely that the connection between smoking and lung cancer is causal than if we found wild fluctuations from sample to sample.

Perhaps a better method to get instance variety is to make sure our sample checks many different types of people. We wouldn't want to check only city smokers, or only country smokers, nor would we check only nervous or high strung individuals.

In effect, an increase in instance variety amounts to a check to determine if some other factor may not be responsible for the apparent significance of the statistics linking cigarette smoking and cancer. For instance, had we found (as in fact we did not) that rural smokers don't get lung cancer any more than rural nonsmokers, we might have suspected that polluted city air is responsible for the lung cancer increase. This suspicion would have been confirmed if we then had discovered that city nonsmokers get more lung cancer than rural nonsmokers. (A good statistical experiment would be weighted between city and country dwellers in proportion to their actual numbers in our society.)

4.   We must also consider higher-level theoretical evidence which might bear on a given statistical correlation. We're more impressed with statistical evidence linking smoking and lung cancer than we would be with statistical evidence linking smoking and, say, cancer of the prostate gland, for theoretical physiological reasons which are obvious.

In fact, in the absence of any pertinent higher-level theoretical evidence, it becomes impossible to know how to increase the representativeness of a sample, and impossible to achieve instance variety. This is because we can divide any sample class into indefinitely many subclasses. For instance, we could divide cigarette smokers according to height, weight, blood type, hair color, sex, age, eating habits, place of residence, etc. But only some of these divisions make sense, and they are precisely those which higher-level evidence makes likely candidates as causes of cancer. Thus, we require representativeness with respect to place of residence because of air pollution, a likely cause of cancer. But we don't bother with height or weight.

5.   Finally, there is negative evidence. Suppose we find that a particularly heavy cigarette smoker (3 packs a day for 50 years) lives to a ripe old age and dies peacefully in bed at age 100 without the slightest trace of lung cancer. Clearly, then, if we are positive of his smoking record, we no longer can believe that heavy smoking over a long period of time *alone* invariably causes lung cancer. But we cannot conclude that there is no causal link between smoking and lung cancer. First, it still is possible that smoking plus some second factor causes cancer, although either of the two alone does not. And second, according to some writers,[8] it still is possible that smoking alone is what they would call a "statistical cause" of lung cancer. That is, according to these writers, it may be that in the absence of any other cause of lung cancer, a certain percentage of smokers always will, and a certain percentage will not, get lung cancer.[9]

Before we leave the topic of inductive logic, one last warning is in order. Statistics are notorious for their great differences in quality, particularly in exactly those areas relevant to *political* disputes. Perhaps the best example of this is statistics on crime in the United States (or anywhere). Such sta-

[8] E.g., Hans Reichenbach. See his *Rise of Scientific Philosophy,* Univ. of California Press, 1953, Chapter 10. Many, perhaps most, philosophers disagree with Reichenbach on this issue.

[9] Technically, what the dispute amounts to is this: Philosophers such as Reichenbach take statistical connections in these cases to be *ontological,* whereas their opponents take them to be *epistemic.* In other words, the former group takes what they call statistical causes to be built into the nature of the universe, while the latter think their use results from our ignorance of the actual causes at work in the universe.

tistics rarely are a true indication of increases or decreases in actual crime, but, rather, indicate the amount of activity which officially is recorded in police records across the nation. But surely we wouldn't want to blindly trust police records on, say, gambling, prostitution, or illegal drug use, given the notorious fact that policemen so often are in on "the take" from such illegal activities. Similarly, we must be wary of crime statistics from areas or times in which crimes committed by nonwhites against nonwhites generally went unreported.

Or consider the F.B.I. statistics indicating that rape increased significantly in the United States during the 1960s. The tendency not to report rape by nonwhites of nonwhites is well known, as is the tendency to hush up rape committed by middle- or upper-class whites against middle- or upper-class whites. How then can we know whether the reported increase is due to an actual increase in rape rather than to an increase in the tendency to report rapes? In fact, there is considerable doubt among historians that *any* of the "traditional" crimes[10] such as murder, rape, ordinary theft, etc., are as prevalent in the U.S. as they were 50 or 100 years ago. (For instance, read almost any account of life in big cities in the U.S. prior to WW I.) And yet, statistics on these crimes almost always indicate a tremendous increase, due no doubt to increased efficiency in the detection and official reporting of crime.

Similar remarks apply to statistics accumulated by means of surveys or polls. What a man *says* he believes or does may bear only slight resemblance to what he actually believes or does. A good example is furnished by two surveys conducted in the early 1950s. One by Chrysler indicated people wanted conservative, functional cars. The other, by GM, indicated the same thing, but also indicated that respondents believed their *neighbors* were interested mostly in racy autos. Chrysler built conservative functional cars and did poorly, while GM built flashy ones "for the man next door" and made a mint.

Clearly, statistics must be used with great care.

---

[10] That is, not including auto theft and other crimes possible only in a technological society.

Appendix B

Answers to Selected Exercises

When consulting these answers, remember that reasonable men may disagree on some of them. Your answers are not automatically wrong because they differ from those given here.

Chapter One

1. *Inconsistency.* Johnson's first statement was that defeat of the communists was essential. Yet he ended up talking about accepting the terms of the 1954 Geneva agreements, which called for elections that the communists might win. He also stated that there could be no military solution in Vietnam. But we could not expect the communists to defeat themselves, so this amounted to an admission that our policy no longer called for their defeat. (Notice that President Johnson never publicly stated that his Vietnam policy had changed.)

2. *Doubtful evaluation.* To answer this correctly, you have to have at least a minimal acquaintance with the fact that the South, especially the deep South, has been resisting the 1954 Supreme Court school desegregation decision, and that the courts hardly could be accused of Draconian edicts when sixteen years after that decision Southern schools still had not complied with the law.

3. *Doubtful evidence,* bordering on *unknown fact.* Presumably, Evans and Novak had no direct access to the goings-on in the North Viet-

namese government. So how did they know about that government's premonitions?

5. *Suppressed evidence.* Ogilvy himself went on to say, "But I was never able to keep a straight face when I said this; if a company's sales had not grown more than sixfold in the previous twenty-one years, its growth was less than average." Ogilvy thus suppressed the evidence which would cast doubt on the conclusion that his advertising caused the increased sales.

9. *Suppressed evidence.* This is another one of those cases in which knowledge of the facts is vital. Lyndon Johnson could not have voted for the 1935 Wagner Act, since he wasn't elected to Congress until 1937 (a fact of which White should have been well aware, having so stated in the very same book, on page 136). It was I. F. Stone who caught White in this error. See Stone's book *In a Time of Torment,* p. 47.

11. *Suppressed evidence.* Stare neglected to tell us three major facts. First, few Americans who eat flaked cereals would otherwise fail to get enough calories in their food; thus the high calorie content of flaked cereals (compared to that of other foods) is not a virtue, and may even be a defect. Second, most of the protein and calcium in a bowl of flaked cereal with milk is in the *milk,* not the cereal. And third, a great deal of the non-caloric food value of the wheat, corn, oats, or rice is removed in the manufacture of these products, and only a part is put back; most of the standard cooked cereals, such as Oatmeal and Ralston, are far higher in vitamins, minerals, and protein than Corn Flakes, Wheaties, etc. (There are some cold cereals on the market that have not had their original food value reduced in manufacture. Granola, Vita Grains with Nuts, and Familia are examples. But they have only limited sales in the United States, chiefly through health food stores.)

14. *Unknown fact.* Of course the AP covered itself by using a "weasel word"—"The President **presumably** had delivered. . . ." But most readers will slide over that indication that what is to follow is mere guesswork.

Chapter Two

1. *Common practice.* Mr. Kugler tried to excuse, or at least mitigate, the failure of the state of New Jersey to deal justly with the poor by appeal to *common practice.*

2. *False dilemma.* The implication of the passage was that the *only* way to finance increased Negro enrollment was to cut back on scholar-ships for poor white students. But there are usually many places to cut a budget; the money might have been cut from administrative or faculty salaries, or obtained by reducing the number of outside speakers brought onto campus or from any number of other places. The selective appropriation of money means that for one reason or another *every* item funded was deemed more important than *any* item not funded.

3. *Ad hominem* argument. The implication is that McCormack was not sufficiently qualified to be Speaker of the House, since he didn't even have a high school education. This constituted an attack on McCormack's formal background, while ignoring an adult lifetime of performance. (The article's point may have been that *no one* with-out a high school education could fill the bill, but that is just foolish, since it would eliminate even such a man as Abraham Lincoln.)

5. *False dilemma* and *begging the question.* The implication is that we can't be "gorged" on sex *and* have love too. But without proof that we can't have both, this is not a true dilemma. The question begged is whether our society *is* gorged on sex, something many would deny.

7. *Straw man.* The amendment, in effect, required *equality before the law* without regard to sex. This means roughly that no law could discriminate *solely* on the basis of sex. But men only could still be drafted, on the grounds that men are more physically suited to the job, and likewise women only might serve as striptease artists, with-out violating the amendment. A law limiting the working hours of women might violate the amendment, but if so one requiring that *physically weak* workers work shorter hours would not. (Such a law would not limit the working hours of burly females, while it would limit those of weak males; but presumably that is the sort of thing women's liberationists are after.)

14. *Straw man* and *ad hominem.* Meany started out to discuss the idea that we should *listen* to the younger generation, but then he switched to the straw idea that we *entrust the government* to them. His argu-ment against young people was *ad hominem* because it attacked their habits (pot-smoking and Woodstock get-togethers), not their views, and it is their views that "these people constantly" suggest we listen to. (What would Meany have thought about the argument that we shouldn't listen to the older generation, on the grounds that they drink more alcohol than the younger?)

16. *Two wrongs make a right.* Mr. Tiger's view is not any less subject to criticism because his critics *also* failed to provide a correct theory.

17. *False dilemma.* An argument against Kaiser, no matter how success-

ful, does not constitute an argument for any other plan, unless it is shown that there is no third alternative. But in this case, there would seem to have been many other alternatives.

Chapter Three

1. *Ambiguity.* Huey Newton meant "manhood" in a figurative sense (he wasn't talking about sexual manhood), but John Corry seems to have taken Newton literally.
2. *Questionable cause* and *exaggeration.* While many would assign some blame for the nation's ills to American educators, it would take a great deal of argument—not provided by Mrs. Mitchell—to convincingly attribute even a major portion of the blame (let alone the total responsibility) to formal education.
8. *Provincialism.* How about the Japanese invasions of Manchuria and China? Western man is preoccupied with Western man.
11. *Ambiguity* and *suppressed evidence.* What does it mean to "have a chance" without a college degree? Rightly or wrongly, most Americans don't want their children to grow up to blue collar or clerical jobs, and (here is the *suppressed evidence*) more and more high-paying and prestigious jobs do require a college degree (why else are most students in college?).
13. *Provincialism.* Eisenring obviously was looking at the matter with the bias of a life insurance man. Who else would say that the discovery of wonder drugs which would vastly increase human longevity is "**fortunately** rather unlikely"?
16. *Irrelevant reason* or *begging the question.* Either President Kennedy *begged the question* by asking other questions (a common ploy) or we must assume he meant that the reasons for climbing mountains or for Rice's playing Texas are the very reasons why we should go to the moon. In the latter case, his reasons are irrelevant; whatever reasons there may be for Rice to play Texas, they have nothing to do with going to the moon. (However, the argument can be construed as saying that we ought to go to the moon for adventure and excitement, the reasons perhaps that we climb mountains and that Rice plays Texas. Construed in this way, the argument is relevant, but the evidence is insufficient to warrant the conclusion, because lots of exciting adventures are not justified. Kennedy would have had to argue that going to the moon is a *justified* exciting adventure.)
18. *Begging the question.* Who says that American colleges are overloaded

with "phony liberals" whose heroes are Che Guevara, etc., or that they "corrupt and pervert the educational process"?

23. This is a typical ambiguous example from daily life. Did Agnew intend a connection between the first part of this paragraph and the last? (The paragraph ended his speech, and in some sense was a summary.) If he did, then the fallacy is *irrelevant reason*. For how could our removing men from Vietnam have had anything to do with the enemy's having paid a heavy price for misreading the American people?

25. *Ambiguity* and *questionable classification*. Did Evans and Novak mean that Miss Davis, like the Weathermen, could have been almost anywhere? Or did they mean that Miss Davis, a Weatherman, could have been almost anywhere? Since there was no evidence at the time connecting Miss Davis with the primarily white middle-class Weathermen, Evans and Novak could always say they meant the former. Yet many readers very likely construed them to be saying the latter. If readers believed she was a Weatherman because of this column, they also committed the fallacy of *questionable classification*.

Chapter Four

4. Plymouth managed to appear to have the largest sales increase in the compact car field because incomparable statistics were compared. Although the Duster was technically part of the Plymouth Valiant line, it was in fact an entirely new entry into the small car field, so that it made no sense to talk of a *sales increase* for it. Ford Maverick figures also were misleading, since Maverick had the advantage of the normal sales increase any successful new model can expect for the first few months of its second year compared to the first few months of its first year. Even so, to compare Valiant and Maverick sales increases was unfair to Maverick. But to compare the sales increases of either Valiant or Maverick with those for Chevy Nova was unfair to the Nova. Nova had been in existence for several years at that time, and so could not be expected to have more than a modest increase in sales. If a comparison had to be made between Nova and, say, Maverick sales increases, it should have been a comparison of second year increases (compared to first) for both models.

6. The fact that the poll correctly predicted the results of the election is irrelevant hindsight, a mere matter of luck. (A coin flip might also have predicted the outcome.) A poll of 64 workers, no matter how

well chosen, cannot provide a reliable estimate for an election involving millions of voters.

8. This demonstrates the fallacy of *hasty conclusion*. We can't generalize from just one instance to the character of an entire people. (Would we like to be judged by My Lai alone?) Along the way, the letter-writer also was guilty of the fallacy of *suppressed evidence;* the Japanese, after all, have produced great art, great music, great intellectuals, etc., all indications that they are no more barbarian than any other supposedly civilized groups. In addition, the letter contains the fallacy of *two wrongs make a right;* it would be barbaric of us to not be concerned about the innocent victims of the atomic bombs we dropped on Japan.

11. This example again illustrates the need to be aware of possible background evidence. One reason that fewer young people voted in the past is that fewer were eligible, due to stringent residence requirements which in particular tended to disenfranchise college students. The new law limited residency requirements to thirty days. The passage also failed to consider the fact that even if proportionately fewer 18–21 year olds voted, their vote still might make a big difference in close elections (three of the six presidential elections from 1948 through 1968 were extremely close).

Chapter Five

1. Here is the *Daily News* editorial with margin notes attached:

The "White Flag Amendment"— which masquerades as the "amendment to end the war" comes before the Senate tomorrow for a showdown vote.

(1) Senate votes tomorrow on McGovern-Hatfield.

This bugout scheme is co-sponsored by Sens. George McGovern (D-S.D.) and Mark Hatfield (R-Ore.). And despite some last minute chopping and changing to sucker fence-sitting senators, the proposal remains what it has always been, a blueprint for a U.S. surrender in Vietnam.

(2) It is a blueprint for U.S. surrender in Vietnam.

It would force a pellmell pullout of American forces there by cutting off all funds for the Vietnam war as of Dec. 31, 1971. It represents the kind of simple—and simple minded—solution to Vietnam for which arch-doves and pacifists (as well as the defeatists and Reds who lurk behind them) have long clamored.

(3)   It would force withdrawal by cutting off funds.

(4)   Doves, pacifists, defeatists, and Communists support the measure.

This amendment wears the phony tag of a "peace" plan. More accurately, it constitutes a first step toward whittling Uncle Sam down to pygmy size in the world power scales; it would fill our enemies with glee and our friends with dismay.

(5)   It's proposed as a peace plan—

(6)   but will really reduce our power around the world,

(7)   and please our enemies, dismay our friends.

McGovern-Hatfield might appear a cheap out from Vietnam. But we would pay for it dearly later in other challenges and confrontations as the Communists probe, as they inevitably do at any sign of weakness, to determine the exact jelly content of America's spine.

(8)   It looks like cheap way out, but will be more expensive when Communists probe this sign of our weakness.

The McGoverns, Hatfields, Fulbrights, Goodells and their ilk would have the nation believe that its only choice lies between their skedaddle scheme and an endless war. That is a lie.

(9)   Proponents pose *false dilemma* between their measure and indefinite war.

President Richard M. Nixon has a program for ending America's commitment in Vietnam, and it is now under way. It involves an orderly cutback in U.S. forces.

(10) But Nixon has a program for ending war which gives VN a fighting chance.

The White House method assures the South Vietnamese at least a fighting chance to stand on their own feet and determine their own future after we leave.

Equally important, it tells the

world the U.S. is not about to pull the covers over its head and duck out on its responsibilities as leader of the free world.

We urge the Senate to slap down the McGovern-Hatfield amendment, and scuttle with it any notion that America is willing to buy off noisy dissidents at the price of its honor.

(11) And tells world we will remain responsible leaders of free world.

(12) Rejection will dispel idea U.S.
(13) will give up its honor to quiet opponents of VN war. So the Senate should reject it.

And here is a summary of the *Daily News* editorial based on the above margin notes (we include unimportant points in our summary for purposes of illustration):

1. *The Senate votes tomorrow on the McGovern-Hatfield amendment.*

2. *If passed, this amendment would result in U.S. surrender in Vietnam.*

3. *It would cut off funds as of December 31, 1971, forcing troop withdrawal.*

4. *Doves, pacifists, defeatists (?), and Communists support the measure.*

5. *It is proposed as a peace plan.*

6. *But it really will just reduce our power around the world.*

7. *It will please our enemies and dismay our friends.*

8. *It looks like a cheap way out, but ultimately will be more expensive when the Communists probe further after this sign of weakness.*

9. *Proponents of the measure say it is our only alternative to an indefinite continuation of the war.*

10. *But President Nixon has a plan for ending the war which gives the South Vietnamese a fighting chance.*

11. *His program will tell the world we intend to live up to our responsibilities as leaders of the free world.*

12. *Rejection of McGovern-Hatfield will dispel the idea that the U.S. would give up its honor to quiet opponents of the war.*

13. *The Senate should reject the McGovern-Hatfield amendment.*

Notice that most of the editorial's heavily emotive or value-charged
expressions are not used in the summary. No such expressions should
be included in a summary of this kind unless their use is supported by
argument.

For instance, the editorial says the amendment would force a "pell-
mell pullout" of American troops, but never explains why. It is hard
to conceive of a troop withdrawal over a period of eighteen months
as a pellmell pullout. (Notice the hidden *inconsistency* in the *Daily
News's* position. The *News* describes President Nixon's program as an
"orderly cutback"; it would never have described it as a pellmell pullout. And yet the President withdrew troops in 1970 at a rate which
would have removed most of our troops from Vietnam by December
31, 1971, *if* the same rate were continued.)

Now we have to evaluate the editorial via an evaluation of the summary. Of the thirteen statements which summarize the editorial, three,
(1), (3), and (5), just give background information; they don't support the editorial's conclusion (13), and hence can be cast aside.
Number (4) (that doves, Communists, etc., support the measure) is
just *ad hominem* argument. The seventh also is fallacious, but interesting. It implies that what pleases our enemies and dismays our friends
must be wrong. This is a nice variation on *appeal to authority*, for it
implies that we can solve our problems by accepting the opinions of
our friends and (in reverse) our enemies. But why should they be better authorities on what we should do than we ourselves?

That leaves eight statements. Two of these, (10) and (11), deny
the content of (9). Four, (2), (6), (8), and (12), are intended to
support the main conclusion (13). On first glance, (6) would seem
to be false, because it is not evident how we would have become weaker
militarily by withdrawing from Vietnam. But the point, made evident
by (8) and (12), was that withdrawal on a schedule would make us
appear weak around the world, and (perhaps) therefore *make* us
weaker relative to the Communists. If this strikes the reader as correct,
then he should accept (6), (8), and (12). Notice, however, that the
News did not give evidence for this very controversial view. Notice
also that the very same objection could have been made against President Nixon's withdrawal proposal, since *any* plan to withdraw without assured victory might look weak in the eyes of the world.

That leaves the second assertion (passage of the amendment would
result in a U.S. surrender in Vietnam). Was this true? It depends on
what would have happened to the South Vietnamese government upon
our withdrawal. But whatever the answer to this question, didn't the
President's plan (if it actually led to withdrawal from Vietnam) run
the same risk of being a surrender?

This last question should make us think about the crucial question, which the *Daily News* glossed over. What, after all, were the differences between the McGovern-Hatfield plan and Nixon's announced program? What was all the fuss about?

In the first place, supporters of the President argued that a hard and fast date for withdrawal of all our troops should not be set. Second, they objected to the particular date set by McGovern-Hatfield (December 31, 1971). The President let it be known at the time that he expected us to be out by campaign time 1972. Proponents of his program argued that withdrawal should be linked to the success of our program of turning the fighting over to the South Vietnamese. They argued that the President was the one who would have the facts needed to make such decisions.

On the other hand, proponents of McGovern-Hatfield were skeptical of our Vietnamization program, and in particular skeptical of the President's intention (or at any rate his political ability) to remove all troops in 1972, unless we miraculously won a total victory by that time.

The problem thus came down to this. Would withdrawal in 1972 give the South Vietnamese government a significantly greater chance than withdrawal in late 1971? Would announcement of a definite withdrawal date adversely affect their chances, or harm our posture around the world? And would the President *really* withdraw all troops from Vietnam by campaign time 1972, even if it became clear that the South Vietnamese government would then lose the war? We now are in a better position to answer these questions, but that's hindsight. The point is that the *Daily News* editorial *begged* all these crucial questions. It supported one plan as opposed to another without ever explaining the real differences between the two, or explaining why the President's program would give the South Vietnamese government a better chance than McGovern-Hatfield.

3. Here is a summary of the Jenkin Lloyd Jones political column (the margin notes have been omitted):

1. *Hubert Humphrey said it is time liberals got on the side of law and order.*

2. *Four days later, as if to illustrate the point (provide evidence for it?), the federal office building in Minneapolis was bombed.*

3. *This building contains a military induction center, and has been a target of antiwar demonstrators.*

4. *Humphrey said that describing all who espouse violence and disruption as "well-meaning" makes the liberal cause less credible.*

5. *Some people mean by "police brutality" any attempt to resist snipers and rioters.*

6. *Talk of police brutality becomes irrelevant (relatively unimportant?) when we discover the size of the Black Panther arsenals and the number of policemen killed (by Panthers?).*

7. *Libertarians who protested the firing by the State of California of the Communist professor, Angela Davis, as a violation of academic freedom have not publicly recanted.*

8. *Since the alleged use of her guns in the murder of four persons at the Marin County Courthouse, these libertarians have been quiet.*

9. *The presidential commission appointed by President Johnson spent $2 million and concluded that completely free pornography has no relation to sex crimes.*

10. *This report ignores FBI statistics showing that rape increased 17 per cent from 1968 to 1969, the largest increase for any major crime except larceny.*

11. *Dr. Victor B. Cline, professor of clinical psychology, claims the report of the president's commission greatly distorts the evidence.*

12. *Humphrey is right that anarchy inevitably brings on repression.*

13. *(Humphrey is right that?) you can't have freedom or social progress without law and order.*

Notice that when stripped of unwanted emotive terms, and put into plain English, the column loses a good deal of its initial appearance of plausibility.

Now we have to evaluate these claims. Assertion (11) clearly is intended to refute the conclusion of the pornography commission stated in (9). It appeals to an expert to support the implicit claim that pornography does cause sex crimes, contrary to the commission report. But this *appeal to authority* is fallacious. First, many other psychologists, perhaps most, as well as most ministers, criminologists, etc., would tend to agree with the commission and disagree with Mr. Jones' psychologist. Where experts disagree violently, it generally is fallacious for the layman to consider any particular expert's *opinion* as good evidence. (His reason and arguments are another matter.) And second, there are some matters, such as religion, politics, and morals, in which, if the issue is important enough, each man must become his own expert, even if those said to be experts are in general agreement. (Just think of yourself living in some fifteenth-century European monarchy where all the "experts"—so far as the layman could tell—took for granted the doctrine of the divine right of kings.)

Assertion (10) also is intended to refute the conclusion stated in (9). FBI statistics on the increase in rape from 1968 to 1969 are presented as good evidence against the commission's conclusion rejecting pornography as a cause of sex crimes. They *are* evidence, given the increase in the availability of what was taken to be pornography at the time. But they are not *sufficient* evidence to warrant acceptance of the theory that pornography *causes* sex crimes. We need to know much more before the quoted statistic becomes more than marginally significant: how the FBI statistics were gathered; the incidence of sex crimes for other years in the sixties during which pornographic material was on the increase; whether the increase in sex crimes was greater in those areas of the country where the increase and pornography was greatest; whether sex crimes increased in other nations (for example, Denmark) which adopted an "anything goes" attitude toward pornography. Some of this information was in the commission's report, but Mr. Jones failed to furnish it for us (because it tends to confirm the commission's findings?).

Assertion (2) (that the federal office building was bombed "as if to illustrate his point"), may *illustrate* the first point, but it doesn't provide good evidence for it. It implies the frequently heard charge that liberal "coddling" of militants is responsible for much recent violence. But it isn't good evidence for this implication because it doesn't show a *causal* connection between liberal attitudes toward militants, in particular, liberal attitudes on the law and order issue, and militant violence.

Similarly, assertion (3) (that the bombed building—containing an induction center—had been a target of antiwar demonstrators) seems designed to support the idea that left-wing radicals committed the bombing, and thus to support the view that liberal attitudes on the law and order issue were responsible for much violence. It does support the idea that left-wing radicals committed the bombing. But it does nothing for the view that left-wing militant violence was caused by liberal softness on law and order.

What we are left with, then, is a series of unsupported assertions. The question now is whether some of them are acceptable on their face or after reflection on the matter, given legitimate beliefs and background knowledge which we bring to bear on Mr. Jones' political column.

In assertion (1), to get his fellow liberals on the right side of the *political issues* of the day, Humphrey made use of a *false dilemma:* you're either for or against law and order, and liberals had better be for. Thus, he masked the real issue between liberals and their opponents, which was not law and order (taken literally—see below). All but the radical fringes were for law and order. The real issues were how best to get law and order, which laws, and whose order. Liberals pointed to police violence and to unequal enforcement of laws in favor of powerful groups and against minorities. They argued against increasing police power as a way to curb violence. Most other groups joined President Nixon in stressing the violence of left-wing radicals, and the need for stronger laws to aid police in curbing that violence.

Assertions (4) and (5), though true, are irrelevant to the main issue. But (6) (police brutality becomes irrelevant) is another matter. Lurking behind it is the fallacy *two wrongs make a right,* the idea that police brutality is justified because it is a response to evils such as the killing of policemen.

Statements (7) (libertarians haven't recanted on their protest of the Angela Davis firing) and (8) (they've been quiet since the alleged use of her guns to murder) both seem to have been true, on independent evidence. But the question whether libertarians *ought* to have recanted was begged. (Many libertarians argued that her firing violated principles of academic freedom, whatever she may later have done.) Statements (7) and (8) both attacked libertarians themselves rather than their positions. Their failure to recant, their silence, tells us nothing of the merits of any positions they may have espoused. To argue otherwise (as Jenkin Lloyd Jones seems to have done) is to use the fallacy of *ad hominem* argument.

That leaves assertions (12) (anarchy leads to repression) and (13) (freedom and social progress require law and order), both of which the reader is likely to accept, and for whose truth there exists almost limitless evidence. But did Mr. Jones mean "law and order" literally? (In its nonliteral use, "law and order" meant harsh measures to obtain literal law and order. It also sometimes was a euphemism for repression of blacks.) He used that expression at the beginning of his article when quoting Humphrey and also at the end. Did he mean it literally in one use and not the other? Whatever the answer to that question, the *reader* should make sure in dealing with the first and last statements in the article that both uses of the phrase "law and order" are given the same interpretation. Otherwise, he should use different expressions in restating the assertions made in the paper. If he fails to do this, he runs the risk of guilt for the fallacy of *ambiguity*.

The point is an important one. When catch phrases like "law and order" are used, the writer (or speaker) often wants one meaning to be used in convincing us that it is good (or bad), and another when talking about his opponent's position. He wants "law and order" taken literally when the reader decides whether to be for or against it, but figuratively when the reader evaluates claims that liberals are against it and thus are criminal coddlers. So he wants to have his cake and eat it, too; anyone who lets him have it both ways commits the fallacy of *ambiguity*.

That gets us to what is probably the point of the political column. In all likelihood, Mr. Jones wanted liberals to be thought of as against law and order in the *literal* sense of that expression. There were two things to be gained from such an identification. First, liberal candidates would be more easily defeated by that label at election time, and second, it would make it much more difficult to sell the liberal position on how to *achieve* law and order, thus leaving the field clear for the more popular idea that harsher police tactics and more stringent laws were called for. His job was made easier by the fact that the liberals were against law and order in the nonliteral sense. He thus played on the usual confusion surrounding ambiguous expressions. Those who want to think straight have to learn not to be taken in by such devices.

Bibliography

1. Fallacies (Chapters 1–5)

Barker, Steven F. *The Elements of Logic* (New York: McGraw-Hill, 1965).

Beardsley, Monroe. *Thinking Straight* (Englewood Cliffs, N.J.: Prentice-Hall, 1970).

Chase, Stuart. *Guide to Straight Thinking* (New York: Harper & Row, 1962).

———. *The Tyranny of Words* (New York: Harcourt, Brace, Jovanovich, 1938).

Copi, Irving M. *Introduction to Logic* (3rd ed.) (New York: Macmillan, 1968).

*Effros, William G. *Quotations Vietnam: 1945–1970* (New York: Random House, 1970).

Fearnside, W. Ward, and William B. Holter. *Fallacy, the Counterfeit of Argument* (Englewood Cliffs, N.J.: Prentice-Hall, 1959).

Fischer, David Hackett. *Historian's Fallacies* (New York: Harper & Row, 1970).

Gardner, Martin. *Fads and Fallacies in the Name of Science* (New York: Dover, 1957).

Gordon, Donald R. *Language, Logic, and the Mass Media* (Toronto and Montreal: Holt, Rinehart and Winston of Canada, Ltd., 1966).

Hamblin, C. L. *Fallacies* (London: Methuen & Co., 1970).

*Hinds, Lynn, and Carolyn Smith. "Nixspeak: Rhetoric of Opposites," *The Nation,* February 16, 1970.

* Asterisks indicate items referred to in the text.

244

Huff, Darrell. *How to Lie with Statistics* (New York: W. W. Norton, 1954).

*Kahane, Howard. *Logic and Philosophy* (Belmont, Calif.: Wadsworth, 1969).

Kamiat, A. H. *Critique of Poor Reason* (New York: privately printed, 1936).

Kytle, Ray. *Clear Thinking for Composition* (New York: Random House, 1969).

Michalos, Alex C. *Improving Your Reasoning* (Englewood Cliffs, N.J.: Prentice-Hall, 1970).

*Morgenstern, Oskar. "Qui Numerare Incipit Errare Incipit," *Fortune,* October 1963.

Moulds, George Henry. *Thinking Straighter* (Dubuque, Iowa: Kendall/Hunt, 1966).

Pitt, Jack, and Russell E. Leavenworth. *Logic for Argument* (New York: Random House, 1966).

Thouless, Robert H. *Straight and Crooked Thinking* (New York: Simon & Schuster, 1932).

2. Advertising and Political Candidates (Chapter 6)

*Baker, Sam Sinclair. *The Permissible Lie* (Cleveland and New York: World Publishing Co., 1968).

*Hopkins, Claude. *Scientific Advertising* (New York: Crown Publishing, 1966).

*McGinniss, Joe. *The Selling of the President 1968* (New York: Trident Press, 1969).

*Ogilvie, David. *Confessions of an Advertising Man* (New York: Atheneum, 1963).

*Rowsome, Frank, Jr. *They Laughed When I Sat Down* (New York: Bonanza Books, 1959).

3. Managing the News (Chapter 7)

Cirino, Robert. *Don't Blame the People* (Los Angeles: Diversity Press, 1971).

*Corry, John. "The Los Angeles Times," *Harpers,* December 1969.

Dinsmore, Herman H. *All the News that Fits* (New Rochelle, N.Y.: Arlington House, 1969).

Hentoff, Nat. Column in the Village Voice, October 22 and 29, 1970 (on *N.Y. Times* treatment of a particular type of news).

*Hersh, Seymour M. *My Lai 4* (New York: Random House, 1970).

Kempton, Murray. "The Right People and the Wrong Times," *New York Review of Books,* April 8, 1971.

McGaffin, William, and Erwin Knoll. *Anything But the Truth; the Credibility Gap—How the News Is Managed in Washington* (New York: G. P. Putnam, 1968).

Rowse, A. E. *Slanted News, A Case Study of the Nixon and Stevenson Fund Stories* (Boston: Beacon Press, 1957).

*Wilson, George. "The Fourth Estate," *Village Voice,* January 1, 1970.

4. Managing Textbooks
(Chapters 8 and 9)

*American Indian Historical Society. *Textbooks and the American Indian* (San Francisco: Indian Historian Press, 1970).

Indexes

Index of persons

Index of publications

Index of topics